CW00430452

Ullrich Kockel, Philip McDermott and Liam Campbell (eds)

Per Scribendum, Sumus

Mairéad Nic Craith (©Andrea Redmond 2020)

Per Scribendum, Sumus

Ethnopoesis, or: Writing Heritage

A Cèilidh in Honour of Mairéad Nic Craith

edited by
Ullrich Kockel, Philip McDermott and Liam Campbell

LIT

Cover image: *Writing Heritage* © Andrea Redmond 2020

This book is printed on acid-free paper.

Bibliographic information published by the Deutsche Nationalbibliothek
The Deutsche Nationalbibliothek lists this publication in the Deutsche
Nationalbibliografie; detailed bibliographic data are available in the Internet
at http://dnb.dnb.de.

ISBN 978-3-643-91357-9 (pb)
ISBN 978-3-643-96357-4 (PDF)

A catalogue record for this book is available from the British Library.

© LIT VERLAG GmbH & Co. KG Wien,
Zweigniederlassung Zürich 2020
Flössergasse 10
CH-8001 Zürich
Tel. +41 (0) 76-632 84 35
E-Mail: zuerich@lit-verlag.ch   http://www.lit-verlag.ch
Distribution:
In the UK: Global Book Marketing, e-mail: mo@centralbooks.com
In North America: Independent Publishers Group, e-mail: orders@ipgbook.com
In Germany: LIT Verlag Fresnostr. 2, D-48159 Münster
Tel. +49 (0) 2 51-620 32 22, Fax +49 (0) 2 51-922 60 99, e-mail: vertrieb@lit-verlag.de

Preface

Marianne Elliott

I first met Máiréad in 1993 when I arrived in Liverpool as the Professor of Modern History. She had been appointed the previous year to the Institute of Irish Studies, established in 1988 with Ullrich ('Ulli') Kockel as its first full-time member of staff. In the aftermath of the Anglo-Irish Agreement of 1985, the British Government had asked the British Association for Irish Studies to advise on the situation of Irish Studies in the British Higher Education sector and I had written the report. The Liverpool Institute was one of the outcomes. Máiréad's courage in leaving her teaching career in Ireland and relocating to an Institute still in its infancy, and still financially insecure, changed her personal and professional life, and I am proud that Liverpool helped launch her as such an impressive and productive scholar.

The Institute also, of course, saw the blossoming of her and Ulli's life together, and a rich intellectual partnership that is tracked in this tribute to Máiréad. As mentioned in the editors' introduction, it was not an easy time to join a British university sector increasingly driven by managerialism. When I took over the directorship of the Institute in 1997, it was a privilege to have Ulli and Máiréad on the very united and productive team in the Institute. After Ulli left at the end of 1999, Máiréad was deputy director, and a formidable one she made, particularly in the very many meetings with those managers when her strong and reflective personality made her the perfect 'good cop'. She had the ability to appear an unthreatening, quiet presence and then to come in with a devastatingly clear, brief and often unanswerable analysis of difficult situations. I was sorry that both she and Ulli had left before we gained financial security at the Institute with the Irish Government's major investment in 2008. Everybody liked Máiréad at Liverpool, and no one missed her more than I did when she moved to the new Academy of Irish Cultural Heritages at Magee in Derry and thus began another significant milestone in her personal and intellectual life. She could not have asked for a more inspiring and warm colleague than Ulster's Dean of Arts at the time, Bob Welsh. I attended the launch of the Academy, when Bob said to me: 'Thank you for Máiréad!' Thus did he appreciate my sense of loss, and what Magee had gained.

Máiréad was a very popular teacher at the Institute, and I witnessed again her commitment to teaching at the Academy of Irish Cultural Heritages when I acted as external examiner for the MA in Irish Cultural Studies. It is a fitting commentary on that gift to see her former students involved in this volume's tribute to her.

But it is as an outstanding researcher that we celebrate Máiréad in this volume, one whose publications have won widespread acclaim and recognition. That research and teaching (and Ulli's as well) stamped the character on Liverpool's Institute as a genuinely multi-disciplinary scholarly enterprise, but one rooted in the sympathetic understanding of Ireland's people, language, culture and heritage, and this she has also brought to Scotland. What a coup for Liverpool's new Institute to have a scholar so rooted in the language and identities of Ireland as Máiréad, and for her then to bring such skills to a wider understanding of linguistic identity throughout Europe. In recognition of her standing, she was fittingly elected a Member of the Royal Irish Academy.

It was Máiréad's research into the Irish Language in Northern Ireland in particular (and indeed Ulster Scots) where I most benefitted from her wisdom, soon appearing in her *Plural Identities, Singular Narratives: the Case of Northern Ireland* (2002) and *Culture and Identity Politics in Northern Ireland* (2003). *Plural Identities* tackled a number of the problems that are still bedeviling the outworkings of the 1998 Good Friday Agreement. It is an impressive work, fully deserving of the Ratcliff Prize. In *Culture and Identity Politics*, she took this debate a stage farther in a truly impressive analysis of some of the most controversial areas in the debate over reconciliation in Northern Ireland (and Ireland): identity politics. In an enlightening survey of the international literature in the area, she showed conclusively – and worryingly – how 'culture' as a concept has the potential to endlessly divide. And she carried us through numerous minefields (ethno-religious traditions, language, education, sport, broadcasting, museums, politics) to offer evidence-based policy lessons for future reconciliation.

Just as she was never phased by the difficult administrative situations in which she has found herself, so Máiréad has taken her linguistic and ethno-logical skills to bear on many of the really big political problems that the world faces today, not least that of human migration and human rights. The range of contributors who here celebrate this remarkable scholar and person will, I hope, show just how much she has enriched and enlightened our lives.

Thank you, Máiréad!

Contents

List of Illustrations

Contributors

Natsuko Akagawa is Senior Lecturer at the University of Queensland. She researches heritage politics, practice and discourse in a global context and is Series General Editor for Routledge Research on Museums and Heritage in Asia. Mairéad was the external examiner of her PhD thesis.

Regina F. Bendix teaches cultural anthropology at the University of Göttingen in Germany. Originally Swiss, she trained in the USA where she also taught for many years before returning to Europe. She had the pleasure of meeting Mairéad for the first time at the EASA congress in Copenhagen in 2002, and enjoyed every meeting since, esp. Mairéad's semester-long stay in Göttingen as a DAAD guest professor. To many more encounters in the future!

Katherine Campbell is a former senior lecturer at the University of Edinburgh, specialising in ethnomusicology (Scots song and Scottish traditional music) and a vocal and instrumental performer, arranger and composer. She has a special interest in the songs of Burns and has recently co-authored a book with Dr Emily Lyle entitled *Robert Burns and the Discovery and Re-creation of Scottish Song*.

Liam Campbell is Heritage Officer with Lough Neagh Landscape Partnership and has published and lectured widely on heritage and environmental issues, especially about the Northwest of Ireland. With undergraduate degrees from NUI Maynooth and Masters degrees from both Queen's University Belfast and Ulster University, he completed his PhD at Ulster under Mairéad supervision.

Cristina Clopot is a postdoctoral researcher at the Wilberforce Institute for the Study of Slavery and Emancipation, University of Hull, England, working on the Horizon 2020 project *European Colonial Heritage Modalities in Entangled Cities*. She completed her PhD at Heriot-Watt University under the supervision of Mairéad Nic Craith and Ullrich Kockel.

Patrick Corbett worked in the oil industry as a geologist until 1988, when he returned to Scotland to undertake a doctorate at Heriot-Watt University, completing in 1993. He stayed on at Heriot-Watt in various academic positions until today; now partially retired, he first met Mairéad as a member of University Court and was delighted to discover a shared interest in poetry.

Vytis Čiubrinskas is director of the Center for Social Anthropology at Vytautas Magnus University, Lithuania, visiting professor at Southern Illinois University, and editor of *Lithuanian Ethnology*, having written a book on anthropological theory, and co-authored and co-edited books on transnationalism, diasporic identity politics and citizenship. He first met Mairéad at EASA in Copenhagen.

Mary Delargy is an independent scholar who previously worked with Mairéad as a research associate on a project investigating diversity in Northern Ireland. Mary has a keen interest in community relations in Northern Ireland and also in Ulster-Scots and the Irish language.

Angelika Dietz studied *Empirische Kulturwissenschaft* and Rhetorics in Tübingen, Germany, before researching for a PhD in Derry/Londonderry, where she was supervised by Mairéad Nic Craith and Ullrich Kockel. Working as a freelancer in cultural works and raising her four children, she has moved several times to Germany, Italy and Greece, and now lives in Backnang, Germany.

Professor Emerita **Marianne Elliott** is a distinguished historian. Until her retirement in 2014, she was Director of the Institute of Irish Studies and first incumbent of the Blair Chair at the University of Liverpool, where she worked with Mairéad from 1997 until 2001. In 2000 she was awarded an OBE for services to Irish Studies and the Northern Ireland peace process, and in 2002 elected a Fellow of the British Academy.

Michaela Fenske is Professor of European Ethnology at the University of Würzburg, Germany. Her research interests include historical anthropology, narrative culture, rural studies, and multispecies studies. Her most recent work explores the return of wild animals like wolves in times of mass extinction. She has collaborated with Mairéad on place-making through historical narratives.

Britta Kalkreuter studied at Trinity College Dublin and Cologne University, where she gained a PhD for a study on the transmission of style in medieval architecture. She has worked in Europe and Asia, researching making-interfaces in the field of design, and Mairéad can take much credit for channelling some of that enquiry back to Britta's 'first love' of heritage research.

Ullrich Kockel has been described as an undisciplined academic. He has held professorships at universities in England, Ireland, Scotland, Lithuania and Latvia. A Member of the Royal Irish Academy, Fellow of the Academy of Social Sciences and former President of the Société Internationale d´Ethnologie et de Folklore (SIEF), he sees his most significant role of all in being Mairéad's *anam cara*.

Jolanta Kuznecovienė is a professor of sociology at the Lithuanian University of Health Sciences. Her research is on migration, transnationalism and diaspora, religion and spirituality. She has known Mairéad since the 2008 SIEF Congress.

Sophia Labadi is Professor of Heritage at the University of Kent. She first met Mairéad at the 2016 Association for Critical Heritage Studies conference in Montreal, and they have collaborated ever since.

Writing Heritage, Anthropologically

Ullrich Kockel, Philip McDermott and Liam Campbell

'[By] writing, we are' – the title of this collection – has been inspired by, but is also a twist on, Patrick Geddes' famous dictum 'by leaves we live'. Geddes arguably was emphasising our bio-ecological dependence on plant matter at a time when diets in industrialised countries were increasingly reverting to the carnivorous habits of prehistoric hunter-gatherers. Writing can, of course, be seen as a form of storytelling. We become by telling stories – our own and others'. The stories of others that we tell are, ultimately, also our stories, whereas these others tell their own, including of us. What can we learn from this about human being-in-the-world, and about the world in which we write ourselves? This is the gateway to fundamental anthropological questions: Who are we? (What makes us 'we', and how do 'we' relate to 'them' – as relate we surely do, ecologically and otherwise?). Writing can thus be seen as an act of *ethnopoesis*, the creation of group identities within a co- and cross-referential cultural ecology. Heritage is a key ingredient linking the individual to such ecological contexts, and writing heritage, therefore, can be regarded as an existential act.

'Writing heritage' can mean different yet interconnected practices of being, expressed through language employed to be read: (1) writing *about* heritage (analytically, 'objectively', from what epistemologists call an *etic* perspective); (2) written heritage narratives (from historiography to biography and memoir, from the factual to the hagiographic); (3) conjuring heritage by writing and rewriting (creative and, at times, subversive non-fiction); (4) the heritage of writing (for example, the history of the book); and (5) writing as heritage (the act and art of writing, often in contrast with oral heritage). Having worked in all five spheres (both academically and practically – not least as a distinguished poet), Mairéad[1] Nic Craith's core intuition of teasing out anthropological insights (in both the narrower disciplinary and the wider philosophical sense of 'anthropology') can be regarded as aspiring towards integrating critical heritage studies (=1), cultural history (=2), literary studies (=4) and philology/folklore (=5) into a creative ethnology (=3) that is political almost by definition. *Ethnopoesis*, (re-) drawing the boundaries of 'community', is where peripheries, archipelagos, edges and other geospatial metaphors are most relevant and of interest. Issues of 'community' and 'place', with a special focus on communication with, about,

---

[1] Shortly before completion of this book, Mairéad decided to return to the original spelling of her name. We followed this here but have left the spelling unchanged in the contributions.

and between cultures (see, e.g., Nic Craith and Kockel 2004; McDermott, Nic Craith and Strani 2016), have been key themes throughout her work, as has the nexus of memory and nostalgia underpinning much of heritage discourse, as her latest inter- and transdisciplinary monograph (Nic Craith 2020) demonstrates.

The present collection grew from a covert meeting at Edinburgh's Scottish Storytelling Centre in November 2018. The co-conspirators concluded that the time had come to celebrate Mairéad's many achievements in, and contributions to, the field of heritage studies over the years. It is usual for a *Festschrift* to mark a significant birthday of the gratulant. Further occasions for a *Festschrift* may include retirement, or some other major anniversary – the gratulant's 'Golden Graduation', 'Silver' or 'Golden Promotion' (PhD), 'Silver' or, rarely, 'Golden Habilitation' (higher doctorate) among them. But in this instance, there are other 'round' anniversaries occurring during the twelve month period within which this book is published that merit and justify a celebration: forty years since Mairéad earned her first degree at Mary Immaculate College, Limerick, that set her on track for her first, successful career in primary teaching; thirty years since she gained her PhD at University College Cork that opened the door to her second career, as an internationally leading researcher and inspiring teacher in higher education. Within twelve months from this book appearing in print, she will have been a professor for twenty years, having held chairs in heritage at the University of Ulster (now Ulster University) and Heriot-Watt University, and honorary/visiting professorships at the universities of Exeter and Göttingen.

Aware that the honouree has had a profound impact on many people over the years – as teacher, mentor, colleague, friend, and fellow researcher – we felt there were good reasons to round up some friends, present and former colleagues, and former PhD students, for a little *cèilidh*.[2] As we initially plotted this publication on a dreich November day, we could barely have imagined the level of warmth with which contributors responded to our call. The contributions here are testament to the impact that Mairéad has had at Liverpool, Ulster and Heriot-Watt, but also in the wider field of heritage, in Europe and beyond.

The ongoing tensions around heritage, its form, its definition and its use are central aspects of the kaleidoscope of contributions to this book. The research essays represent the breadth of themes that Mairéad has explored in her own writing, and the authors frequently identify new directions shaped in their own work through the honouree's influence. Other contributions note Mairéad's support and mentoring or illustrate the author's appreciation of Mairéad's work

---

[2] In Scots Gaelic culture, *cèilidh* refers not just to dancing, but to a gathering where music and poetry, songs and stories are shared to celebrate community.

through prose, music and artistic representations. This, we feel, captures the spirit of the honouree's life and work perfectly, and demonstrates the influence that she has had, within academia and beyond.

We could have grouped the contributions by genre but felt that this would be too rigid a structure. Instead, we opted for a line-up that reflects thematic foci and explorations that have shaped Mairéad's journeys, which also map on to the places where she has worked as an academic. Importantly, the contributors to this volume come from a range of disciplinary perspectives, indicative of the breadth of Máiréad's academic interests. This was evidenced when authors submitted work using a range of referencing styles from across the arts, humanities and social sciences. As editors, we considered standardising these styles to a modified Harvard format, to obtain 'consistency'. However, we concluded that this would not be in the spirit of our project, which aimed to highlight the gratulant's transdisciplinary approach. The use of different styles is maintained, therefore, as a reminder of the scope of Mairéad's work.

The first section, capturing Mairéad's time as Lecturer in Modern Irish at Liverpool, opens with a painting by her first PhD student, Janet Leyland, depicting the building where the Institute of Irish Studies was located when Mairéad joined it in 1992, leaving a secure job as a primary teacher in Ireland for the vagaries of an increasingly commercialised and managerialised higher education sector. Ullrich Kockel recalls stations and turning points on their individual and shared journeys of discovery, a trajectory that reveals a common curiosity about islands, liminal spaces both off and on shore – from the Great Blasket in Co. Kerry, to the Gaelic and other linguistic and cultural 'islands', surrounded by another language or culture, across Europe. Cornwall and Catalonia, although both attached to a 'mainland', might be considered 'islands' in these terms. Philip Payton reflects on the inspiration he drew from Mairéad's work on Northern Ireland for his own study of Cornwall. A poem by Colin Williams considers the themes of language, forced migration and exile through the life story of a Catalan woman. Throughout her time at Liverpool, Mairéad was involved with the European Centre for Traditional and Regional Cultures ECTARC (whose Director in the early 1990s, Franz-Josef Stummann, features prominently in Kockel's contribution) and the European Bureau for Lesser Used Languages – arenas in which she met, and worked with, the contributors in this section.

After nine years at Liverpool, Mairéad was appointed to a Chair at the University of Ulster's newly established Academy for Irish Cultural Heritages (AICH). Her professorship, originally designated as 'Irish Language and Literature', became 'European Culture and Society' when she took up the directorship of the Academy a few years later, setting out her research programme in her inaugural lecture (Nic Craith 2008). Throughout her time at Ulster, her research interest in language as heritage was complemented by a renewed interest in literature, landscape and memory. In many – often unexpected – ways, Ulster enabled Mairéad to develop new interests and branch out in multiple disciplinary directions while holding it all together in what Richard Kearney (1985), writing about *The Irish Mind*, once described as 'creative confluence'. One of her favourite quotes from the Bible is Isaiah 40:31, and so the soaring golden eagle, painted by her PhD-student Andrea Redmond, provides a suitable metaphor to open the second section. The contributions in this section illustrate the plurality of heritage captured in the Academy's title, but also the scope of heritage as an evolving process over time and space. Language, literature and memory were key themes of Mairéad's time at Ulster, and the contributions represent these, reflecting heritage at both the local and the global level. William Logan considers how heritage functions as a language by examining how individuals, communities and entire nations structure the past. The language of identity politics is also highlighted by Pól Ó Dochartaigh, who examines the complexity of identities in post-Brexit Northern Ireland. Philip McDermott shows how language, a vehicle of tradition and heritage, is often also a symbolic political tool used for inclusion and exclusion. Regina Bendix contemplates the very nature and status of language, but especially the deep intertwining of language varieties as they relate to notions of personal and cultural belonging.

From different angles, Salis, Delargy and Wulff address the more overt form of 'writing heritage' in different literary genres. Drawing on nineteenth century gastronomy books, Loredana Salis describes female authors as creative writers who act as intercultural mediators in culinary traditions. Mary Delargy focuses on the emergence of a political pamphlet tradition in Irish, noting that such texts can be drawn on to challenge contemporary views of the Irish language. Helena Wulff's essay on the writer Éilís Ní Dhuibhne relates closely to Mairéad's interest in intercultural biography, exploring how a bilingual author chooses which language to write in, and how this relates to identity, culture and power. Michaela Fenske and Ulrich Marzolph pick up the culinary theme and weave their literary and historical narrative around the staple of Irish heritage, identity and memory – the humble potato.

The impact of migration on people's identification of and with particular heritages, the political dimensions of heritage, and the discourses associated with migrant heritage, feature in several contributions. Christian Ritter explores the ways digital media in everyday life have transformed ordinary writing about heritage, especially in more permanent migration contexts, such as the German

Lutheran congregations in Ireland, and in the more transient movement of tourists. The theme of transient migration is also illuminated in the short autobiographical piece by Angelika Dietz, who 'walks us through' her experiences as a migrant in Athens. Vytis Čiubrinskas and Jolanta Kuznecovienė discuss how (post-)ethnic identity in the United States is characterised by pride in the narratives of ethnic heritage, ideas that are constantly circulating in public discourse, with particular reference to migrants claiming Lithuanian ancestry.

Memory as a theme is also explored in chapters by MacKinnon, Campbell, and Walters. Iain MacKinnon's poem 'Go to Your Grandfather's House', speaking of creativity, memory and language, is inspired by family conflict over engagement with the past. Similarly, Liam Campbell's essay interweaves elements of family history with the memory of landscape, place and also the process of 'forgetting' and recovery. Victoria Walters engages with the notion of memory and intangible heritage as reflected in the Portuguese music tradition of *Fado*, raising questions about how intangible heritage might be recorded through art, and who has the right to create memory in that way.

Alastair McIntosh's essay mirrors Andrea Redmond's image of the soaring eagle, offering a deeply personal reflection on Mairéad's role as an educator who supports the development of her students. Alastair compares his experience of supervision to hospitality where the communal expansion of mind was a key element. Those among the contributors to this collection who were PhD students of Mairéad's (as two of us were) will appreciate how she fulfilled this pastoral role that is so central to the development of scholarship.

An unexpected congregation of circumstances conspired to bring Mairéad to Scotland and her second Chair, at Heriot-Watt University, after eleven years in Ulster. Her inaugural lecture in Edinburgh as Professor of European Heritage and Culture[3] was described by one audience member as 'a breath of fresh air in the Scottish heritage debate'. The 'topical transdisciplinarity' Rūta Muktupāvela and Valdis Muktupāvels note in their contribution here (p. 177), 'transcending boundaries of disciplines and research fields, bridging the gap between science and art, between academic and popular discourse', has become a true hallmark of Mairéad's work. Anthropologists and others talk of working in 'the field'. But 'field' is actually too solid and fixed a concept for this, and indeed for Mairead's work. The boundaries are rather more 'leaky', fluid. Water has been an underlying theme in much of Mairead's oeuvre that has influenced some of us in our approach to life, work, and searching for the source. As the late John O'Donohue (2010: 45) observed, '[water] takes on the shape of whatever contains it: jug,

---

[3] Subsequently redesignated Cultural Heritage and Anthropological Studies.

stream, well, river, lake, ocean, tears, rain, mist or moisture. In this sense water holds a wonderful imaginative invitation in it.' The invitation is to make sense of the *shoormal*,[4] a liminal land-/waterscape and multivariate space of meaning.

The third section of this collection opens with Natsuko Akagawa's visual poem *Live [いきる =ikiru]*, which, following the genteel Victorian garden in England and the golden eagle soaring over the rugged northwest of Ireland, invokes a vision of growth and rootedness at a time of significant challenges – thus aptly capturing Mairéad's time in Scotland, where the geopoetic and archipelagic perspectives in her work have found a fertile cultural ecology in which to unfold.

Natasha Sumner explores the restoration of a 'lost' documentary film, highlighting the close intertwining of identity and language, key themes in Mairéad's work, at multiple levels of representation. From a different angle, Nigel Rapport's philosophical meditation on literature and the common good addresses the writing of heritage in the tension between individual and collective.

Air for Mairéad is a piece of music, commissioned by Margaret Mackay and composed by Katherine Campbell, that at once celebrates Mairéad's influence in Scotland and expands the notion of 'language' to embrace artistic expression, picking up a track laid by Walters in the previous section, and introducing a suite of contributions similarly infused with an artistic spirit. Smith's contemplation of inscriptions on the building that houses his place of work, the Scottish Storytelling Centre, opens up a historical window that tells a story about language and identity as it is linked to tangible heritage. Artistic practice as research is explored in the three-part, mixed-genre contribution by Rūta Muktupāvela and Valdis Muktupāvels, the centrepiece of which is the telling of a mythical story about the creation of a 'folkoratorio' by practice-based research. Closely related to their approach are Mairi McFadyen's insightful observations on meaning in birdsong and folksong, a multi-layered exploration of the embodiment and ecology of music and lyrics.

The migrant experience has been a recurrent theme in Mairéad's work and throughout this book, as has memory – both individual and collective. There is in this context almost always an undercurrent of trauma, however slight, and a set of contributions from colleagues and PhD-students at Heriot-Watt illustrates this. In a personal reflection drawing from her doctoral fieldwork, Vitalija Stepušaitytė presents 'home' as the ultimate 'Not-Yet' where the little and big traumata of jarring memories that line our displaced lifeworld may be overcome. Cristina Clopot, taking her personal experience as a case study, discusses

---

[4] *Shoormal* is a Shetlandic term for the tidal edge between land and sea.

the shaping of a European identity, threatened by politics, and its deliberate recovery, as a process of 'making' one's heritage and at the same time learning about it. Kerstin Pfeiffer's reading of a Medieval mystery play in a contemporary context shows how past texts can be adapted performatively in the present to express concerns about the future. Taking Rachel Seiffert's *The Dark Room*, a novel about dislocations in post-War Germany, as a case study, Maggie Sargeant examines representations of memory, identity and heritage in the traumatic light of a dark past. Returning to the theme of migrant heritage, Katerina Strani, drawing on her own family experience, shows complexities of heritage in the everyday in terms of the 'incredible lightness of being'. Britta Kalkreuter discusses examples of how design anthropological research on textiles heritage is helping to mediate social tensions and conflict.

As the second section of this book concludes with Alastair's appreciation of Mairéad's support for students, Sophia Labadi's 'Homage à Máiréad' pays tribute to her encouragement of academics in the early stages of their career. And in a geopoetic spirit, Patrick Corbett's poem, referencing green pastures (old, new and utopian) celebrates Mairéad's transdisciplinary intuition, bringing together Arts, Humanities, Social Sciences and STEM subjects, not least through the medium of poetry – a fitting tribute to an award-winning poet.

When Mairéad set out on her first, tentative expedition, to Liverpool, many years ago, she could hardly have expected this *cèilidh* to celebrate her work and the inspiration she has been for us all. With the other contributors, we hope that our shared offering will encourage and inspire her to continue writing heritage, anthropologically, as she is embarking on yet another expedition.

References

Kearney, R. (1985), *The Irish Mind: Exploring Intellectual Traditions* (Dublin: Wolfhound).

McDermott, P. M. Nic Craith and K. Strani. (2016), 'Public Space, Collective Memory and Intercultural Dialogue in a (UK) City of Culture', *Identities* 23(5): 610-627.

Nic Craith, M. (2008), 'Intangible Cultural Heritages: The Challenge for Europe', *Anthropological Journal of European Cultures* 17(1): 54-73.

Nic Craith, M. (2020), *The Vanishing World of* THE ISLANDMAN: *Narrative and Nostalgia* (Basingstoke: Palgrave).

Nic Craith, M. and U. Kockel eds (2004), *Communicating Cultures.* (Münster: LIT).

O'Donohue, J. (2010), *The Four Elements: Reflections on Nature* (London: Transworld Ireland).

First Expedition: Liverpool

Abercromby Square (© Janet Leyland 2019)

My ink and watercolour wash depicts Abercromby Square, sketched on location from just inside the Square's communal gardens, known to original inhabitants of these residences as 'The Shrubbery'.

The Square was designed at the beginning of nineteenth Century, with most residences completed by the 1820s. Built to attract the wealthier mercantile classes, the north, south and west sides of the square each had a Greek Doric Porch in the middle. Now owned entirely by the University of Liverpool, No. 11 was the original home of the Institute of Irish Studies during my postgraduate years in the 1990s.

Janet Leyland

Islands at Sea, on Land and in the Air
Elemental Voyages from Nostalgia to Utopia

Ullrich Kockel

> *Ik drööm vun een Eiland up See,*
> *Dat drifft unnern Wind, wild un free.*
> Helmut Debus[1]

Leaning on the bolted lower half of the door and gazing into the distance, I could just about make out the contours of the island in the mist, like the back of a gigantic whale, about to be beached in the sound. Behind me, Heiko, sitting on the steps to the loft, plinged on his guitar and Inge was making a pot of tea while Reiner, huddled close to the smouldering turf fire, talked of someone I had never heard of, a local man who had written a famous autobiography, in Irish, about living on that very island. The Great Blasket. And then about the deer that the Taoiseach (prime minister) at the time of my visit, Charles Haughey, had flown across to the smaller island behind that one, Inishvickilaun, so that he could watch the animal through his panoramic sitting room window. Or so the local myth went.

Nobody lives there now, Reiner said. On the big island. Pity. Why not, I said. What would it take? Well, said Reiner, you tell me. What do we send you to university for? I thought about it, gazing at the shadow in the mist. The following winter I was back, researching the ecology of the Great Blasket, for a BA dissertation[2] trying to work out a scheme for resettling it in a sustainable way.

That same year, a graduate in philosophy and Irish started an MA by research at University College Cork,[3] looking at the library of that *Islandman* Reiner had talked about one misty evening in a small cottage on the hillside east of Dunquin. And so commenced two intellectual journeys that should converge a decade later in the great English port city of Liverpool, reputedly the real capital of Ireland.

****

---

[1] Transl.: 'I dream of an island on (the high) sea, drifting in the wind, wild and free.' From Debus, H. (1981), 'Ik drööm vun een eiland', on: *As een Strom* (Worpswede: Atelier im Bauernhaus).

[2] Kockel, U. (1984), *A Blasket That Might Be? A Utopian Proposal*. Schriftenreihe der Deutsch-Irischen Gesellschaft Bremen 3.

[3] Nic Craith, M. (1988), *An tOileánch Léannta* (Baile Átha Cliath: Clóchomhar).

Islands. What is it about them? Anyway, aren't Continents just that – (big) islands? When is an island not an island? Islands, Franz said, it's all about islands. Can't you see? Franz, like me, is German. After I had started my postdoc research fellowship at Liverpool, I discovered that he had taken up the directorship of something called the European Centre for Traditional and Regional Cultures, located (of all places) in Llangollen, Wales. I wrote to him and we met. It turned out he had lived in Ireland and worked with some of the great names in Irish ethnology and folklore. So we started teaching Irish ethnology together, at the newly-founded Institute of Irish Studies, where I had the honour of holding the only full-time position at the time, as a research fellow. Another of the many hats Franz wore was as the secretary for culture with the Assembly of European Regions, a role in which he worked with someone called Sandy whom he described as 'the president of the Western Isles'. It was one evening after one of our seminars, when we stopped off at my local pub, the Ring-O-Bells in West Kirby, that Franz revealed his conviction. He never explained, just looked at me over his pipe, with curiously raised eyebrows – don't you see, boy, what it is all about? Islands!

****

Leaning on the railing at the edge of Crosby beach, long before Anthony Gormley made it *Another Place*, we scanned the horizon for ships approaching from the haze. You should translate your book into English, I said, bring it to a wider readership. May be, Mairéad said, looking pensive. Some day, yes. Walking along the sea front, talking research, was one of our favourite pastimes. A few years earlier, we had joined Liverpool University 's Institute of Irish Studies as lecturers. Now we were spending many evenings on Crosby promenade bouncing ideas off each other, probing intellectual puzzles, in the process laying the foundations for her third and fourth book. You know, she said one day, I'm all about language. That was indeed what her first two books had been about. But then she went on to write two books on the conflict in Northern Ireland, where language was just one topic among others (and more books on different themes since).

****

Islands. Bloch wrote a lot about them, didn't he? But then, he would, given his focus on Utopia (does Atlantis ring any bells?). This is Ernst I am talking about, not Marc or any other Bloch. A favourite philosopher, certainly in my book, if little known in the Anglophone world. Islands as the location of the future, of our visions and desires, are a common trope in European cultures, and possibly beyond that. There is something edgy about them. Even if we recognise that we all, all of humanity, de facto live on an island of some sort. That is where the concept of offshore islands comes in. Of course, all islands are offshore. Australia is off the shore of New Zealand and Papua New Guinea (and vice-versa), if by some distance. But there seems to be a threshold of size beyond which an island becomes mainland. That threshold is, of course, entirely relative. So, what determines when an island becomes a mainland, and when a mythical location of the future? The only instance where an island seems to have managed being both, so far, is Britain, which is both *the* Mainland *per se* off the coast of which lies the rest of the world, including that nebulous area called Europe, while Britain simultaneously bears the secret abode of the once and future king, who will return and lead his people to a glorious future...[4]

****

Leaning at the bar in the Swiss restaurant on another island, Man, we discussed the local culture with the blow-in chef-owner. We had been visiting for a few days to explore with heritage professionals in the island how their cultural resources might be developed. It had been an interesting introduction to the politics of heritage. Yes, the chef-owner said, heritage is big here. Very big indeed. And very, very personal. We already knew that, having been shown the transcripts of the Irish Folklore Commission's wax cylinder recordings just long enough to register that they had been typed on fairly rough paper that was reaching the end of its useful life. Here was a problem for archivists. At this juncture, Hypertext Markup Language – HTML, as it is known now – was just making inroads in academia and was seen as the salvation for archives like this. Sadly, this was not a language either of us could speak then. They're a peculiar lot, said the chef-owner, the Manx. But they do like *Rösti*.

****

Islands. What does that designation tell us about them? A leisurely trawl of the *Online Etymological Dictionary*[5] reveals the following terms:

> **isolated (adj.)**
> 'standing detached from others of its kind,' ... rendering into English of French *isolé* ..., from Latin *insulatus* 'made into an island,'...

---

4 Rumours that the return of a blonde-mopped king and his grumpy-looking wizard has already happened in 2019 are vastly exaggerated.

5 Available at https://www.etymonline.com/word/ (accessed 19 August 2020). Although not an academic work, this is a diligently compiled reference source, modest inconsistencies of dating notwithstanding, and serves here as a prompt for reflections.

insula (n.)
Latin, literally 'an island' (also, in ancient Rome, 'a block of buildings') ... In anatomical use, ... 'detached or standing out by itself.'

insulate (v.)
... 1530s, 'make into an island,' from Late Latin *insulatus* 'made like an island,' ... Sense of 'place in an isolated situation, cause (someone or something) to be detached from surroundings' .... Electrical/chemical sense of 'block from electricity or heat' (by interposition of a non-conductor) ....

Islands are places apart, on the edge. Interesting nuances are worth noting here, however. An island is not simply detached, but 'from others of its kind', which suggests that its position might well be otherwise, and has been made what it is by what must have been, by implication, a deliberate act. By whom? And why? Moreover, islands are not all necessarily surrounded by water – blocks of flats in ancient Rome, for example. And one might wonder whether the arrival of the verb 'insulate' into English could reflect a growing 'island consciousness' under the Tudors, following England's loss of its territories on the European mainland, a wound that the best efforts of the Houses of Stuart, Oranje, Hannover and Sachsen-Coburg have not been able to heal (nor have those efforts succeeded in bringing the Sceptred Isle any closer to the mainland, either physically or even just ideologically).

But how detached are islands really? Ultimately, all islands are situated on, connected with, a larger land mass. That is true not only of the *insulae* in ancient Rome, which obviously were built on (mostly) dry land, but also of islands that are surrounded tightly by water – whether in a stream, a lake or the ocean – and are (with few atypical exceptions) outcrops of the land underneath the water.[6] Only mythical and artificial islands, like the one Helmut Debus sings about, tend to float freely.

****

Leaning against the churchyard wall on a minor elevation in a small Bohemian town, I surveyed the town- and landscape below. So, I think, that is how a former language island (*Sprachinsel*) looks today, traces of the culture that came with the language still evident in the architecture and other material heritage. This

---

[6] One might ponder why, for example, river islands are 'in' the water in both German and English while lake and high sea islands are (immersed?) 'in' the water in High German and English, but (floating?) 'on' it in Low German. But that is a question for another day.

part of Europe, stretching all the way between the Danube and the Volga, was once full of these islands with their fuzzy edges. German 'salvage ethnology', especially in the late nineteenth and early twentieth century, was obsessed with them – islands of 'German' language and culture. Strikingly, the designation was not applied to other areas of Medieval and Early Modern German settlement in Central and Eastern Europe, such as the Baltic. Is that something to do with power relationships or broader class relations? The Teutonic Knights and Sword Brethren colonising the Baltic after the Crusades, supported by the Hanseatic merchants, were in a different category from the peasants and craftsfolk that floated down the Danube in their wooden boxes or followed the call of 'Mother dear-Tsarina' Katherina to cultivate the expanding Russian frontier. Different also from the Jewish traders that Kazimierz, last of the Piast kings, invited to Poland – their *shtetl* did not merit the romantic accolade *Sprachinsel* either, nor was Yiddish fully acknowledged as a Germanic language until later. Power relations define where and what is or is not an island, when, and for how long.

Mairéad's research on intercultural writers[7] has drawn extensively on interviews with authors from such *Sprachinseln*, as my own subsequent work on expellees from Central and Eastern Europe[8] inevitably has done. These projects marked for both of us the expansion of our research horizon from a primary focus on Ireland. Yet the ultimate archipelago comprising islands both off and on shore continued to loom in the background – the Irish *Gaeltacht*, to which we have kept returning over the years, especially to *Corca Dhuibhne* with *An Blascaod Mór*, the Great Blasket.

Other islands on land, intriguingly named, come to mind: Scotland's Black Isle, or Ireland's Inishowen (island of Owen). Our friend Liam Campbell grew up close to the latter and tells us that the elders at that time had stories about the land- and waterscapes of the area being very different when they were young. Land is solid, while water is not. Yet water erodes land, floods it, turns it into a soggy swamp. Land may temporarily redirect the flow of water, but ultimately, water wins – if ecological need be, with rising sea levels.

****

---

[7] Nic Craith, M. (2012). *Narratives of place, belonging and language: an intercultural perspective* (Basingstoke: Palgrave).

[8] Kockel, U. (2019), 'Commemorating vanished "homelands": displaced Germans and their Heimat Europa.' In: Ullrich Kockel, Cristina Clopot, Baiba Tjarve, and Máiréad Nic Craith (eds): *Heritage Festivals in Europe: Performing Identitites* (London: Routledge), 188-204.

Islands. They have been steady companions on our journeys together, especially the Hebrides and Scotland's Northern Isles – holiday destinations the former, mainly work-related the latter. Scotland's *Gàidhealtachd*, like its Irish counterpart, is an archipelago partly on land, but as I surmised earlier, all islands tend to be on land, so thinking about them in terms of waterscape may be misleading. Or maybe not. Since Liam Campbell's doctoral research on the Foyle catchment, 'waterscapes' have pervaded my own thinking and influenced Mairéad's. It has not escaped us that during that period there has been a synchronous cascading of approaches using 'waterscape', *shoormal*, and other similarly liminal, watery concepts; it feels like one of those instances of an idea whose time has come.

****

Leaning against a rock while catching my breath after climbing the 'Hill of the Back to Ireland' on Iona, I can confirm St Columba's conclusion: that larger island is not visible from here. Neither are Atlantis, Hy Brazil, or any of the other mythical islands of hope. A special island for many people, Iona is often described as 'a thin place', a portal to an elsewhere that is actually right here. On a pilgrimage there, giving thanks for my first Chair, at UWE Bristol, my mind wanders back to another place where I had a similar sense of spiritual liminality: Kloster Andechs, a monastery overlooking the Ammersee lake in Bavaria – an onshore island, yet close to water. The thought drifts off in a rising sea mist as a soaring eagle cries in the sky above.

****

Islands. That's where it all began. With one rugged island off the coast of Kerry, which we finally visited together in 2018, the year of our Silver Wedding: the Great Blasket. And that book was finally written – not just an up-dated, English-language version of the original, as I had once suggested, but a new work, building on its predecessor. Taking the old story to a new level of both description and analysis. That journey has rekindled our shared interest in liminal places, worlds on the edge, towards fresh departures into cultural heritage, ethnography, creative ethnology, and beyond. Islands. That's what it's all about.

… ní bheidh ar léithéidí arís ann …
Tomás Ó Criomthain[9]

---

[9] Transl.: 'The likes of us will not be seen again.' Quoted from Ó Criomthain, T. (1929), *An t-Oileánach* (Baile Átha Cliath: Clólucht an Talbóidigh), p. 265.

'Plural Identities'
Hybridity and the Case of Cornwall

Philip Payton

In 2002, Máiréad Nic Craith published what, for me, is perhaps her most important book: *Plural Identities—Singular Narratives: The Case of Northern Ireland* (Nic Craith 2002). Her purpose in this book was to explore the politics of cultural traditions in Northern Ireland, looking beyond the widely accepted duality of 'Catholic/Nationalist' and 'Protestant/Unionist' to discover a multiple complexity in which apparently oppositional identities might overlap or even share cherished myths and narratives. Moreover, this complexity was dynamic, open to continued negotiation, with shifting as well as blurred boundaries between ostensibly distinct traditions. Religious belief, cultural and linguistic symbolism, and other ethnic signifiers turned out to be less exclusive than conventional wisdom might suggest, so that 'Celtic', 'Ulster-Scots', 'English' and other supposedly distinct categories were best understood as political constructions designed to suit particular historical situations. Ironies, paradoxes and contradictions were commonplace. Thus, for example, Catholic/Nationalists and Protestant/ Unionists could each assert a 'Celtic' identity, albeit with varying narratives, while both groups energetically laid (oppositional) claim to the Ulster folkloric, Cú Chulainn.

In her book, Máiréad attempted to look beyond such competing narratives, asking whether it was possible to posit a non-threatening common heritage in Northern Ireland, so that competing groups might at last admit their commonality, embracing a multicultural hybridity (my word, not hers) as a means constructing a more secure and less adversarial future. For Máiréad, this meant reconceptualising the two traditions model, encouraging people to understand and appreciate the real extent of their shared heritage, and thus the vast repertoire of cultural resources at their disposal. Although I readily shared Máiréad's aspirations, her analysis led me to ponder anew the nature of hybridity, as I understood it, asking questions about the origins of separate 'traditions', the political power relations that often lay behind them, how they might be resolved, and what the consequences (intended or otherwise) of such resolution might be. I wondered, in particular, how the situation Máiréad had described in Northern Ireland might read across to the sometimes equally complex questions of identity and tradition in Cornwall.

Coincidentally, in the same year that Máiréad's book appeared, my *A Vision of Cornwall* (Payton 2002) was published—an intentionally eclectic and deeply personal book that attempted to explain, if not resolve, many of the complexities and contradictions of modern Cornwall. Aware of each other's work, Máiréad and I had compared notes from time to time, but essentially, we worked in parallel, not side by side but independently at a distance. It was a measure of this close but not close academic relationship, that together but separately in our twin examination of 'traditions' we had both alighted upon the work of Robin Cohen, a sociologist, who had suggested that the boundaries between modern identities were often 'fuzzy'. Thus, for example, according to Cohen, the 'shape and edges of British identity are . . . historically changing, often vague and to a degree, malleable—an aspect of the British identity I have called a "fuzzy frontier"' (Cohen 1994: 35).

For Máiréad, the 'fuzzy frontier' was an insight that helped her to unpick the 'conundrum of Britishness' in Northern Irish identities (Nic Craith 2002: 156). It was an approach that, unwittingly, I had echoed in my own discussion of Cohen's 'fuzzy frontiers', where, searching for a useful comparison to assist explanation of the ambiguities of Cornish identity, I had also applied the concept to Northern Ireland. 'There are Ulstermen', I wrote, 'who are proud to don the green shirt to play for Ireland in the 'Six Nations', not least in the hope of defeating England, but who politically are opposed to a united Ireland and support the Union with Great Britain' (Payton 2002: 48). In the same way, I proposed, it might be possible for Cornish people to be simultaneously both 'English' and 'non-English'—a 'fuzzy frontier' that allowed the Cornish to hope that England would beat France at rugby union, at the same time enabling them to imagine that, when Cornwall played Yorkshire or Gloucestershire or whoever in the county championship final at Twickenham, the contest was actually between 'Cornwall and England' (Payton 2002: 47).

The 'fuzzy frontier' of Cornish identity is not, of course, only a contemporary phenomenon. In his classic *The Cornish Miner*, first published in 1927, A.K. Hamilton Jenkin told the perhaps apocryphal but nonetheless telling story of Peggy Combellack, an elderly teacher at a nineteenth-century 'dame school' in Cornwall. It was said that Peggy 'dedn't knaw grammar, but she knawed georgraphe, rithmetic, and the whole of the halfabet' (Hamilton Jenkin 1972: 252). She also knew a thing or two about Cornwall and was concerned that her young charges should share in her knowledge. According to Hamilton Jenkin (1972: 274-5):

'Hes Coornwall a nashion, hes he a Hiland, or hes he a furren country?', an old school-dame, Peggy Combellack, would ask.

'He hedn't no nashion, he hedn't no highlan, nor he hedn't no furren coun-try', the brightest of the scholars on one occasion answered.

'What hes a then?' asked Peggy.

'Why, he's kidged to a furren country from the top hand', was the reply, which was heard by the whole school with much approval, including old Peggy herself.

The anecdote is revealing at several levels. The unselfconscious use of the Cor-nish dialect word 'kidged' ('joined'), readily understood by the other pupils as well as Peggy herself, is emblematic of separate (non-English) identity, being derived from the Cornish-language *kyja*—to join or unite. The 'furren country' to which Cornwall is joined 'from the top hand' (the northeast) is, of course, England. Thus, by logical extension, Cornwall is not actually part of England, and yet while Cornwall might seem 'furren' to outside observers, it is not foreign as far as its own inhabitants are concerned. Cornwall is clearly not an island, as the young scholar recognises, but in asking the question, Peggy is suggesting that Cornwall is *almost* an island, surrounded by sea on three sides and almost cut off by the River Tamar on the fourth, its peninsular life in many ways akin to existence on a small island. Similarly, in making her tentative suggestion that Cornwall might be a nation, we see more than an echo of the assertive sense of Cornish identity noted by contemporary observers. In 1851, for instance, Wilkie Collins had informed his readers that in Cornwall 'a stranger is doubly a stranger . . . where the national feeling is almost entirely merged in the local feeling, where a man speaks of himself as Cornish in much the same way as a Welshman speaks of himself as Welsh' (Collins 1851: 124). Yet our young scholar rejects the idea that Cornwall is actually a nation, a conclusion approved by Peggy and his classmates. England may be a foreign country to which Cornwall is merely (and rather tenuously) joined, but this does not necessarily make Cornwall a nation in its own right.

This conundrum lies at the heart of modern Cornish identity, emblematic of a hybridity where Cornwall and Cornishness may vacillate between different traditions to a degree that observers find puzzling, yet which often poses no conscious contradiction for its practitioners. Here Cohen's 'fuzzy frontiers' are at work. John Vernon, for example, has mused on the 'ambivalent position of Cornwall in the English imagination, and of England in the Cornish imagination— of the Cornish as English but not English', of 'Cornwall's place on the margins of England and Englishness' (Vernon 1998: 153). More recently, Bernard Deacon has offered a more sustained analysis of what he terms Cornwall's 'unsettling' hybridity, describing 'a kind of halfway house between English county and Celtic nation', where Cornwall's Janus-like identity is the result of the colliding influence of 'two traditions' over the past millennium—one 'Celtic', the other 'English'—presenting us today with a 'post-industrial paradox': Cornwall as 'nation, region and county all wrapped up in one' (Deacon 2007: 2 and back cover notes).

To the 'fuzzy frontiers' of 'Cornishness' and 'Englishness' was added that of 'Britishness', sometimes treated as synonym for 'Englishness', and yet at other times a catch-all umbrella term for all the island peoples, so that one could be both 'Cornish and British' while being simultaneously 'Cornish but not English'. Ian MacBride, in his contemplation of this 'British problem', referred not to 'fuzzy frontiers' but to 'ethnic allegiances co-existing in concentric circles, with different patterns existing in different contexts' (politics, religion, sport, and so on), pointing to 'the persistence of such concentric loyalties within the United Kingdom . . . [and thus] the unresolved nature of Britishness itself' (MacBride 1996: 1). This analysis, among other things, explained why an Ulster loyalist might be keen to play rugby for an all-Ireland team, or why a Cornish nationalist might support England against France. 'Fuzzy frontiers', it turned out, could operate at concentric levels, heightening ambiguities while extending the repertoire of possible identity choices for various ethnic or national groups.

Added to this complexity, as Bernard Deacon noted, was Cornwall's putative 'Celtic' identity, on the one hand distancing Cornwall from England and on the other claiming common cause with the other 'Celtic nations' of Scotland, Ireland, Wales, Brittany and the Isle of Man. Robin Cohen recognised the ambiguity inherent in the label 'Celtic', observing that the 'Celtic fringe ... is a familiar but inexplicit internal boundary. For the English, the boundary is marked by irresolution, uncertainty, incongruity, derogation or humour'(Cohen 1994: 12). This was doubly so for Cornwall, where emerging concepts of 'Celticity' in the nineteenth century had to compete with powerful imperial narratives that celebrated 'Britishness' and 'Englishness'. The Cornish (like the Welsh) might take pride in their status as 'Ancient Britons', more British than the English, but fretted sometimes that this placed them beyond the bounds of Imperial fraternity. In 1859, for example, in an echo of old Peggy Combellack's conundrum, the chairman of the West Cornwall Railway could declare that before the opening that year of the Royal Albert Bridge across the Tamar, Cornwall was 'neither within nor without the borders—but now we are part of England (cheers)' (Corin 1998: 20).

The unequal power relationship evident here was made explicit in the short story 'Inconveniences of Being a Cornishman', which appeared in Charles Dickens' periodical *All Year Round* in 1861. As Simon Trezise has noted in his treatment of the story, the fictional narrator, called Pendraggles, 'is made to deny Cornwall's genuine links with other Celtic countries' but at the same time 'finds it impossible to resist the stereotypes thrust upon him by his English companions' (Trezise 2000: 60). A tormented and exasperated Pendraggles complains (Trezise 2000: 60):

> I wonder how often, and in how many varieties of ways, I have had forced upon me that stale, flat insipid joke about the wise men having from the *east*. I wonder how often I have had to declare to well-meaning people, that Cornwall is *not* a queer country, that we do *not* speak the language of Wales and Brittany, that we are only one day's post from London, and that we regularly read the Times.

However, as Trezise also observed, there was on occasion reaction against such denial and stereotyping, as in Charles Kingsley's 1848 novel *Yeast*, where the protagonist, Paul Tregarava, a Cornish gamekeeper whose 'dark curls' mark him as 'Celtic', displays the inner strength of his Cornish Methodist convictions, exhibiting moral, physical and intellectual superiority over his Anglo-Saxon neighbours in southern England: 'They are not like us Cornish: they are a stupid pigheaded generation at best, these south countrymen' (Trezise 2000: 63-4). Such assertions of superiority became commonplace on the international mining frontier, where the 'myth of Cornish Jack', a central plank of the Cornish transnational identity that emerged during the nineteenth century, asserted the innate supremacy of the Cornish miner over competing groups in the workplace (Payton 2020: 6) . Yet in Cornwall itself, especially after the passing of the era of industrial prowess, as the mining industry declined in the latter half of the century, so the derogation experienced by the fictional Pendraggles (evident even in his 'Cornish' name) became ever more commonplace.

In the late twentieth century, Allen E. Ivey investigated the nature of contemporary Cornish identity. He identified in particular the 'Cornish paradox'— the insistence on the part of English individuals and institutions that Cornwall was an integral part of England and yet their simultaneous belief that the Cornish were 'not really English' (Ivey and Payton 1994: 156). As Ivey recognised, this paradox was a powerful mechanism of discrimination, on the one hand allowing Cornish claims for separate status or treatment to be dismissed out of hand (often with more than a hint of ridicule) but on the other encouraging the patronising portrayal of the Cornish as a rustic and passive 'other'. As one of the many recent in-migrants to Cornwall observed in 1985, the Cornish were 'the postman ... the milkman ... the shopkeepers who are ... a joy to pass a few words with to brighten the day' (*West Briton*, 7 January 1985).

Here Cornish hybridity was less about 'fuzzy frontiers', or even the choices offered by 'concentric circles' of loyalty, but was rather the discriminatory product of what appeared to be subtly imposed contradictions. It was not so much the collision of two distinct traditions but instead the dominance of one tradition over the other, a classic 'Catch 22' situation in which the Cornish were denied their individual or collective identity but nonetheless still treated as 'other'. It was a situation that had eased, perhaps, by the early twenty-first century, helped indirectly by the Peace Process in Northern Ireland and the emergence of devolutionary self-government in Scotland and Wales. In February 2000 Tony Blair, the British prime minister, could assert that it 'is intrinsic in the nature of the [UK] Union that we have multiple allegiances; we can comfortably be Scottish and British or Cornish and British or Geordie and British or Pakistani and British' (*The Times,* 12 February 2000). The journalist Andrew Marr, meanwhile, had gone further to muse that we 'can be Cornish-English-European, or Jewish-Welsh, or Yorkshire-Chinese', such was the diversity of possibilities in turn-of-the-millennium multicultural, devolutionary Britain (Marr 1999: 162).

Acceptance of such diversity appeared to underpin the British government's decision in 2002 to add Cornish to the list of indigenous United Kingdom languages that it was prepared to recognise under the Council of Europe's Charter on Regional and Minority Languages (Payton 2017: 310). Similarly, in 2014 'national minority status' was granted to the Cornish by the British government under the aegis of the Council of Europe's Convention for the Protection of National Minorities, ostensibly affording the Cornish the same status and protection in the United Kingdom as the Scots, Welsh and (Northern) Irish (Payton 2017: 328). However, for those who had imagined that such 'official' recognition of separate identity would translate into policy designed to safeguard that identity, there was disappointment in September 2017 when the British government announced proposed Parliamentary boundary changes in which, for the first time, the Tamar border would be ignored, the existing North Cornwall constituency scheduled now to be replaced by a new Bideford, Bude and Launceston constituency, straddling parts of both Cornwall and neighbouring Devon (Payton 2017: 332). Hybridity, with its attendant ambiguities and uncertainties, had re-emerged in this new institutional guise, where an apparently unequivocal recognition of separate identity had almost immediately been compromised by proposed legislation that appeared to sidestep the implications of such status. For

Cornwall, in a very real sense its political 'frontier' was shortly to become very 'fuzzy'.

Hybridity, it seemed, remained deeply ingrained in the Cornish condition, even in the first decades of the twenty-first century as the United Kingdom slowly re-invented itself, with 'Britishness' increasingly open to doubt and dispute. Within this flux, Cornwall and the Cornish remained something of an enigma, not falling neatly or happily into the new categories that were appearing—a battleground perhaps for conflicting visions, constructions, imaginings of Cornishness, Celticity and Britishness, and a problem too for those politicians and planners attempting to manage the constitutional evolution of the UK state. Added to the long-standing ambiguity of Cornish identity, was the perpetuation of Ivey's 'Cornish paradox', not least for the ever-increasing demands of the 'tourist gaze', much of it constructed today through television series such as *Doc Martin* and *Poldark* (Moseley 2018). The 'gaze' required that the Cornish be imagined as 'other'. However, there were limits to this 'otherness', a strong English proprietorial sense of ownership insisting that Cornwall remained an integral part of England. To admit otherwise was fraught with difficulties and danger, not only subverting an imagined England but also prompting the re-writing of Britain's national story. As James Vernon warned: 'Crossing the border to Cornwall threatens to unpick not only English history, but British history as well' (Vernon 1998: 169).

References

Cohen, R. (1994), *Frontiers of Identity: The British and Others* (London: Longmans).

Collins, W. (1851), *Rambles Beyond Railways: Or, Notes in Cornwall Taken A-foot* (London: Richard Bentley).

Corin, J. (1988), *Fishermen's Conflict: The Story of Newlyn* (Newton Abbot: David & Charles).

Deacon, B. (2007), *A Concise History of Cornwall* (Cardiff: University of Wales Press).

Hamilton Jenkin, A. (1972), *The Cornish Miner* (Newton Abbot: David & Charles).

Ivey, A. and P. Payton (1994), 'Towards a Cornish Identity Theory', in: P. Payton (ed.), *Cornish Studies.* Vol. 2 (Exeter: University of Exeter Press), 151-163.

Marr, A. (1999), *The Day Britain Died* (London: Profile).

McBride, I. (1996), 'Ulster and the British Problem', in: R. English and G. Walker (eds), *Unionism in Modern Ireland: New Perspectives on Politics and Culture* (Basingstoke: Macmillan), 1-18.

Moseley, R. (2018), *Picturing Cornwall: Landscape, Region and the Moving Image* (Exeter: University of Exeter Press).

Nic Craith, M. (2002), *Plural Identities –Singular Narratives: The Case of Northern Ireland* (New York: Berghahn)

Payton, P. (2002), *A Vision of Cornwall* (Fowey: Alexander Associates).

Payton P. (2017), *Cornwall: A History* (Exeter: University of Exeter Press).

Payton P. (2019), *The Cornish Overseas: A History of Cornwall's Great Emigration* (Exeter: University of Exeter Press).

Trezise, S, (2000), 'The Celt, the Saxon and the Cornishman: Stereotypes and Counter-Stereotypes of the Victorian Period', in: P. Payton (ed.), *Cornish Studies* Vol. 8 (Exeter: University of Exeter Press), 54-68.

Vernon, J. (1998), 'Border Crossings: Cornwall and the English (imagi)nation', in: C. Cubitt (ed.), *Imagining Nations* (Manchester: Manchester University Press), 153-172.

Newspapers
The Times
West Briton

For Mireya—a Life Span Exile

Colin H. Williams

Justice can always be accomplished
because it has no expiration date.

But in my homeland the struggle goes on.

We were secrets all, sentenced *in absentiam!*

My family, Folch and Serra,
up to our souls in Republican hopes,
The Second Spanish Republic breeched-birth our destinies
and made us refugees in our own homes.

Coup d'état not coup de grace became my end.

Barcelona opened to Franco, half a million less,
Refuged in France notwithstanding the loss.

Mortgaged to democracy and bankrupt through loyalty
The affront of the new state!

I have finally accessed the Justice account
Their lies and tissues, their scams and crabbed reality.

It is time to reconstruct history,
To remap geography,
For time and space to be reframed
And justice to raise its pendant once again.

My family needs its story,
Exoneration and memory
The just for the unjust
The crimes retold, remembered and repulsed
Archives store the bitter crimes
Spew out the buried consciousness
And cleave to a form of narrative which sentences father to death.

Justice can always be accomplished
because it has no expiration date.

The family camped in France,
Lost honour, goods and meaning,
Exodus was never more forgiving.
A baby brother, Toulouse born, alone among the women,
Maria Júlia Serra Peraire, her sister
Monste Serra Peraire, myself
Mireya and my brother Santiago.

Escaping from the pain, the boat was fully laden,
We were forced to flee but could not board the deck.

Ironic kindness took us up, Uncle Francisco's border
patrol safeguarded back to Barça, where deep in hiding
we survived, jailed in Jaume Solé's home.

The menfolk could not hide, shot on sight—they fled to sea
They took the boat *Nyassa*, bound for liberty
At Casablanca's port the men discovered death, but
pressed by fate they flew the Coup, and cheated destiny.
The Nazi war had bled them dry and Franco's dance not run its course.

Emilio, Francisco, Jaume,
Luciana, Jordi and Luci
partners in the macabre-
refugee discounts for a one-way trip
in Columbus' wake and Magellan's new ship.

We took the Marquis de Comillas, ocean bound from Bilbao,
Havana offered respite, but the plane was duty bound,
so Merida became
Mexico City encamped on military ground.

The family then dispersed these many years
populated the New World for its breath
And all the NAFTA lands saw Folch and Serra grow,
in Cuba, América, Canada, Mexico.

But coffin graved the eldest lost in deep Habana soil,
All medics gone to earth to root the change of new birth come to pass.
And I, I struggled home these forty years and licensed twice in name and law
Gained a new identity and fought for space to be

Dr Folch Serra, Catalan by birth and Spanish by edict.

I met the 'others', those who stayed and reaped the gains,
We dined and laughed and reminisced
Forgiven not forgotten, diaspora tales
As *Primera trobada dels Folch* was established as fact.

How would our grandchildren write these lines?
What pictures come to mind?
Representation without justice—just more crimes
So that *Arriba, ABC* and others need to honour the dead and let
La Vanguardia Española fight the good fight.
Falange Española, monarchist and tongue, strictured under torture.

Archivo Guerra y Exilo becomes my solace, my Wikipedia and my faith,
So conscientious were the bureaucrats that truth and dignity were mired in the clay.

Fils et Filles de Republicains Espagnoles et Enfants de l'Exode
operates a sister service for the fallen dead
and those who must remain.
But Companys and Aguirre, as Ravensbrück and Belsen,
are memorialised with governments in exile
for hollowed bones in hallowed graves.

The shadow of the Veteran Captain and Provident Legislator
cooled the Civilized Right and created a bunkered-army
opposed to peaceful change, but duty-bound to guard 'democracy from above'.

The young, the *desencanto* and the *pasotas,*
Ranged against the old dogs in new collars.

Convergence, conciliation and 'taxi parties'
forged the amnesty based on amnesia, but
Ruptura democrática became a negotiated rupture.

Yet 'Democracy without adjectives', a form of
democratic pluralism could not hold the
Pacto del olvido, broken iconoclastic claims, or.
Constitutional divorce and national water
for the fish to swim in autonomous depths.

Where was the statecraft when I fled?
Where the international justice when we bled?
Where the recompense for stolen lives?
Where the record of the exiled tribes?

Scabbard lives in Bezalú, Banyoles,
Vic, Cornella del Tern.

Vox popular vs vox Pujolar
It never ends!

Seny i rauxa so the anthem goes
But no sense and no reason play for us.
It is time to reconstruct our history
To seek the moral victory
To legally exonerate the just
and Honour their Exiled Memory.

It is time, my time, my life, my truth,
My *Pacte de pàtria*!

This poem is inspired by the life and family trajectory of my very close Catalan friend, Dr Mireya Folch Serra, who was born November 14, 1937 in Tarragona. Survivors in the family, having been exiled from Catalonia in February 1939, dispersed as refugees to Mexico, the USA and Cuba. Her grandfather, Dr Jaume Serra i Hunter was born on January 7, 1878 in Manresa and died in Cuernavaca, Mexico on December 7, 1943. A university philosopher, he was the first democratically elected Rector of the University of Barcelona on June 9, 1931 and became the President of the Parliament of Catalonia. Her father, a medical doctor, was condemned to death for crimes he did not commit, never returned to Spain and died in exile in Mexico City, 1978.

Mireya has recently retired as an academic from the University of Western Ontario, Canada. We met many years ago at the European University Institute, Florence, as we were both interested in the geographical context of minority nationalism, particularly the Catalan struggle for independence. It was my great honour to accompany Mireya on field excursions in Catalonia and when she was honoured in her home city of Girona when the local newspaper, *Diari de Girona,* mounted an exhibition recording the experiences of the Catalan disposed and featured Mireya's family as one of its case studies.

Given Máiréad's passion for justice and plight of 'the other', this Catalan trajectory is offered as an individual's experience of dislocation and re-adjustment to a life not of her choosing – sadly, the harsh reality of so many in today's world where dignity and mutual respect are in such short supply.

Second Expedition: Ulster

Golden Eagle over Lough Barra (© Andrea Redmond 2019)

The painting *Golden Eagle over Lough Barra* reflects my interest in the natural flora and fauna of the area. In 2001, Golden Eagles were reintroduced to the area of Lough Barra in County Donegal, Ireland, which now hosts a number of breeding pairs. This painting came from an encounter with an eagle in the summer of 2019, when it was observed fishing wild salmon in the Lough near to my cottage. The metaphor of the eagle soaring (Isaiah 40:31) became a motto for Máiréad during her time at Ulster; it can very well be applied to Máiréad's teaching and support of her students, and thus it is an apt illustration for this book.

Andrea Redmond

Heritage (as) Language
Its Limitations and Limits

William Logan

It is now well recognised that heritage exists in the mind. Heritage significance is an attributed rather than an inherent property of places and things. Heritage is how people as individuals, communities and nations seek to structure the past; in this sense it acts like language. This paper summarises my interest in the similarities and interconnections between heritage and language—heritage language, heritage as language and the limitations and limits facing heritage as the result of language failings. This interest grew out of working with Máiréad Nic Craith, initially through the Academy of Irish Cultural Heritages in Derry/Londonderry, subsequently at my university in Melbourne where, in December 2002 she gave a brilliant address on cultural citizenship, and through reading some of her many publications on linguistic heritage, language rights, power and politics.

Language

Linguists argue that no language is 'better' than another in that they all perform their purpose of allowing people to communicate about themselves and the world around them. There are, however, prestigious and less prestigious language forms–Queen's English and Cockney, Geordie or Scouse in England, the middle-class English found in Australian cities and the 'ocker' forms of provincial areas and the Outback. So, too, with heritage: historic places, artefacts and documents, oral traditions and expressions, performing arts, social practices, knowledge and crafts—all types of heritage expressing notions of the past and modern-day connections with it. But a similar kind of differentiation has occurred in the realm of heritage, with palaces, cathedrals and archaeological sites often being more highly regarded than humbler historic villages and vernacular buildings, and classical music and dance termed 'high art' in contrast to indigenous and folk versions.

While the conception of heritage has widened since the 1980s, there is nevertheless a World/national/local hierarchy in the way heritage management operates globally. Some heritage sites are inscribed as 'World Heritage' under the UNESCO World Heritage Convention 1972. Other heritage elements are selected as representative of the intangible cultural heritage of humanity and registered under UNESCO's Intangible Cultural Heritage Convention 2003. Some documents are recognised through the UNESCO's Memory of the World (MOW) program. Only heritage artefacts do not have a UNESCO normative instrument, although the International Council on Museums (ICOM) was for many years housed within UNESCO Paris headquarters.

To understand why some heritage items are inscribed on heritage registers and others are not it is necessary to recognise that the creation of 'heritage' is the result of a process that is essentially political in the sense that it is based on the distribution of decision-making power in society. Places are nominated to official lists because they reflect the narrative endorsed by the authorities responsible for them, and that, in turn, almost always conforms to the vision of the society held by the political regime in power and its supporters. In authoritarian states, the ideology of the regime in power determines the official heritage and other views of the past are sidelined or hidden. Ideological renditions continue to provide a basis for wars, ethnic cleansing and genocide within and between states. Myanmar is an outrageous case in point (Logan 2018a), but cultural inequalities and denial of human rights exist in many other countries, including some, like China, that seek to hide such injustices from the world, claiming that these are internal matters.

Even in the more democratic states like the United Kingdom and Australia, however, contradictory versions of the past underpin so-called 'culture wars' or 'history wars'. Máiréad Nic Craith demonstrates this in her studies of culture, identity politics and cultural citizenship in Northern Ireland (Nic Craith 2014). Her book on the subject contrasts the experiences of Protestant Unionists with those of Catholic Nationalists, the former having a longstanding commitment to a form of equal citizenship in which each person has individual rights whereas the latter have been more concerned with obtaining political recognition of their cultural distinctiveness and communal structure. The culture wars in Australia have many similarities, with the argument of the Indigenous Australian minority evolving into the *Uluru Statement from the Heart* (2017) that argues that reconciliation with the dominant settler population requires the establishment of a 'First Nations Voice' enshrined in the Australian Constitution. In both Northern Ireland and Australia, the struggle continues in changing political circumstances—Brexit in the former case and the unexpected re-election of a conservative national government in the latter.

Nevertheless, in Australia, the debate has moved on since the period under the earlier conservative government of Prime Minister John Howard (1996-2007) when scorn was directed at academics writing about the decimation of the Aboriginal and Torres Strait Island peoples by a combination of white people's guns, diseases, arrogance and apathy. Howard called this 'black arm band history' and took steps to shape the national narrative the way he and his party wanted through interventions in educational curriculum development and museum curation (Logan 2019: 155). In the face of such long-running insensitivity, Indigenous Australians have insisted on taking primary responsibility for defining their own heritage and many heritage items are now well protected under Indigenous leadership. This culminated in 2019 when Budj Bim in south-western Victoria was inscribed on the World Heritage List, the first of Australia's 20 properties to have been recognised solely for its Aboriginal values following a campaign led from the outset by the local Indigenous people themselves.

Australia ICOMOS has accepted the Indigenous Australians' right to tell their story since 2001 (Australia ICOMOS 2001). UNESCO has since 2003 argued that it is imperative that the values and practices of the local communities, together with traditional management systems, are fully understood, respected, encouraged in management plans if the heritage resources are to be sustained into the future. After a long struggle to gain a direct indigenous voice in World Heritage Committee deliberations (see Logan 2013), the International Indigenous Peoples' Forum on World Heritage (IIPFWH) was launched at the World Heritage Committee 42nd Session in 2018.

This heritage trajectory is in line with the move in human right perspectives, notably the shift from first and second to third generation human rights. The first two perspectives, with their emphasis on the individual were often criticised as Western in origin and character, whereas third generation collective cultural rights have been closely associated with Indigenous peoples, commonly living as minorities within European settler societies in the New World (Logan 2016: 180). Some international law scholars and human rights activists think that the balance has shifted too far toward collective rights, arguing that it has become increasingly difficult for an individual or nuclear family to retain their essential identity and dignity while rejecting elements of the collective culture (Logan 2014: 162).

This concern is highlighted in Australia by Stan Grant, a self-identified Indigenous Australian, award-winning journalist and influential commentator on Indigenous issues, who argues in his book *On Identity* that 'identity does not liberate; it binds' (Grant 2019: 43). Part of his powerful little book deals with Ireland but it is mostly about the continuing insistence in Australia to separate people into types. He particularly rails against the requirement in censuses and other bureaucratic programs to tick a box if you are Aboriginal or Torres Strait Islander (p. 22): 'One box that, I'm expected to believe, holds all that I am. In that box all the blurred lines of my confounding, contradictory, complicated family history are dissolved into one definitive statement of being. What life can be reduced to this?' By ticking the Indigenous box Grant is forced to deny, betray his white grandmother. 'In that box I am being asked to choose when I would rather embrace it all' (Grant 2019: 23).

Limitations

Just as language performance is not set in concrete, the conception and language of heritage also evolve over time. In today's more inclusive approach, attention is given to vernacular buildings, indigenous and minority cultures, cultural landscapes and historic urban landscapes. Heritage identification and management can be bottom up (led by the heritage owner) or top down (led by the heritage expert), or both together. The question that arises from all this, however, is whether there is too much heritage today. Much is valued, protected and used for a variety of reasons that have little to do with the heritage itself. More fundamentally, if it is understood that most historic places, practices and artefacts have meaning to some people, underlying their cultural identity, then heritage encompasses so much that the concept is perhaps in danger of losing its own meaning. It may be that the notion of a hierarchy of significance is still needed to avert this danger, provided this is a hierarchy based on the number of people for whom a place or practice is meaningful and not based on Western (Eurocentric) prejudices, or money, caste and class.

Regrettably there is no single forum in which such issues can be debated and conclusions drawn. UNESCO deals with most forms of heritage but its programs are separate, coming under different Conventions or proclamations. While it has moved strongly into indigenous heritage it has a rival in the Geneva-based World Intellectual Property Organization (WIPO) which also deals with traditional knowledge and traditional cultural expressions but works mainly through legal regimes aimed at protecting intellectual property (IP). Even within academia there are differences between scholars according to their discipline in the way they use the concepts and associated terminology. Archaeologists, historians, geographers and political scientists tend to refer to 'cultural heritage', for instance, whereas anthropologists, economists and law scholars see it as 'cultural property'. In her 2004 paper 'Culture and Citizenship in Europe: Questions for Anthropologists', Máiréad Nic Craith showed disciplinary divergence, too, with anthropologists focussing on culture rather than citizenship and the sociologists neglecting the cultural dimension of citizenship.

This diversity is perhaps of no consequence in itself, merely part of the world's rich linguistic tapestry (Logan 2018b: 22). There is a problem, however, when the concepts and terms making up the 'language of heritage' are differently understood and used from one institution to another, one discipline to another and one culture to another. Misunderstandings lead to inefficiencies in communication about heritage between those working in the field, in management teams and in policy-making bureaucracies. In trying to implement international models of best heritage conservation practice, national and municipal governments, community groups and heritage practitioners struggle to keep up with the international discourse and its confusing use of key concepts and terminology.

Limits

Over the last year, I have been working with the Korean National Commission for UNESCO (KNCU) on a project in which the role of language is again central—here the language used in interpreting heritage places, specifically World Heritage properties. Albeit in a different part of the world and in a more applied vein, the KNCU project starts like Máiréad's work with the acceptance that we do not all agree on what makes a historic place or artefact or an intangible cultural element significant. This is particularly true where the heritage reflects bitter conflicts and associated atrocities in the past and where tensions continue to be felt today. Memories of an international or civil conflict do not end with the ceasefire. They continue on and are an important element of the intangible cultural heritage that we must now consider in World Heritage nomination and management practices. It becomes critical to find the right language to build bridges to peace as UNESCO's Constitution requires rather than exacerbating tensions.

In the World Heritage context there have been a number of cases where interpretation strategies adopted by nominating States Parties to the Convention have not reduced tensions but, just the opposite, have inflamed tensions. Some of the most difficult cases have occurred in East Asia and represent unfinished business from conflicts in the first half of twentieth century. The 'Sites of Japan's Meiji Industrial Revolution: Iron and Steel, Shipbuilding and Coal Mining' inscribed 2015 is a case in point. Inclusion of the Hashima industrial ruins, off the coast of Nagasaki, was particularly controversial because of the Republic of Korea's claim that forced Korean labour had been used. An agreement was brokered under which interpretation for visitors at the Hashima site would include reference to Korea's claim.

Other cases of problematic attempts to interpret sites of conflict come to mind such as Jerusalem, and Preah Vihear in Cambodia. Such difficulties, moreover, do not only apply to the protection of heritage places. In October 2015, UNESCO listed a set of Chinese documents relating to the 1937 Nanjing Massacre on the Memory of the World register. Japan withheld its annual dues of around USD30 million. This forced the UNESCO Executive Board in October 2017 to adopt a resolution calling on UNESCO to try to avoid aggravating political tensions among Member States in line with its fundamental aim of working towards mutual understanding. A new procedure was established to take into account the views of all concerned nations when historical and political sensitivities are involved.

How can the tensions around the inscription and interpretation of such sites be resolved? Sensibly, a spate of nominations relating to recent war sites led to a temporary halt in their processing until the relevant issues could be considered.[1] The World Heritage Committee at its 2018 meeting in Manama, Bahrain, agreed that a 'comprehensive reflection' should take place and that at its 2020 session a decision would be taken on 'whether and how sites associated with recent conflicts and other negative and divisive memories might relate to the purpose and scope of the World Heritage Convention' (Decision 42 COM 8B.24). This formalised the proposal made by the Committee's Advisory Body on cultural heritage matters, ICOMOS, in its April 2018 discussion paper entitled *Evaluations of World Heritage Nominations related to Sites Associated with Recent Conflicts* (ICOMOS 2018) which had canvassed the challenges of evaluating such sites.

What UNESCO policies can we fall back on? Strictly speaking, UNESCO has until recently had very few 'policies' in the cultural heritage area. The World Heritage Convention is implemented through a set of *Operational Guidelines* (UNESCO 2017). There is a language problem here in that 'guidelines' merely guide. By contrast, like its conventions, UNESCO's policies are mandatory and apply to all Member States. In 2015, however, the United Nations adopted a post-2015 sustainable development agenda that incorporated, among other things, the need for action on the peace and reconciliation front. As a member of the UN family of institutions, UNESCO recognised that it had a responsibility to promote this agenda and to ensure that all of its programs adhered to sustainable development principles. A *Policy for the Integration of a Sustainable Development Perspective into the Processes of the World Heritage Convention* (hereafter WH&SD policy) was drafted and approved by UNESCO's General Assembly in November 2015 (Larsen and Logan 2018).

---

[1]   Some of this increase was related to the centenary of World War 1, such as the 'Funerary and Memorial Sites of the First World War (Western Front)' nominated by Belgium and France in 2018. The Tentative Lists, however, held another eight places relating to more recent conflicts sites, including the Gelibolu/Gallipoli battle zones from the World War 1, the Normandy beach sites where allied troops landed in World War 2, genocide sites in Rwanda, a torture and extermination camp in Argentina and a Russian battlefield memorial.

This policy and several ICOMOS documents[2] are starting to articulate a number of principles for use in interpreting World Heritage and other cultural heritage sites in ways that help reduce tensions in post-conflict situations. The policy, for instance, calls for States Parties to the World Heritage Convention to use inclusive approaches promoting the engagement of multiple stakeholders. States Parties should consider Tentative List additions and nominations for World Heritage listing that 'have the potential to generate fruitful dialogues between States Parties and different cultural communities...' (para 30iii) and they should adopt cross-culturally sensitive approaches to the interpretation of World Heritage properties...' (para 30iv). In order to build bridges to peace in the minds of men it is essential to overcome suspicion, fear and hostility towards those different from ourselves. Site interpretation needs to explain these differences in terms that visitors can understand and, as visitors are of various types (adults with specialist education relevant to the site, adults with more general background knowledge, and children with more limited vocabulary, etc.), interpretation needs to take many forms and not simply rely on interpretative panels bearing technical descriptions. More usually needs to be told than just the narrative about the conflict that is officially approved by the regime in power.

In fact, it is hard to find good examples of the interpretation of sites related to recent, or even ancient, conflicts, which highlights the many difficulties hindering the reconciliation between former enemies. Chief among these difficulties are that international, national and local community contexts are constantly shifting and that national interest nearly always dominates interpretation strategies. In some cases, simply not enough time has elapsed since open conflict ended for reconciliation to be possible. I used to think that the best examples worldwide were the Culloden and Tower Museum in Derry/Londonderry. In its main hall, Culloden organises the story as seen by each of the antagonists—English and Scottish—opposite each other, with a more neutral view down the middle. At the Tower Museum, the Protestant Irish story faces the Catholic Irish. In both cases, the aim is to be inclusive and to encourage visitors to understand both histories. Whether, in fact, this physical arrangement simply enables visitors to follow their prejudiced pathway remains to be tested. Is it a case of being able to draw the horse to water but it refusing to drink? Máiréad's study of the development of a bi-cultural infrastructure in Northern Ireland in spheres such

---

[2] *Interpretation of Sites of Memory* (International Coalition of Sites of Conscience 2018); *ICOMOS Charter for the Interpretation and Presentation of Cultural Heritage Sites* (ICOMOS 2008); *Vimy Declaration for the Conservation of Battlefield Terrain (Draft)* (ICOMOS 2009); *ICOFORT Charter on Fortifications and Related Heritage: Guidelines for Protection, Conservation and Interpretation (Draft)* (ICOMOS 2019).

as language, media and museums, raises the same concern: have these developments dissipated difference or worked to essentialise cultural communities (Nic Craith 2004)?

With regard to the management of World Heritage sites, what else might UNESCO do? The *Operational Guidelines* are being revised to incorporate the WH&SD policy. The World Heritage Committee might be persuaded to require in new nomination dossiers an Interpretation Plan that outlines the interpretation strategy to be used, showing the significance of the heritage site in an international context and, where relevant, telling the various sides of the story and highlighting the message of reconciliation and peace. It needs to be emphasised, however, that the success of these efforts ultimately depends on UNESCO's Member States and, in relation to World Heritage, the States Parties to the World Heritage Convention. It is here that real limits are imposed on the implementation of UNESCO's objective of building bridges to peace: it can monitor, but it has little power to enforce. It is, after all, an intergovernmental organisation—an IGO—made up of Member States that jealously guard their independence and put their national interest first. The system depends on goodwill and cooperation and UNESCO's chief mode of operation is to inspire: to find the language to challenge and encourage its Member States to embrace peace and sustainable development, to engage in intercultural dialogue, to maintain the culture of their minorities and to avoid reviving or exacerbating tensions.

So far, such a language has not been found. The KNCU project demonstrates yet again that politics overrides heritage—that politicians make use of heritage when it suits them and often prevent heritage from being interpreted in ways that encourage peace. In East Asia, it is still too soon to expect the various, previously warring States Parties to achieve reconciliation. Indeed, the past 12 months has seen considerable deterioration of the situation. The erection in 2011 of a statue of Korean comfort woman opposite the Japanese embassy in Seoul was deliberately provocative and Japan has sought to have it removed. It has been subject to attacks and is now guarded 24-hours a day by Korean volunteers. This keeps wartime bitterness in the public consciousness rather than letting memories of the war fade away. It is also part of wider Korea-Japan disputation over territorial boundaries and trade, with a tit-for-tat cancelling of each other's favoured trading nation status. Similar conflicts continue to simmer between Japan and China. Meanwhile, China insists that the fate of the Tibetans and Uyghurs and their cultures is an internal matter for Beijing to control through mass internment and re-education. No interference from international human rights and heritage bodies is to be countenanced.

The task of using heritage as a means of achieving peace and security in the world is, thus, clearly fraught with enormous difficulties. As detailed elsewhere (Logan 2018c), I am frankly pessimistic about the ability of UNESCO's heritage programs to achieve either reconciliation between former enemies or peace and security for minority cultures under authoritarian regimes. This said, however, there have been some important advances in the heritage field, especially in relation to managing indigenous heritage, and perhaps the WH&SD policy, when fully implemented, will provide a new set of more useful directives. The task of seeking to foster peace and reconciliation through heritage work remains an ethical professional objective that is still worth supporting.

References

Australia ICOMOS (2001), *Statement on Indigenous Cultural Heritage*. Available at: https://australia.icomos.org/wp-content/uploads/Australia-ICOMOS-Statement-on-Indigenous-Cultural-Heritage.pdf (accessed 30 August 2019),

Funerary and Memorial sites of the First World War (Western Front) (Belgium, France). Paris: UNESCO. Available at: https://whc.unesco.org/en/decisions/7137/ (accessed 30 August 2019).

Grant, S. (2019), *On Identity* (Melbourne: Melbourne University Press).

ICOMOS (2008), *ICOMOS Charter for the Interpretation and Presentation of Cultural Heritage Sites*. Available at: https://www.icomos.org/charters/interpretation_e.pdf (accessed 29 August 2019).

ICOMOS (2009), *Vimy Declaration for the Conservation of Battlefield Terrain* (ICOFORT Draft). Available at: http://www.veterans.gc.ca/eng/remembrance/memorials/overseas/first-world-war/france/vimy/declaration (accessed 29 August 2019).

ICOMOS (2018), *Evaluations of World Heritage Nominations related to Sites Associated with memories of Recent Conflicts. ICOMOS Discussion Paper*. Available at: https://www.icomos.org/images/DOCUMENTS/World_Heritage/ICOMOS_Discussion_paper_Sites_associated_with_Memories_of_Recent_Conflicts.pdf (accessed 29 August 2019).

ICOMOS (2019), *ICOFORT Charter on Fortifications and Related Heritage: Guidelines for Protection, Conservation and Interpretation (Draft)*. Paris: ICOMOS.

International Coalition of Sites of Conscience (2018), *Interpretation of Sites of Memory*. Available at: https://whc.unesco.org/en/activities/933/ (accessed 30 August 2019).

Larsen, P. and W. Logan eds (2018), *World Heritage and Sustainable Development: New Directions in World Heritage Management* (London: Routledge).

Logan, W. (2013), 'Australia, Indigenous Peoples and World Heritage from Ka-
    kadu to Cape York: State Party Behaviour under the World Heritage Con-
    vention', *Journal of Social Archaeology* 13: 153-76.
Logan, W. (2014), 'Heritage rights: avoidance and reinforcement', *Heritage and
    Society* 7: 156-69.
Logan, W. (2016), 'Collective rights in Asia: Recognition and Enforcement', in A.
    Jakubowski (ed.), *Cultural Rights as Collective Rights: An International Law
    Perspective* (Leiden: Brill Nijhoff), 180-203.
Logan, W. (2018a), 'Ethnicity, Heritage, Human Rights and Governance in the
    Union of Myanmar', in J. Rodenberg and P. Wagenaar (eds), *Cultural Con-
    testation: Heritage, Identity and the Role of Government* (New York: Pal-
    grave Macmillan), 37-60.
Logan, W. (2018b), 'UNESCO Heritage-speak: Words, Syntax and Rhetoric', in C.
    Antons and W. Logan (eds), *Intellectual Property, Cultural Property and In-
    tangible Cultural Heritage* (London: Routledge), 21-49.
Logan, W. (2018c), 'Heritage, Sustainable Development and the achievement
    of peace and security in our world: ambitions and constraints', in P. Larsen
    and W. Logan (eds), *World Heritage and Sustainable Development: New Di-
    rections in World Heritage Management* (London: Routledge), 134-52.
Logan, W. (2019), 'Blowing hot and cold: Culture-related activities in the de-
    ployment of Australian soft power in Asia', in S. Labadi (ed.), *The Cultural
    Turn in International Aid: Impacts and Challenges for Heritage and the Crea-
    tive Industries* (London: Routledge), 152-170.
National Constitutional Convention (2017), *Uluru Statement from the Heart*.
    Available at: https://www.referendumcouncil.org.au/sites/default/files/
    017-05/Uluru_Statement_From_The_Heart_0.PDF (accessed 29 August
    2019).
Nic Craith, M. (2004), 'Culture and Citizenship in Europe: Questions for Anthro-
    pologists', *Social Anthropology* 12: 289-300.
Nic Craith, M. (2014), *Culture and Identity Politics in Northern Ireland* (Basing-
    stoke: Palgrave Macmillan).
UNESCO (2015), *Policy for the Integration of a Sustainable Development Per-
    spective into the Processes of the World Heritage Convention* (online). Avail-
    able at: http://whc.unesco.org/en/sustainabledevelopment/.(accessed 30
    August 2019).
UNESCO (2017), *Operational Guidelines for the Implementation of the World
    Heritage Convention*. Paris: UNESCO. Available at: https://whc.unesco.org/
    en/guidelines/_(accessed 30 August 2019).
UNESCO (2018), *Decision: 42 COM 8B.24*. World Heritage Committee.

Post-Brexit Identity in Northern Ireland

Pól Ó Dochartaigh

In discussion many years ago with a colleague and friend from Bangor, Co. Down, a liberal unionist of Northern Irish and Scottish descent, I casually referenced the well-known origins of the Irish tricolour as representing the orange and green traditions, Protestant and Catholic, Unionist and Nationalist, cemented together by the white band of peace. He immediately retorted: 'Orange doesn't represent me and never has. I am not an Orangeman!' It was a challenge to the usual simplistic reductionism of identities in Northern Ireland.

The Good Friday Agreement (GFA) of 1998 embedded binary notions of identity in an international treaty and in the devolved structures that were created on the back of that treaty. One might rightly wish to tread carefully in criticising that treaty, given that it provided a till now comparatively peaceful way forward after thirty years of murderous conflict, but it was, nevertheless, a treaty full of creative ambiguity. As Fintan O'Toole (2018) put it: 'The agreement tries to replace either/or with both/and,' and in so doing, it sought to be inclusive rather than exclusionary. That in itself is a noble principle for which its chief author, John Hume of the SDLP, and his collaborators in the Ulster Unionist Party under David Trimble, have subsequently paid a heavy political price. Unionists gained recognition, not least from the Irish government, which, following a referendum, removed the constitutional claim to the North, that the North's status as a part of the UK could only be changed by majority consent in the North, as part of a two-stage process that would require consent in the South also for unification. Nationalists in the North were able, because of the status of both states as members of the EU customs union, to behave in their daily lives as if the border was no more than a minor irritant involving some slightly different road signs.

Yet ambiguity can only hold for so long. Mandatory coalition, for example, sits uneasily in a true democracy, and the institutions have collapsed on several occasions in the twenty-two years since 1998. Conflicting wishes for the Agreement itself are also a cause of continued tension. Unionists and Loyalists generally have wished to see the agreement as an end point in terms of the constitutional status of Northern Ireland, the minor renegotiations of 2006 at St Andrews and early 2020 in Belfast notwithstanding. Nationalists and Republicans, by contrast, have regarded it as a staging post or, to use a historically loaded term, a stepping-stone. Therein lies a fundamental ambiguity that was brought out very publicly by the American-British writer and political activist Bonnie Greer on BBC's *Question Time* on 3 October 2019 in the context of a Brexit discussion of the so-called 'backstop', where she described the GFA as a 'truce' that came about 'because the United States of America and the EU sat down with this country [the UK] to make it happen' (Anon. 2019). Most commentators have spoken of the 'peace' achieved under the 1998 agreement, but Greer's use of the term 'truce', in the context of a debate about the implications of Brexit for Northern Ireland, captured the fragility and potential ephemerality of that arrangement. Moreover, her referencing of the EU points to what is arguably the biggest threat to date to the GFA, namely, the reinstitution of customs and financial checks between the UK and the EU.

When the Brexit debate was carried on over a brief few months in the spring and early summer of 2016 in the UK, Ireland barely featured. Some Remainers referenced what they saw as a potential threat to the GFA in Brexit, while Leavers, if they replied to this at all, consistently dismissed the argument. Yet the discussions since then have exposed fault lines that arise because the Brexit that the UK seems intent on choosing, which involves customs borders between the UK and the EU, requires the imposition of border checks, the absence of which the GFA was predicated upon. The constitutional integrity of the UK is threatened on two fronts, Scotland and Northern Ireland, and at this point, early 2020, it is impossible to predict where it will lead.

A threat to the continued existence of the UK is also a threat to the continuance of British identity, something that affects the entire UK and not just Northern Ireland. Moreover, the threat to that identity has been subject to some basic misunderstandings. In the long run-up to the 2014 referendum on independence for Scotland, the then leader of the British Labour Party, Ed Miliband, warned the Scots that 'if they leave the UK they won't be British any more' (Anon. 2012). The psychology of that argument could fill many books, but at the time, I wrote in response that Miliband was surely missing the point that, in the event of the break-up of the UK, the English would not be British either, because 'claiming to be British with no Scots is a bit like claiming to be married with no wife' (Ó Dochartaigh 2012).

When Britishness as a modern concept achieved new force in sixteenth-century England, a primary motivation was the fanciful perception that both Scotland and England 'derived from a united, pre-Roman British monarchy'; the argument was given an evangelical twist in the 1540s under Henry VIII and Edward VI, and the Scots initially resisted it (Ryrie 2006: 82-3). Even with the formalisation of Britain as a political term when, in 1604, King James VI and I styled himself 'King of Great Britain', the title was rejected by both the English and Scottish parliaments (Croft 2003). It was not until 1707 that a 'Kingdom of Great Britain' was created following the union of the parliaments and a century of familiarising the terms 'Great Britain' and 'Britishness', and it was very much based on a shared Protestant identity, theological and organisational differences between Calvinism and Anglicanism notwithstanding. Catholics in England were sceptical of this new-found Britishness until well into the seventeenth century, which from an Irish perspective is well after the Plantation of Ulster (see Highley 2002). Linda Colley has gone further and argued that British identity was forged in war and empire-building in competition with the Catholic powers of Europe, and that 'Britain could be imagined as the Protestant Israel, God's very own chosen island' (Colley 2014: 18). A core part of this, according to Niamh Dillon (2019: 215), was a 'belief in the rational superiority of Protestantism over other religions, and conviction in the racial superiority of British people over those they colonised'.

All of this could by now have become a matter of supreme indifference to Ireland were it not for the events of the early twentieth century that gave the United Kingdom new, reduced contours and led to a partitioning of Ireland, not least because of the existence of competing identities in what became Northern Ireland.[1] The GFA was, dare I say it, an honest attempt to reach an accommodation between those identities, but the challenges that now emerge in the wake of Brexit have resulted in no small measure from the failure of both sovereign governments to live up to consequences of that treaty. Identity, and insecurity about identity, are at the core of these challenges.

In her book *Plural Identities—Singular Narratives*, Mairéad Nic Craith (2002) studied the evolution of identity in the contested space that is Northern Ireland. Her very wide-ranging points were well-made, considered, and, when they looked forward, reflected the optimism of the first few years after the signing of the GFA. The word Brexit had not yet been invented, to indicate just one of the many changes that have happened either more rapidly than could be anticipated or, indeed, entirely unexpectedly. The Republic of Ireland has moved much further from its foundational Catholicism than anyone could have foreseen just twenty years ago to become a society in which the role of the Catholic

---

[1]   The idea that Ulster Protestants are all descended from settlers from England and Scotland is a myth, as the widespread presence of Gaelic Irish surnames among their number might indicate. Some are native Irish converts from the earliest years of the Plantation of Ulster. The presence of multiple such names in *The Session Book of Templepatrick Presbyterian Church, 1646-1743*, held by the Public Record Office of Northern Ireland in Belfast, is just one early illustration of this.

Church has been marginalised, and there are echoes, albeit at a slower pace, of that change among the Catholic community in Northern Ireland, too.

Despite the success of the GFA, failures may be noted that have nothing to do with Brexit. The UK, for example, has failed to incorporate the identity provisions of the GFA into its nationality laws, and has gone to court to assert that its 1981 Nationality Act trumps the GFA, so that anyone born in Northern Ireland is a British citizen, despite the assurance in the GFA that anyone in Northern Ireland can identify as 'Irish or British, or both'.[2]

For its part, the Republic has failed to reflect in its language the fact that by giving up its claim to the whole of the island, the state forfeited the right to simply call itself 'Ireland'. One reads on an almost daily basis the nonsensical expression 'Ireland and Northern Ireland', which semantically includes the six counties of Northern Ireland twice but legally implies that when you cross the border going North you leave Ireland. This is exclusionary towards those in the North who consider themselves to be Irish. Among the logical consequences, if we accept the phrasing, would be that all-Ireland teams in rugby, hockey, and other sports ought to be renamed 'Ireland and Northern Ireland'.

In her final chapter in which she searches for a 'common ground' in the North, Máiréad considers common Europeanness, regional identity, an 'Ulster' identity and suggests that the development of a 'Northern Irish identity' might prove attractive (Nic Craith 2002: 194f.). We should not, in the wake of the 2016 referendum, dismiss the common Europeanness, for many in the Unionist community quite clearly consider themselves to be European and are as resentful as any Northern nationalist of Brexit. Indeed, as the figures below show, Northern Irish Protestants, alongside the Scots, identify somewhat more strongly as European than either the English or the Welsh. It also needs to be said, repeatedly,

---

2   For the relevant commitment, see 'Constitutional Issues, clause 1.vi' of the text of the GFA, at: https://www.dfa.ie/media/dfa/alldfawebsitemedia/ourrolesandpolicies/northernireland/good- friday-agreement.pdf (accessed 15 January 2020).
For the 1981 British Nationality Act, which in Part 1, clause 1(1) confers citizenship on anyone born in the UK to a parent who is British or settled in the UK, see http://www.legislation.gov.uk/ukpga/1981/61/pdfs/ukpga_19810061_en.pdf (accessed 15 January 2020). The court case is that of a Derry woman, Emma De Souza, who is seeking settled in the UK status for her American husband based on his marriage to an Irish citizen in Northern Ireland. The UK government has insisted that in order to do this, she must first renounce her British citizenship. See Patrick Smyth, 'Derry woman puts her finger on a bizarre Brexit anomaly', *Irish Times*, 16 Feb 2019, at: https://www.irishtimes.com/news/ireland/irish-news/derry-woman-puts-her-finger-on-a-bizarre-brexit-anomaly-1.3795544 (accessed 15 January 2020).

that the EU is not Europe, even if it is the clearest political manifestation of Europeanness. We are all of us Europeans, the insular habit of referring to the mainland as 'Europe' notwithstanding.

Máiréad rightly indicated that an 'Ulster' identity is a loaded one that is unlikely to gain cross-community acceptance. For most Northern nationalists, 'Ulster' is a term associated primarily with three apparently paradoxical things: the GAA, the Irish language, and Unionism. It comes as a surprise to many Unionists that there is a strong Ulster Irish dialect and loyalty to it among Northern Nationalists that sets them slightly apart from the rest of Ireland, and there is also a fiercely contested provincial championship in Gaelic Football in Ulster that is generally regarded as the most competitive of the four provinces. But that is a different Ulster, a nine-county province that disregards the political border between the North and the Republic. For most Unionists, 'Ulster' is synonymous with 'Northern Ireland', and in the political sphere it is an essentially Unionist term.[3] In that respect, Máiréad was correct to suggest that it is unlikely to gain broad support.

The regional identity that could be cultivated, and which in opinion polls went through a period of increased popularity, especially among young people, she suggested, is 'Northern Irish', and that identity has certainly shown sporadic increases in popularity in opinion polls. Yet even that apparently neutral and potentially ambiguous term, because someone who is Northern Irish can regard this as a subset of either Irishness or Britishness, is, in fact, not genuinely cross-community. In fact, as the tables below indicate, no term is at this level.

The most comprehensive post-Brexit opinion poll on identity, carried out across the UK in spring 2018 by LucidTalk in NI and YouGov in GB on behalf of the BBC, included a question in which respondents could offer multiple senses of identity, ranging from town, county, region, through various countries up to Europeanness. We will now focus on the four options in Table 1 below, which relates to Northern Ireland only. A number of things stand out in this survey. One is that, of the four main identities, Irish is the most popular and British the least. The second point is that Irish identity scores significantly higher than average among the younger age group (18-44) and Britishness significantly lower. A third point is perhaps slightly surprising: Northern Irish rather than British is the most popular option among over-45s. Also surprising, when set beside earlier opinion polls, is that 'Northern Irish' scores lower in the 18-44 age group

---

[3]   Occasional exceptions to this rule, such as the Republican splinter organisation *Saor Uladh* (Free Ulster), founded in east Tyrone in the early 1950s, merely serve to reinforce the point by the fact that they are relatively unknown and ephemeral.

than among over 45s. Each of the four identities scores more than half of the population in the 45+ age group, while in the 18-44 age group only 'British' fails to do so. Summarising the findings, it can be said that younger people and Catholics in Northern Ireland identify as more Irish and European than the average, while older people and Protestants feel more British and Northern Irish.

Table 1: Identity in Northern Ireland (May 2018)[4]

Identity	All	Protestant	Catholic	Other	Age 18-44	Age 45+
Irish	**58.6**	29.3	**96.3**	51.5	**65.4**	52.8
Northern Irish	57.9	81.8	27.3	63.1	54.5	**60.7**
European	56.7	30.9	82.4	**68.9**	61.8	52.3
British	46.7	**82.9**	3.9	46.1	39.2	53.1
Responses to the question: 'How strongly, if at all, do you identify as being...?'						

What is also notable, in contrast to many of the findings of twenty and even ten years ago, is the virtual unanimity of the Catholic population in identifying itself as Irish, whereas 1 in 6 Protestants does not identify as British. Notable, too, is the fact that the percentage of Protestants identifying as Irish is very similar to the percentage of Catholics identifying as Northern Irish. It is important to note, as the figures indicate, that this survey did not force anyone to choose a single identity, and it is clear that much of the population in Northern Ireland is comfortable with multiple identities.

Table 2: English and Protestant Northern Irish Identity in the UK
(March-May 2018)

Identity	England	NI Protestants
British	82	83
English	80	--
Northern Irish	--	82
European	26	31

---

4   LucidTalk May 2018—Northern Ireland Tracker Poll, Report of 6 June 2018. Available at: https://2514bea3-91c5-415b-a4d7-2b7f18f64d4f.filesusr.com/ugd/ 024943_ d536561565de 48c7a893fb22fec0ce50.pdf (accessed 5 January 2020). Based on 1,336 responses (see report p. 5 for the methodology), the figure captures those who identified either 'very strongly' or 'fairly strongly' with the given identity. I have put in bold the most popular identity for each population category.

In those terms, Protestant Northern Irish identity most closely echoes the percentages expressed by people in England, except that they feel slightly more European (Table 2). When set beside figures from the three countries of Great Britain as recorded in a parallel survey by YouGov (Table 3), it is clear that Northern Ireland identifies as the least British and most European of all the constituent parts of the UK. It also has the lowest percentage of the population that strongly identifies as being from the territory it inhabits:

Table 3: Identity in the UK (March-May 2018)[5]

Identity	England	Scotland	Wales	N. Ireland
British	82	59	79	47
E/S/W/NI[6]	80	84	62	58
European	26	31	22	57

In all four parts of the UK, it is clear from the figures that a significant proportion of the population is content to have plural identities. The Northern Irish poet John Hewitt captured his sense of multiple identity in an interview in 1974 (quoted in Longley and Ormsby 2007: xx-xxi), where he expressed views that suggest that he may well have felt able to tick all four of the boxes in Table 1 if he were still with us:

> I'm an Ulsterman, of planter stock. I was born in the island of Ireland, so secondarily I'm an Irishman. I was born in the British archipelago and English is my native tongue, so I'm British. The British archipelago consists of offshore islands to the continent of Europe, so I'm European.

Hewitt's Ulster, if we are to go by his poem 'Ulster Names', is definitively the six-county variety (Hewitt 2007: 135). In another poem, 'Freehold', he identifies with 'historic Ulster', which for all his ability to embrace a multi-layered identity, he recognises is a battlefield (Hewitt 2007: 133):

---

[5]   Mark Devenport, 'Fewer NI people feel British than other UK regions—survey', *BBC*, 8 June 2018, cited at: https://www.bbc.com/news/uk-northern-ireland-44398502 (retrieved on 5 January 2020). The results in Table 2 are derived from YouGov surveys conducted in March-May 2018 and published by the BBC. The figure given represents the percentage in that territory who identified either 'very strongly' or 'fairly strongly' with that category.

[6]   This row gives the figure identifying as 'English' in England, 'Scottish' in Scotland, etc.

Mine is historic Ulster, battlefield
of Gael and Planter, certified and sealed
by blood

Of course, as Benedict Anderson (2006) has written, communities are imagined, and some require more of an imagination than others do, while the circumstances that lead to their imagining vary widely. And as John Hewitt and others have implied, there is in everyone a hierarchy of identities, from local to regional to national and beyond, and different hierarchies can exist side-by-side in otherwise cohesive communities. To take just one example: Most Germans have a strong regional identity that almost none, a few traditionalist Bavarians excepted, would dispute is a subset of German national identity. Those Bavarians who might dispute this would simply elevate their own identity to the level of national, displacing Germanness to a cultural and linguistic space. At the opposite end of this spectrum, there is also a minority opinion in the German-speaking countries that defines the nation by language and that nebulous concept known as 'race', a view that reached its epitome in the Third Reich. The key point here is that whatever hierarchy an individual adopts and shares with like-minded individuals, there is usually a single nation in that hierarchy, which in this example can be Bavarian, German or pan-German. This is largely uncontroversial until it strays into the realms of essentialist, often racist and/or sectarian attempts to define nations.

The binarism of the GFA excludes 'Northern Irish' from being a national identifier. Few beyond the fringes of extreme loyalism have ever argued for an independent Northern Ireland, though economically it may well have been possible in the early twentieth century, when the area around Belfast was the economic driver of all of Ireland's economy. The GFA, however, defines the choice as being 'Irish or British, or both'. That creates a simple question for those who might define themselves as Northern Irish (or Ulster): is your identity a new national one, or a subset of Britishness or of Irishness? The results of the 2018 survey suggest that it is most closely, though not exclusively, linked to Britishness, with only limited appeal amongst those who regard themselves as Irish.

If this is the case, then, in the context of Brexit and the possible break-up of the UK, a further question becomes pertinent, one that by extension faces all four constituent parts of the UK. To paraphrase Joyce in *Ulysses*: What is my nation? The ambiguity surrounding the concept that is inherent in the British state, 'the confected nation state', as Jeremy Black (2017) has called it, is less problematic while the state exists. That ambiguity has rarely been better encapsulated than in the words of Edward Carson, Dubliner and Unionist leader, who saw his Irishness in unity with 'the great English nation and the great Scottish nation, and the great nation of Great Britain' (quoted in Hennessey 2008: 258). Yet the time has already arrived when such ambiguity is inadequate.

Britishness is, in effect, a multinational identity masquerading as a national one. The masquerade functioned while the building of an empire was in full flow, with Scottishness (think whisky, fighting Highlanders in kilts and Harry Lauder) and Welshness (think chapel, coalmines and language) very much subsidiary elements in the English-led imperial project. This is rhetorical, of course, but it holds a core of truth, and regional differences became politically irrelevant in this context. It is only in the late 20th and early 21st centuries that Scottishness and Welshness emerged from this embrace with the potential to become established as self-confident and independent national identities.

Britishness in Ireland has meant something different. To be sure, many Irishmen submerged their identity (think whiskey and porter, fighting men, and Catholic lyricism or Protestant Bible) in the imperial project. Beyond the confines of Ulster, however, few called themselves British as a result, and most who did were of planter or Anglo-Irish stock and called themselves 'West Britons', in imitation of the seventeenth-century coinage 'North Britons' for Scotsmen. (It might be noted that the term 'South Britons' for Englishmen never passed into widespread usage.) Before the partition of Ireland, 'Britishness' united two diverse groups: the largely Anglican Anglo-Irish tribe and the predominantly Presbyterian Ulster Protestant population, both of whom were content to see themselves as both Irish and British (see Ó Dochartaigh 2010: 312f.).

Partition sundered them, and today the descendants of those Southern Protestant Unionists who remained after independence have become what Roy Foster has recently called 'an element in Irish life whose Irish identity is unequivocal' (Foster 2019: xxi). Britishness in Northern Ireland, propped up by the union with Great Britain, is now confronted with a rapidly changing environment that carries its own dangers. Fundamentally, it has often seemed that the 'N' in the abbreviation 'N. Irish' has stood as much for the word 'Not' as it has for 'Northern'. Britishness there, since partition, has often seemed as much about denying Irishness as affirming Britishness, doing so along largely confessional lines, and in that respect, it sits in contrast to English, Scottish and Welsh identity, all of which, at least in the modern era, transcend such divides. There is no shared civic identity in Northern Ireland, and if the UK breaks up then the state with which Unionists identify will be gone, whereas the state with which nationalists identify will not. In such circumstances 'British' will be about as meaningful as a national identity as Scandinavian or Soviet; it will be either a geographical or an historical term, but no longer a 'national' one in any contemporary sense. British identity in Northern Ireland will become an orphan identity.

At the height of empire, Britishness was about assimilation into the dominant English language and culture, allowing only for the retention of a few elements of quaintness. Undoubtedly, individuals from all the corners of these islands influenced the development of that empire, but they, in effect, became honorary Englishmen, and the terms 'England' and 'Britain' were used interchangeably. It is ironic that the final stages of the reverse of empire are being induced by the rise not of some narrow, small-nation, romantic nationalism in the so-called Celtic Fringe but by a retreat by the dominant partner from a bigger union, frustrated, it would seem, because it could not dominate it as it had once dominated the empire.

As a consequence, if that time comes, it will be for those in Northern Ireland to reflect and possibly redefine their Britishness. Their history since the Plantation has not been one of unequivocal loyalty to the concept. The kin of those Ulster British were in the vanguard of the American independence movement as they fought the armies of King George for freedom from Britain. Barely a generation later, many of them—especially Presbyterians—were similarly in the vanguard of the United Irish movement that sought to establish an independent republic in Ireland in the wake of the French Revolution. Protestant nationalism has a long tradition in Ireland, and even in the modern era in Northern Ireland— examples since the 1970s have included the SDLP politician Ivan Cooper, the Irish Independence Party politician John Turnley, and the INLA member Ronnie Bunting.

Moreover, loyalty to the Crown has often been expressed in contractarian terms, leading to frustration at the perception that it is not reciprocated, which in turn can lead to a potentially anti-democratic approach, whereby disobeying parliament is not disloyalty because loyalty is directly to the monarch, not parliament (Nic Craith 2002: 102-5). Unionists have on occasion become 'Queen's rebels' in order to protect their position, a position that nationalists pejoratively refer to as 'loyalty to the half-crown', i.e. loyalty to oneself (O'Leary 2019: 358). If the UK does indeed break up, then positioning themselves as 'Queen's rebels' to protect their national identity will be fundamentally contradictory. That may force a reconsideration of the current hierarchy of identities that include Ulster and/or Northern Irish as a subset of British, as it may no longer be tenable. It would be incumbent on all others to create the space for them to do so.

That does not, though it may seem I am hinting at it, automatically assume assimilation into an Irish identity that they may be reluctant to embrace. The Republic of Ireland is a more pluralist place than at the foundation of the state, and any new constitutional arrangement, if it comes, must reflect that. The discourse in this regard in the Republic has barely begun—yet begin it must. As Máiréad rightly wrote almost twenty years ago, and as my friend from Bangor clearly indicated, there have always been plural identities in Ireland. Post-Brexit, we should be ready, in all of Ireland, to move into the realm of plural narratives.

References

Anderson, B. (2006), *Imagined Communities* (London: Verso 2006).

Anon., 'Scots will not be British if they vote for independence, says Miliband', *Guardian*, 7 June 2012. Available at: https://www.theguardian.com/politics/2012/jun/07/scottish-independence-ed-miliband (accessed 5 January 2020).

Anon., 'Brexit: Bonnie Greer says "Ireland owes the UK nothing"', *Irish Times*, 4 Oct 2019. Available at: https://www.irishtimes.com/news/world/uk/brexit-bonnie-greer-says-ireland-owes-the-uk-nothing-1.4040054 (accessed 3 January 2020).

Black, J. (2017), 'Great Britain: The confected nation state', in P. Furtado (ed.), *Histories of Nations. How their identities were forged* (London: Thames & Hudson), 166-73.

Colley, L. (2014) *Acts of Union and Disunion* (London: Profile).

Croft, P. (2003), *King James* (Basingstoke: Palgrave Macmillan), 59-68.

Devenport, M. (2018), 'Fewer NI people feel British than other UK regions—survey', *BBC*, 8 June. Available at: https://www.bbc.com/news/uk-northern-ireland-44398502 (retrieved on 5 January 2020).

Dillon, N. (2019), '"We're Irish, but not that kind of Irish": British Imperial Identity in Transition in Ireland and India in the Early Twentieth Century', in I. d'Alton and I. Milne (eds), *Protestant* and *Irish. The minority's search for place in independent Ireland* (Cork: Cork University Press), 213-28.

Foster, R. (2019), 'Preface: The Protestant Accent', in I. d'Alton and I. Milne (eds), *Protestant* and *Irish. The minority's search for place in independent Ireland* (Cork: Cork University Press), xx-xxiv.

Hennessey, T. (2008), 'The evolution of Ulster Protestant identity in the twentieth century: nations and patriotism', in M. Busteed, F. Neal and J. Tonge (eds), *Irish Protestant Identities* (Manchester: Manchester University Press), 257-69.

Hewitt, J. (2007), 'from IV The glittering sod', J. Hewitt, *Selected Poems*, ed. M. Longley and F. Ormsby (Belfast: Blackstaff), 133-4.

Hewitt, J. (2007), 'Ulster Names', in J. Hewitt, *Selected Poems*, ed. M. Longley and F. Ormsby (Belfast: Blackstaff), 135-6.

Highley, C. (2002), '"The lost British lamb": English Catholic exiles and the problem of Britain', in D. Baker and W. Maley (eds), *British Identities and English Renaissance Literature* (Cambridge: Cambridge University Press), 37-50.

Longley, M. and F. Ormsby (2007), 'Introduction', in J. Hewitt, *Selected Poems*, ed. M. Longley and F. Ormsby (Belfast: Blackstaff), xi-xxv.

LucidTalk May (2018) *Northern Ireland Tracker Poll*. Report of 6 June 2018. Available at: https://2514bea3-91c5-415b-a4d7-2b7f18f64d4f.filesusr.com/ugd/024943_d536561565de48c7a893fb22fec0ce50.pdf (accessed 5 January 2020).

Nic Craith, M. (2002), *Plural Identities Singular Narratives. The Case of Northern Ireland* (New York: Berghahn).

Ó Dochartaigh, P. (2012), 'Letter to the Guardian', 12 June. Available at: https://www.theguardian.com/uk/2012/jun/12/the-search-for-englishness (accessed 5 January 2020).

Ó Dochartaigh, P. (2010), 'Ostpolitik, Nordpolitik: Partition and National Identity in Germany and Ireland', *German Life and Letters* 63(3): 311-330.

O'Leary, B. (2019), *A Treatise on Northern Ireland, Volume I: Colonialism* (Oxford: Oxford University Press).

O'Toole, F. (2018), 'The Good Friday Agreement is so much more than a "shibboleth"', *The Guardian*, 10 April. Available at: https://www.theguardian.com/commentisfree/2018/apr/10/good-friday-agreement-brexit-identity (accessed 3 January 2020).

Ryrie, A. (2006), *The Origins of the Scottish Reformation* (Manchester: Manchester University Press).

Language, Power and Identity Politics
Continuing Challenges for Today's Europe

Philip McDermott

Languages are always entangled with political, social and cultural power. In 'Europe and the Politics of Language' (2006), Nic Craith explored these very questions with a particular consideration on how the redrawing of borders, the mass movement of people and processes of historical memory have shaped the ways that languages are viewed, categorised and attributed with status. Moreover, the positioning of certain languages in this hierarchy denotes how speakers can be considered as 'within', 'without' or at the periphery of Europe. As Nic Craith notes, '[w]hile Europe as a concept is vague, there is no doubt that it serves as a social space in which there are clear boundaries between insiders and outsiders' (Nic Craith 2006: 18). These questions continue to have relevance as we move towards the third decade of the twenty-first century and the themes investigated in 'Europe and the Politics of Language' have arguably become more pronounced in the decade since it was published. Tensions between the forces of globalisation and more parochial forms of populist nationalism have intensified and as a consequence fluid and diverse identities have been pitted against more hardened discourses of monocultural belonging which are primarily rooted in [a] place. Attempts to deal with these conflicting notions of belonging are amongst the most fraught challenges in today's liberal democracies and fall within the well-trodden debate termed by Baumann (1999) as the 'multicultural riddle'.

Assessing the social positioning and status of languages at any given time, therefore, provides a prism through which we can understand the ever changing political, social and cultural dynamics of Europe. The affinities that we have to the language(s) that we speak may differ greatly to the perceptions that we have of languages spoken by others. Languages can in such circumstances become symbolic of an 'other' and in many cases such perceptions continue to be exacerbated by wider social debates on national identity and belonging. Therefore, claims that nationalism in the age of late modernity has waned appear to be premature particularly when we assess the various linguistic policies that multiple nation states continue to implement in the twenty-first century (McDermott 2011, 2017). Language, power and wider issues of identity politics, as a result, provide a critical means through which we can continue to understand interpretations of place, debates around recognition, social justice, and even the tensions and antagonisms that emerge between groups in periods of conflict (McDermott and NicCraith 2019).

This chapter revisits themes initially explored by Nic Craith in *Europe and the Politics of Language*, such as discourses of inclusion, exclusion and belonging; statehood and citizenship; linguistic hierarchies; and language borders. Complex debates, such as these, continue to help us interpret and reinterpret the political dynamics of linguistic diversity. Drawing on some European examples, the chapter considers how major political shifts in the past two decades have continued to impact on minority/minoritised languages. I especially consider the centrality of the nation to the concept of linguistic belonging which has consolidated just at the period when some felt this ideology, frequently touted as a relic of modernity, was on the wane. Each case discussed in this article provides the reader examples for reflection on how wider macro level trends will always have an impact at the micro level of the individual speaker.

Linguistic Tensions of the Global and the Local

The twentieth century witnessed the extraordinary expansion of transnational networks relating to trade, cultural engagement and communication. The emergence of the 'global language' can be considered as either a consequence or a resultant factor of free market ideas, imperial aspirations, ambitions of cultural superiority or a combination of all three. The unequal power processes evident within globalisation have inevitably generated tensions in economic, cultural and political power which have also shaped the linguistic categories of the 'global', 'national' and 'regional/minority' languages. With the rise in transnational migrations we have also witnessed the category of 'migrant' or 'heritage' language which is perhaps even more marginalised in political discussion and societal acceptance (McDermott 2011). Such discourse, Nic Craith notes, creates 'hierarchies of legitimacies' that create a sense that global and majority languages are 'naturally advantaged rather than socially constructed'; by contrast, 'minority languages are deemed to be inherently handicapped and unworthy of state respect or planning' (Nic Craith 2006: 58).

A socially constructed notion of 'languages of worth' and languages of 'lesser worth' is thus instilled and normalised. Philipson (2003), for instance, uses the example of how political and cultural transnational bodies such as the EU have channelled the prioritisation of English in their operation and how this has largely gone unquestioned. The perception of this 'linguistic imperialism' is that it is quietly situated within processes of cultural and societal oppression. Phillipson, like Nic Craith, pleads for a reassessment of how we view languages in the present through a critique of the past. Instead we should 'be aware of the deeds of our ancestors', and we should 'also be prepared, following Proust, to be sceptical of appearances and to approach the territory of the languages of Europe with a critical eye' (Phillipson 2007: 65-66). Given the changes to the political landscape in the past decade, perhaps this critical eye is needed now more than ever to challenge processes and discourses which have solidified the perceived superiority of majority identities at the growing expense of the 'outsider'.

Language and the Politics of Belonging in Contemporary Europe

In the conclusion to *Europe and the Politics of Language*, Nic Craith notes that 'while some languages in the twenty-first century are infinitely more privileged than others, this is no indication of any inherent quality in the languages themselves. It is merely an inevitable consequence of state planning for languages and access to power' (2006: 187). These sentiments are as applicable in 2020 as they were in 2006, and this chapter now provides insight into more recent examples where the linguistic hierarchy continues to determine senses of belonging both *to* and *in* Europe.

Examples from countries which were previously ardent advocates of multilingualism show that a favourable status toward this concept can change as political dynamics alter. The politics of exclusion can suddenly impact on communities which had earlier attained some level of linguistic recognition. For instance, the 1970s through to the 1990s were characterised by a reaction at the grassroots level against the processes of globalisation. The subsequent rise in 'a Europe of the Regions' placed emphasis on the 'local' within the member states of the EU. Supporters of regional and minority languages (e.g., Basque, Irish in Northern Ireland, Welsh, and Sámi) became adept at using the supranational agenda of organisations such as the Council of Europe and the EU to gain significant sympathy for their causes. In circumventing the state such locally focused movements acquired support from Brussels or Strasbourg which led several national governments to improve the status of lesser-used languages. Globalisation, somewhat paradoxically, provided benefits for local or regional cultures in a process which Roland Robertson (1994) termed 'glocalisation'.

The economic, political and cultural landscape of Europe has of course shifted since this period. Interconnected events in the last two decades such as the 9/11 attacks, the so-called 'War on Terror', the international financial downturn and the refugee 'crisis' have raised further questions around national identity and belonging – which can of course take a linguistic focus. Events like these have created fertile ground for both anti-globalisation sentiment and a reversion to the myth of the 'monocultural' nation originally grounded in the period of the Enlightenment. From Britain to Hungary, from Finland to the Netherlands and from Portugal to Germany, linguistic rights have faced a much less sympathetic hearing than previously. Policies supporting the development of language minorities or even advocating the maintenance of multilingualism for migrant minorities have increasingly been placed under the microscope. It is important to note that this is not only about governments changing policy but about a growing discourse of exclusion that has been advocated by right wing populist parties that have apparently capitalised on growing anti-globalisation sentiment. In such circumstances, the environment for speakers and supporters of minority language movements has been an increasingly questioned one.

Finland is just one example of where an increasing vote for right-wing populist parties has led to a wider questioning in public discourse of linguistic rights for groups such as Swedish-speakers and the Sámi minority. Since 1991, the Sámi language Act has offered protections for speakers of various Sámi languages especially at the municipal level. Support for education initiatives and coverage in public broadcasting was also improved at this time. These 'rights' for Sámi -speakers are described by Pietikäinen et al. (2019: 295) as follows:

> [T]he indigenous people have the right, guaranteed by two language Acts to use their Sámi language when dealing with the authorities. Furthermore, in Sámiland, official announcements, proclamations, notices and signs must be written in the three Sámi languages spoken in the area and authorities are obliged to advance use of the Sámi languages in their activities. Municipal authorities must use indigenous languages alongside Finnish in records and other main documents. By law, authorities in the homeland must ensure that personnel in their offices have the necessary language skills to serve Sámi-speaking customers in their own language.

This description illustrates how the Sámi languages as a marginalised and peripheralised element of Finnish culture nonetheless benefitted from legislative change. The Sámi Language Act, while not going far for many, perhaps provided an initial platform through which to redress the historical and economic processes that marginalised the language in the first place. Nonetheless, the existence of an indigenous national minority can, when political circumstances change, be appropriated as a symbol of national disunity – and language diversity is frequently a target within this discourse. This proved to be the case during the emergence of the right-wing populist True Finns Party at the beginning of the 2010s. In 2011, the party increased its share of votes to 19 per cent, consolidating this in the 2015 election (Wahlbeck 2016: 579) and again in the 2019 poll. The party also held several ministerial portfolios from 2015-2017 which provided a more direct input into national policy.

In particular, True Finns have consistently built their campaign on an anti-group rights stance. The allocation of rights to minorities (both indigenous and immigrant) have been upheld as examples of an 'anti-democratic' process. The provision of additional linguistic rights to the Sámi, it is argued, fragments the ideal of a monolithic Finnish identity. In their 2011 manifesto, the party asserted that the Finnish language is a fundament feature in the Finnish nation. They noted that as a unifying linguistic element of the state: 'We must treasure the Finnish language. Cultural appropriations must be targeted to reinforcing Finnish identity. Pseudo-artistic postmodernists can find their funding in the free market. The Finnish Broadcasting Company must be Finnish and deliver high quality' (True Finns Party 2011, cited in Wahlbeck 2016: 580). While the party maintains a solid support base there is potential for the previous attempts at promoting linguistic diversity in Finland to be challenged and ultimately deconstructed.

Finland provides only one example where such approaches have emerged and where the idea of linguistic diversity as a national norm has been questioned more widely. In Hungary, which has a historical commitment to multilingualism, the changing political dimensions of the past decade appear to be a driving force in this regard. The advisory committee for the Council of Europe's Framework Convention on National Minorities recently reported on growing levels of anti-minority sentiment. The attribution of such negative views were particularly associated with the populist 'one nation' ethnic framework promoted under the premiership of Viktor Orbán. The prioritisation of hungarian ethnicity and language it appears has clear ramifications in a country with 12 other official linguistic minorities. The adverse impact on minority language speakers was especially identified by the committee, which comprises several international human rights experts. Their report noted 'with regret that ethnicisation of society and perceived tensions concerning the authorities' approach to commemoration of historical events' has 'had a negative effect of diminishing the presence of and interest in existing diversity within Hungarian society, resulting occasionally in self-censorship, including in the media in the languages of national minorities' (CoE 2016: 33). In this case an evocation of a singular ethnic past has been drawn on by political elites in ways which consciously 'for-

get' aspects of Hungary's multilingual history. While longstanding legislation remains at the national level, the political rhetoric of Hungarian ethnocentrism
severely undermines its effectiveness.

These are certainly more extreme cases which allude to a retreat from the
promotion of linguistic diversity and the ethos of multiculturalism more generally. However, perhaps this merely follows wider trends which are played out in
more subliminal ways. As early as 2004, in the wake of 9/11, Christian Joppke
pinpointed a growing scepticism among nation states in the west towards the
notion of cultural plurality (2004: 239). This 'retreat from multiculturalism' has
witnessed an aggressive growth in monolinguistic assimilation policies aimed at
migrants particularly. Such policies aim to promote the majority/national language to newcomer communities, and to their children especially, through majority language acquisition programmes. Language fluency in the majority language has also become a prerequisite for citizenship in several European states
where language programmes for linguistic assimilation are funded heavily by
the state while little focus is placed on supporting multilingualism.

Discussing the implementation of language tests for immigrants in Britain,
Anne-Marie Fortier (2018) argues that these approaches are deeply embedded
in historical processes of dominance. Drawing on the example of the UK, she
notes that British citizenship tests are akin to a 'form of assessing and judging
English language skills in ways that devalue other Englishes as well as other languages' (1265). Fortier's work indicates that language tests merely mirror already pre-existing prejudices. Native speakers of languages other than English
are most devalued. However, the dialects of English spoken by migrants from
previous British colonies are also highly degraded. Such examples are also relevant in other former colonial powers such as France and Belgium where 'non-
European' dialects of French, and particularly those from variants from Africa,
hold less cultural prestige which is played out through the testing regimes.

A recent forum edition of the *Anthropological Journal of European Studies*
concentrated on the theme of linguistic diversity in contemporary Europe. The
research papers produced, primarily by early career researchers, provided current examples of the continuation of linguistic inclusion and exclusion. Rühlmann and McMonagle's discussion on Germany notes that even migrants born
in the country face questions relating to their linguistic proficiency. Moreover,
their multilingual abilities (e.g in German and Turkish) are frequently sidelined
and ignored in the public space. This is especially true in institutional settings
such as education and where such discrimination, they argue, mirrors the wider
racial hierarchies of German society. Consequently, the authors argue that a
more critical race perspective should be applied in the context of plurilingualism

in Germany because perceptions about languages are often connected to racism. They do note however, that given the historical connotations between the word 'race' and National Socialism this is no easy task (Rühlmann and McMonagle 2019). The issues that the authors identify, despite the specific nuances of the German situation, are all too familiar in many European countries.

A further example of continued contemporary challenges relating to inclusion and exclusion is elaborated by Szelei (2019) who discusses the value attributed to the languages of migrant communities in the Portuguese education system. In her study, she argues that a primary focus again is placed on the acquisition of the majority language, Portuguese. This notion of the 'national' language as a key symbolic and actual marker of inclusion is one which is replicated elsewhere where limited focus is placed on the language skills that migrants bring with them. As Szelei (2019: 101) notes, little attention has been placed on

> multilingualism more broadly, including minority and migrant languages, or to complementing perspectives regarding the importance of students' home languages, their multilingual repertoires and linguistic identities. While the teaching and learning of Portuguese is a major concern in compulsory education, minority and migrant language lessons tend to be organised by communities, embassies, NGOs or other organisations outside formal education.

Therefore, while the private space of the family home provides the main platform for a child's linguistic heritage, the civic spaces of socialisation such as education remain places where there is continual scepticism regarding multilingualism which is mirrored in education policies throughout the continent (McDermott, 2008).

Conclusion

The examples described above illustrate key points relating to the inclusion of those who speak languages which are perceived to 'belong' vis-a-vis those whose languages are viewed as not belonging and excluded. These exclusionary processes need not necessarily involve the most overt forms of discrimination but may be manifested in ways which are subliminal, under the surface, and hidden from the experiences of the majority. Indeed linguistic 'othering' continues to be legitimised through processes of public policy as an authoritative and normalising discourse. Nic Craith, in a pragmatic assessment of the situation in the mid-2000s, noted that scholars and policy makers should advocate a 'multicentric language policy that will cater to the settled, nomadic and migrant life-styles that are a feature of contemporary society' (2006: 187). These sentiments are arguably more relevant in a Europe which has witnessed continued polarisation of political ideologies in the aftermath of major global events. Under these conditions it is imperative that scholars continue to apply a critical lens to language planning so that exploitative linguistic nationalisms are challenged. Discussion about the role of languages and their position in contemporary Europe should continue as a vital point of deliberation if the multilingual realities of the public sphere are to be defended and adequately reflected, not merely in scholarly debate, but also in the applied elements of language planning.

References

Baumann, G. (1999), *The Multicultural Riddle: Rethinking, National, Ethnic and Religious Identities* (London: Routledge).

CoE (2016), *Advisory Committee on the Framework Convention for the Protection of National Minorities: Fourth Opinion on Hungary*. Council of Europe. Available at https://rm.coe.int/CoERMPublicCommonSearchServices/DisplayDCTMContent?documentId=09000016806ac04b (accessed 20 December 2019)

Fortier, A. (2018), 'On (Not) Speaking English: Colonial Legacies in Language Requirements for British Citizenship', *Sociology* 52(6): 1254-1269.

Joppke, C. (2004), 'The Retreat of Multiculturalism in the Liberal State: Theory and Policy', *British Journal of Sociology* 55(2): 237-257.

Kelly, M. ed. (2018), *Languages After Brexit: How the UK Speaks to the World* (Basingstoke: Palgrave).

McDermott, P. (2008), 'Acquisition, Loss or Multilingualism? Educational Planning for Speakers of Migrant Community Languages in Northern Ireland'. *Current Issues in Language Planning*, 9(4): 483-500.

McDermott, P. (2011), *Migrant Languages in the Public Space: A Case Study from Northern Ireland* (Münster: LIT).

McDermott, P. (2017), 'Language Rights and the Council of Europe: A Failed Response to a Multilingual Continent?', *Ethnicities* 17(5): 603-626.

McDermott, P. and M. Nic Craith (2019), 'Linguistic Recognition in Deeply Divided Societies: Antagonism or Reconciliation', in G. Hogan-Brun and B. O'Rourke (eds), *The Palgrave Handbook of Minority Languages and Communities* (Basingstoke: Palgrave), 159-180.

Nic Craith, M. (2006), *Europe and the Politics of Language* (Basingstoke: Palgrave).

Phillipson, R. (2003), *English Only Europe? Challenging Language Policy* (London: Routledge).

Phillipson, R. (2007), 'English in Europe: Threat or Promise?', in M. NicCraith (ed.), *Language, Power and Identity Politics* (Basingstoke: Palgrave), 65-82.

Pietikäinen, S., H. Kelly-Holmes and M. Rieder (2019), 'Minority Languages and Markets', in Hogan-Brun, G. and B. O'Rourke (eds), *The Palgrave Handbook of Minority Languages and Communities* (Basingstoke: Palgrave), 287-310.

Robertson, R. (1994), 'Globalisation or Glocalisation?' *Journal of International Communication* 1(1): 33-52.

Rühlmann, L. and S. McMonagle (2019), 'Germany's Linguistic "Others" and the Racism Taboo', *Anthropological Journal of European Cultures* 28(2): 93-100.

Szelei, N. (2019), 'Português Língua não Materna and Linguistic Misrecognition in Portugal's Schools', *Anthropological Journal of European Cultures* 28(2): 101-108.

Wahlbeck, Ö. (2016), 'True Finns and Non-True Finns: The Minority Rights Discourse of Populist Politics in Finland', *Journal of Intercultural Studies* 37 (6): 574-588.

Language of the Heart
Franz Hohler's *S'Totemügerli*

Regina F. Bendix

When a colleague tells of a plan to take up a position in German-speaking Switzerland, sooner or later I will find an opportunity to acquaint him or her with Franz Hohler's performance of his story *S'Totemügerli*. The Swiss author and comedian conceived of this legend-like story in Bernese dialect in 1967 and performed it to great acclaim for more than fifty years.[1]

On first listening, *S'Totemügerli* appears to be a legend, both in intonation and the atmosphere created. It takes rather more intensive relistening to trace in the narration an account of two villagers, out late at night in a backcountry valley. They are deep in argument with one another when they encounter a supernatural creature. It is a Totemügerli—a fictional creature not even the most eager of legend and folk belief scholars has ever heard about—who enlists their assistance. In the familiar logic of legends, the two men have no option but to help. One of them manages to escape but he is a changed man forever after; the other is never seen again, and it is suspected that he was transformed into a Totemügerli himself. Rather than sinking into shudders and awe as one might expect of a legend, the audience tends to laugh uproariously throughout the performance—a puzzle I hope to address with the following brief musing on dialects and what pleasures they bestow on the speakers of these generally not written idioms.

I pick up an echo that a number of Máiréad Nic Craith's scholarly contributions have evoked in me. With, among many others, her work on bilingual authors who write in languages other than the one that they grew up speaking (2012), as well as with her repeat attention to an Irish memoirist and his transformation of the oral into the written (e.g., 2020), she has drawn attention to the deep intertwining of varieties of language and personal and cultural belonging. Franz Hohler and scores of other Swiss songwriters and rock bands, poets and novelists have not just given me ongoing delight and a deep sense of being

---

[1] A version was aired by Swiss TV for the 50th anniversary of Hohler's original in 2017: https://www.youtube.com/watch?v=OlY_minvSSg (accessed 2 September 2019). The program contained additional versions and homages of this broadly known and much appreciated spoof story (cf. https://www.srf.ch/sendungen/hoerspiel/50-jahre-totemuegerli-eine-hommage-mit-franz-hohler-und-gaesten, accessed 2 September 2019).

part of a creative mesh of similar yet diverse Swiss dialects. They have also encouraged reflection on the persistent aesthetic celebrations as well as political efforts to keep dialects in circulation, even strengthen them, as varieties of non-standard and generally non-written language.

Swiss intellectuals have fought for the idiosyncrasy and inspirational qualities of their dialect as compared to standard German ever since efforts took shape to arrive at a shared, purified standard German in the 18th century. With print achieving a broader place in social, political, and literate lives, there was also experimentation with new print genres such as literary and political magazines. The Swiss scholars J. J. Bodmer and J. J. Breitiger, in particular, created themselves such outlets where they, among other topics, devoted themselves to combat the pedantic strictures proclaimed by the 18th century German poet J. C. Gottsched. Against the latter's insistence, they pushed for the value of linguistic variety, having themselves begun to write in a variety of German coloured by some elements of their native Zürich dialect. In one of their statements, published in a, for their time, broadly circulating journal, they pointed to the creative obstacles imposed by an insistence on standardised choice rather than 'natural flow' of language:

For the writer who has to first acquire this foreign dialect [i.e. the new standard German], the so called naïve [natural] writing style is made impossible; how could one express the language of the innermost heart in a studied standard? Where could the non-native speaker find in this standard those expressions and terms linked to house and family which have a completely different effect— as they are for all times tied to serene memories of childhood and youth—than those learned from books (cited after Crüger 1888: XXXV, my translation).

Against Gottsched's notion that German literature was only just getting created and citing this as a reason for a shared standard, Bodmer was able to shore up his position by pointing to historical precedent. He had succeeded, assisted by Breitinger, to find manuscripts of works by medieval minnesingers. Performers, such as Walther von der Vogelweide, had written in dialects such as Swabian or Upper German. Bodmer could thus strengthen his position for the use and preservation of dialects in an era where educated Germans considered any dialect to belong at best to the uncultured speech of peasants (Trümpy 1955: 14). While, ironically, in particular Bodmer carried forth his literary and historical writing increasingly in standard German, Swiss resistance to let go of their many varieties of dialect continued through the centuries. Franz Joseph Stalder initiated the research and publication of a Swiss dialect handbook in the early 19th century and led the way toward dialectological scholarship (Stalder 1806-12; 1819). The dictionary, called *Das Schweizerische Idiotikon*, grew into an ongoing, funded enterprise and is now accessible over a website.[2] Empirically based studies on how dialect fares vis-à-vis standard have received continuous scholarly attention, with schooling, media, military, church and bureaucracy as particular areas potentially 'endangering' dialect fluency (Schwarzenbach 1969; Ramseier 1988; Christen 1998; Oberholzer 2018).

In the 1960s—which happened to coincide with my childhood, there was a growing number of chansonniers—or, in today's nomenclature, singer-songwriters. In clubs in the capital city of Berne, Mani Matter and a number of others enthralled audiences with clever lyrics that used the compelling vocabulary of dialect to depict the comedy of human interaction, Swissness, and everyday absurdities (e.g., Matter 1967, 1969, 1973). Matter died in a car accident aged only 36, but his oeuvre lives on and has inspired many other Swiss singer-songwriters as well as rock musicians to create and perform in dialect. Franz Hohler emerged as author and comedian during the same time. He was known for his cabaret work where he performed while accompanying himself on his cello—with the warm deep sound of the string instrument complementing funny and weird stories and songs. There is, for instance, his brief text that recommends that one might organise a move the way that hedgehogs do:

Igel Züglete[3]

Wüsset dir, wie s d Igle
Mache, wenn si zügle?

Si stecken ihri Sächeli
Uf ihri spitze Stächeli

Ihri Tischli und ihri Bänkli
Ihri Stüehli und ihri Schränkli

Ihri Chüsseli und ihri Tüechli
Ihri Bildli und ihri Büechli

Ihri Lämpli und ihri Bettli
Und ihri Trottinettli

Ihri Cöütschli und ihri Thrönli
Und ihri Grammophönli
Ihri Tassli und ihri Pfännli
Und ihri Sitzbadwännli –

So göh si is neue Hüsli—tripp trapp!
Und strychen ihre Hushalt a de Wänden ab!

Oh, wäre mir doch Igle
De chönntemer besser zügle!

When Hedgehogs Move House

Do you know how hedgehogs
do it when they move?

They stick their little things
Upon their little pointy spines

Their little tables and their little benches
Their little chairs and their little closets

Their little pillows and their little towels
Their little pictures and their little books

Their little lamps and their little beds
And their little scooters

Their little sofas and their little thrones
And their little gramophones
Their little cups and their little pans
And their little bathtubs

Thus they go to their new little house- trip trap!
And strike off their belongings on the walls!

Oh I wish we were hedgehogs
Then we would be better able to move house!

---

[2]   Schweizerisches Idiotikon (https://www.idiotikon.ch/, accessed 22 September 2019).
[3]   The song appeared on Hohler's album Kompakt (Bern: Zytglogge 1989), available on Spotify.

Hohler's praise of hedgehog efficiency linguistically gains a great deal of its humour through the extreme use of diminutives—something many Swiss German speakers unconsciously slide into, not just but especially when speaking with children. At once making fun of this speaking habit and depicting hedgehog life anthropomorphically, the song appeals on several levels, to young and old. Likewise, *S'Totemügerli* enjoys a broad following across generations who take delight in the breadth of intertextual and performative allusion. Hohler titled it 'Es bärndütsches Gschichtli'—a little story in Bernese dialect. It is recognisable as such to the listener, because in Hohler's performance, the words, names and turns of phrase all are convincingly Bernese-sounding. Yet a good 70% of the text consists of verbs, nouns and adjectives that do not actually exist. This is, indeed, the reason for having chosen the hedgehog song as a translatable example, as *S'Totemügerli* is quite untranslatable. A written passage out of it looks as follows[4]: 'Düpfelig u gnütelig si si blybe schtah wie zwöi gripseti Mischtschwibeli'.

A listener familiar with Swiss German dialect might try to guess what this sentence means—e.g., 'they stood still awkwardly and slightly shocked like two hurt dung creatures.' But everyone recognises the whole story as a fantastically innovative example of gibberish (in Bernese: Gromolo). With it, Hohler manages to at once tease and celebrate the Bernese dialect and its speakers, to invoke excessively serious dialect story telling as one might have heard it in radio broadcasts, and yet keep up a certain amount of pride in the listeners who savour all the layers he appeals to. Born 1943 in Biel, indeed located in the canton of Berne, Hohler grew up in Olten in canton Solothurn, went to high school in Aarau in canton Aarau, and studied in Zürich. Each of these cantons has its own dialect; many of them will have additional regional dialects. Like many Swiss, Hohler thus accumulated early on familiarity and speaking knowledge of similar yet different dialects of Swiss German. He performs the story in the inflections and the 'sitting on the vowels' typical of Bernese and his word inventions sound deceptively close to actual Bernese. The joy of the listener consists in moving from bewilderment ('why can't I understand this story?') to recognition: 'oh, this is Bernese but it is not, and this is a legend, but it is not!'

---

[4]   The full text is available as part of a set of teaching materials for Swiss high school teachers: https://www.mittelschulvorbereitung.ch/contentLD/DE/Div21fBernd Gschicht.pdf (accessed 2 September 2019). Discovering that this story made its way into high school curricular materials is worthy of reflection beyond this short essay. It certainly supports my sense that the Swiss insistence on valuing their spoken language to the point of representing it in print remains alive and well.

The performance then also encapsulates everyday linguistic life in Switzerland: riding a train or listening to the radio, one sorts what one hears into dialects and possible regional upbringing of speakers, perhaps just unconsciously, but it is a facet of language diversity one is accustomed to. Naturally, dialects have shifted and some have also assimilated to one another, particularly in the densely populated mid-country, from Zurich to Bern and beyond, and due to migration as well as commuting. Yet just as increased bureaucracy and increased media presence far into the years after WWII pushed for more standard German in public discourse, the poetic, literary, and sung resurgence and embrace of dialects since the 1960s bespeak a certain amount of pride in the particularity of the Swiss linguistic landscape. Hohler's *S'Totemügerli* maintains just enough ironic distance to keep the love of dialect from that kind of danger of linguistic patriotism (which is at any rate impossible in a nation that is quadrilingual by constitution). Multilinguality in the ear, in the brain, and in the heart may indeed be one of the recipes toward the kind of cosmopolitan politics that would seem the safest path away from populist aberrations.

References

Christen, H. (1998), *Dialekt im Alltag: eine empirische Untersuchung zur lokalen Komponente heutiger schweizerdeutscher Varietäten* (Tübingen: Niemeyer).

Crüger, J. (1888), *Joh. Christoph Gottsched und die Schweizer Joh. J. Bodmer und Joh. J. Breitinger* (Darmstadt: Wissenschaftliche Buchgesellschaft).

Matter, M. (1969), *Us emene lääre Gygechaschte. Berndeutsche Chansons* (Bern: Kandelaber).

Matter, M. (1973), *Mani Matters Sudelhefte* (Zürich: Benziger).

Matter, M. (1967), *Alls wo mir id Finger chunnt* (record) (Bern: Zytglogge).

Nic Craith, M. (2012), *Narratives of Place, Belonging and Language: An Intercultural Perspective* (Basingstoke: Palgrave).

Nic Craith, M. (2020), *The Vanishing World of the Islandman. Narrative and Nostalgia* (Basingstoke: Palgrave).

Oberholzer, S. (2018), *Zwischen Standarddeutsch und Dialekt: Untersuchung zu Sprachgebrauch und Spracheinstellungen von Pfarrpersonen in der Deutschschweiz* (Stuttgart: Franz Steiner).

Ramseier, M. (1988), *Mundart und Standardsprache im Radio der deutschen und rätoromanischen Schweiz* (Aarau: Sauerländer).

Schwarzenbach, R. (1969), *Die Stellung der Mundart in der Schweiz* (Frauenfeld: Huber).

Stalder, F. (1806-12), *Versuch eines schweizerischen Idiotikon* (Aarau: Sauerländer).

Stalder, F. (1819), *Die Landessprache der Schweiz oder schweizerische Dialekto-logie* (Aarau: Sauerländer).

Trümpy, H. (1955), *Schweizerdeutsche Sprache und Literatur im 17. Und 18. Jahrhundert* (Basel: S. Krebs).

No Ordinary Instructions
Nineteenth-Century English Gastronomy Books and the Female Art of Cooking

Loredana Salis

Gastronomy books reflect and are the reflection of the way in which food shapes received social roles. Focusing on nineteenth-century English cookery manuals compiled by women, this study investigates their creative role as writers of recipes as well as intercultural mediators within the culinary tradition of their country. Through the art of cooking, publishing female experts in food preparations could perform new roles, beyond the traditional ones as natural guardians of culinary treasures, the nurturers and managers of all things domestic. Their recipes were no ordinary instructions but explorations of and experimentations with common tastes and eating habits that helped facilitate the encounter between diverse local and exotic food ways.

Nineteenth-century English culture saw a significant production and mass circulation of women-authored gastronomy manuals the study of which furthers our understanding of the period with a special interest into the ideological function of food and food ways. Victorian culture 'understood cooking as a highly politicised act', Susan Zlotnick reminds us as she takes the view that British women publishing cookery books contributed to 'the construction of [...] imperialism' by domesticating it at a time when 'national identity [...] appeared most vulnerable'[1]. Focussing on 'Victorian domestic cookbooks and the curry recipes they contain', Zlotnick charts the naturalisation of ethnic food at the hands of British women who helped incorporate it 'into the national diet'. Accordingly, cookbooks facilitated imperial assimilation, rather than hybridisation. For Caroline Lieffers, Victorian cookbooks represented 'sites where knowledge was constructed through simplification, interpretation and contradiction'[2]. Addressing

---

[1] Speaking of Indian cuisine most especially, Zlotnick maintains that 'the Englishwoman at home could remake the foreign into the domestic by virtue of her own domesticity [...] In being brought back to England and located within the domestic sphere [...] curry would be naturalised, converted from the exotic into the familiar (and the familial) through its association with the woman's domain of the home and the kitchen'. Susan Zlotnick, 'Domesticating Imperialism: Curry and Cookbooks in Victorian England', *Frontiers: A Journal of Women Studies*, Vol. 16., No. 2/3, Gender, Nations and Nationalisms (1996), pp. 51-68: 62-63, 54.

[2] Caroline Lieffers, 'The Present Time is Eminently Scientific': The Science of Cookery in Nineteenth-Century Britain', *Journal of Social History*, Vol. 45, No. 4 (Summer 2012), pp. 936-959: 947.

the demand to combine 'technical skills and expert knowledge in the kitchen' cookbooks compiled by women occupied a central role in recasting domestic art as domestic science. However different in their aim and focus, both studies situate food at the crossroads between gender and colonial discourse and conceive of recipes as powerful cultural and narrative spaces, if not as 'communities' proper, to use Janet Theophano's wording[3]. In such terms, these scholarly works and ideas provide a stimulating starting point for the present investigation. More specifically, they inform the following reflection on the creative role of women as writers of recipes *and* as intercultural mediators within the culinary tradition of their country. It is my contention that through publishing and mastery in the art of cooking nineteenth-century female food experts came to perform new roles, beyond the traditional ones as natural guardians of culinary treasures, to become the nurturers and managers of all things domestic. Their recipes were no ordinary cooking instructions, but rather explorations of and experimentations with common tastes and eating habits that helped facilitate the encounter between local and exotic food ways. By focusing on Victorian gender roles and gendered narratives, I shall examine the way in which food interacted with and somehow impacted on the social history and the cultural dynamics of the time. To that end, *English Cookery Books to the Year 1850*, an inventory of English books on cookery and domestic economy, proves to be a useful tool. The volume embraces over three centuries of English culture as seen from the perspective of food recipes and their transcription, and it thus records the changes occurring in society in relation to who cooked and how, when, why and for whom food was prepared between the 1500s and 1850[4].

Gastronomy manuals circulating in England during that 350-year period span were intended for use within the private realm of the household, and their readership would have been *mostly* of the female sex: mostly but not exclusively, that is, since early cookery books catered for a mixed public of men and women. With time, the former specialised in food making in the public sphere such as court kitchens and restaurants while women became gradually confined

---

3   Janet Theophano, *Eat My Words: Reading Women's Lives through the Cookbooks They Wrote*, New York: Palgrave, 2002. 'Cookbooks as Communities' is the eloquent title of chapter 1 in her study. Theophano expands on this concept and provides definitions of cookbooks which are relevant to the present investigation: for her cookbooks are 'maps of the social and the cultural worlds they [*women*] inhabit' (p. 14); 'a record of the relationships that comprised at least a portion of a woman's social universe' (p. 14) and 'a source of collective power enabling women to create and maintain vital links and mutual support among themselves and their households, by fostering communication, social interaction, and the exchange of ideas' (p. 21)

4   Arnold Whitaker Oxford, *English Cookery Books to the Year 1850*, Oxford: OUP, 1913.

to the private self-contained space of the house kitchen[5]. By the 1800s, the gendered codification of roles in relation to food-making came to replicate the dominant ideology of the separate spheres although early traces of significant changes were already in place that situated women, primarily middle-class women, somewhere else within the confines of the domestic realm, if not beyond. Domesticity was re-formulated in relation to the empire and to scientific advancement, as noted by Zlotnick and Lieffers above, with food proving functional to an emancipatory process that granted women access to the editorial market in a much more significant and active way than it had in the previous century. As more female experts began collecting, writing and publishing cookbooks, a popular literary genre developed parallel to fiction which, to cite Theophano, offered them a unique opportunity to 'develop their concepts of the feminine ideal and their opinions on social and political issues ranging from education to temperance to religion'[6]. Some female authors, the majority, published anonymously and signed their work simply 'By a Lady'; others used their married name (e.g. Mrs Robinson, Mrs M'Ewan, Mrs Child, Mrs Mary Holland, Mrs Beeton), or, more rarely, 'came forward' and exposed themselves to public view, as unmarried women (Miss Crawford, Esther Copley and Eliza Acton, the latter being the first modern professional cookery book author)[7]. In the hands of these 'professed' cooks, to recall the title of Mrs Mary Holland's volume (1830), domestic literature, and recipes most especially, became cultural and narrative sites where the imaginative and creative hunger of emerging female professionals could be nourished and whence the taste of readers would be educated. Women authoring gastronomy books, in other words, came to mediate

---

[5]   Queens and kings of England often employed men as their head chefs. This was the case with Richard II, whose chef compiled the first 'recipe book' we are aware of, a vellum roll named *The Forme of Cury*. A century later, *The Booke off Noble Cookry*, appeared. This was the first book of recipes ever to be printed, and it was largely influenced by the French cooking tradition. Cf. Alan Davidson, 'Food': The Natural History of British Cookery Books', *The American Scholar*, 52 (1), 1983, pp. 98-106, p. 98. Under Queen Victoria, the royal kitchens were in the hands of chef Charles Elme Francatelli, who compiled several cookery books including *The Modern Cook* (1846), *A Plain Cookery Book for the Working Classes* (1852), *The Cook's Guide, and Housekeeper's & Butler's Assistant: A Practical Treatise on English and Foreign Cookery* (1867).

[6]   Theophano, *p. 6.*

[7]   Cf. Oxford, *English Cookery Books to the Year 1850*, cit. The expression 'coming forward' follows Carol Bock's depiction of authors leaving the solitary confinement of the domestic space and exposing themselves to public view by entering the literary market. Carol A. Bock, 'Authorship, the Brontës, and Fraser's Magazine. Coming Forward as an Author in Early Victorian England', *Victorian Literature and Culture*, 29 (2001), 54-69.

between the demands of the private sphere and those of their profession, between their traditional roles as family nurturers, educators, and care givers and
the equivalent functions they learned to perform for their readership. This was
a significant change from the previous century, when cookery books were also
produced by female experts, but the extent of their circulation and influence
upon the nation's food culture was not as prominent as it would be in Victorian
times.

It is worth recalling that the history of English gastronomy literature is
linked to the history of normative 'how to' manuals where recipes appeared at
first as part of 'conduct' and 'etiquette' books meant to duly instruct readers, as
early as the 16th century, in the execution of various culinary pursuits. The notion of *mens sana in corpore sano* represented a fundamental aspect of one's
training to the point that, as Davidson points out, 'whoever was in charge of the
kitchen [...] was as much concerned to match the qualities of the consumers as
to pay attention to flavours [*and*] degrees of doneness'[8]. This approach to gastronomy was a legacy of the medieval theory that four elements correspond to
the four humours that characterise the human being, hence the need to combine gastronomic and medical skills in the kitchen. Good cooks, and certainly
good housewives, were expected to be knowledgeable about nutrition as well
as about the potential medicinal effects of the ingredients they deployed. They
had a certain degree of responsibility towards guests; literally, it behoved them
to nurture people's health through a careful selection and preparation of food,
and the supply of what Victorian cookbook author Jane Stokes referred to as 'a
judicious mixture of bone-forming, strength-giving [...] and warmth-giving material'[9]. The medicine of food gradually came to be 'destroyed by the growth of
railways', Oxford nostalgically and provocatively maintains,[10] nonetheless it was
still regarded as crucial to the art of cooking 'through the first quarter of the

---

[8]   Davidson, *Food*, p. 99.

[9]   Jane Stoker, *Home Comfort: A Complete Manual of Domestic Economy*, London, 1876, p. 132,
      cited in Lieffers, p. 946.

[10] Oxford in the 'Preparatory Note' to *English Cookery Books to the Year 1850*. Arnold Whitaker
      Oxford was a collector with a special interest 'in the combination of cookery with medicine'.
      In an earlier publication, he had noted that 'medicine and cookery are often found united in
      very attractive little volumes in the seventeenth century', after which their combination gives
      way to different criteria for creating recipes. Cf. A. W. Oxford, *Notes from a Collector's Cata-
      logue with a bibliography of English cookery books*. London, John and Edward Bumpus, 1909.
      To Oxfords' attentive and nostalgic eye, the onset of industrialisation and of the age of reason
      marked a shift towards a diverse conception of food-making and of food consuming.

nineteenth century'[11], when it evolved into a complex set of skills that included also economics and chemistry.

Female gastronomy and gastronomic literature developed from an exclusively domestic dimension to a clearly popular and public field of expertise in the nineteenth century, as is especially evinced in the work of Eliza Acton (1799-1859) known mostly for *Modern Cookery, in all its Branches* (1845), and Mrs Isabella Beeton (1836-1865), author of the celebrated *Book of Household Management* (1861). Acton and Beeton were professional cookbook writers whose modern narrative styles changed the way in which recipes were compiled and received. The former was the innovative author of four gastronomy books that placed significant attention to details and introduced a distinctive schematic format entailing 'a list of ingredients and their weights and measurements as well as the precise cooking time'[12]. Acton paid due respect to produce seasonality while also testifying the fact that thanks to its increased wealth Britain was now able to import all sorts of foodstuff, and therefore could aspire to a richer and more varied diet all year round. Mindful of the diverse requirements of readers from religious persuasions other than the dominant one, she sampled all her recipes herself, and was among the first to include foreign and Jewish recipes in her volumes[13]. Her cuisine was at once traditional and experimental, a careful negotiation between domesticity and internationalism, between national identity and the need to 'intermingle', rather than to assimilate the exotic[14].

About fifteen years later, Mrs Beeton replicated Acton's quantitative summary and gradually introduced a diverse layout to her recipes with ingredients being listed *before* the cooking instructions (as opposed to the traditional order, i.e. ingredients appeared after, or at the end). Beeton simplified the traditional paragraph-style narrative with a 'plain cooking method', i.e. a more schematic set of instructions giving quantities in numerical form ('a quarter of a pound' became ¼ Lb), followed by cooking time, costs and number of portions. *The Book of Household Management* responded to its author's 'discomfort and suffering [...] brought about by household mis-management' and was clearly designed to

---

[11] At the height of the era of the railway, *The Modern Housewife*, by Alexis Soyer, included recipes dedicated to the sick: 'receipts for the economic and judicious preparation of every meal of the day, *with those of the nursery and sick room*, and minute directions for family management in all its branches' (180, *emphasis added*).

[12] Lieffers, pp. 940-941.

[13] George Kiloh, *Eliza Acton*, Battleford District Historical Society (BDHS) August 2017, available online at http://btckstorage.blob.core.windows.net/site15733/Web%20M/M%20 2017ELIZA%20ACTONv2.pdf (accessed 30 September 2019).

[14] Eliza Acton, *Modern Cookery in all its Branches*, London, 1845, p. xii.

be 'more than a Cookery Book'[15]. The revolution was 'slow and uneven', as Lieffers notes, but it proved nonetheless efficient in introducing 'systems of order and constituent analysis'[16] and, most importantly for us here, in locating women at the centre of a narrative shift whose effects persist to this day.

By the time Acton and Beeton were teaching readers to cook with accuracy, gastronomy books and their female authors had digested and assimilated the 'closet' rhetoric of several companions and manuals which, especially in the seventeenth and the eighteenth centuries, had assigned women the role of warden of 'rich cabinets stored with all manner of rare recipes' as Hannah Wolley put it in her volume of recipes, the first to be published by a woman in Britain, in the year 1670.[17] As early as then, in fact, cookery books aimed at *instructing* women on how to become 'experienced housekeepers', if not 'complete' and impeccable 'lady's assistants', which suggests their ideological value in terms of containment and construction of gender roles.[18] Indeed, the development and dissemination of didactic literature, including gastronomy books, may reflect a strategy of containment, if not self-containment still during the nineteenth century[19], and for some women that is probably what it came to signify as George Eliot famously lamented in an attack to contemporary 'silly' female writers.[20] Similarly, though more recently, Elizabeth Langland has contended that 'middle-

---

[15] Beeton adds generous sections dedicated to 'the natural history of the animals and vegetables we use as food', 'the nurse' and 'the nursery', 'homeopathy', and a 'legal memoranda'. Cf. Beeton, 'General Contents', in *The Book of Household Management*, pp. 3-4.

[16] Lieffers, p. 943.

[17] Hannah Wolley, *The Queen-Like Closet*, London: Printed for R. Lowndes, 1670.

[18] The term *instructor* appears in the title and subtitles of a number of manuals, eg. *The Ladies' Delight or Cook-Maids best Instructor* (1770); *The Cook's Confectioner's Guide or Female's Instructor, in Cookery, Confectionary, Making Wines, Preserving, Pickles, &c.* (1800); *The Family Friend* or Housekeeper's Instructor (1802); *The Housekeeper's Instructor* (1804); *The Female Instructor* (1815). Cf. Whitaker Oxford, *English*, pp. 104, 126, 132, 143.

[19] Following Frederic Jameson's notion that 'all ideologies are strategies of containment' through which society 'provides an explanation of itself and suppresses the underlying contradictions of History. *Literature as well as literary criticism is necessarily ideological.* Whereas literature seeks to disguise ideological conflicts beneath its language or through its mechanism of censorship, a genuine criticism reveals the traces of censorship in literature, and also recognises the historical origins of its own interpretive concepts or categories'. This kind of criticism is what Jameson calls metacommentary, or dialectical criticism. Emphasis added. Cf. Frederic Jameson, *The Political Unconscious. Narrative as a Socially Symbolic Act*, Ithaca, NY: Cornell U.P., 1981, p. 10.

[20] George Eliot, 'Silly Novels by Lady Novelists', appeared first in the *Westminster Review*, in October 1856, and reprinted in *George Eliot. Selected Essays, poems and other writings*, ed. A.S. Byatt and Nicholas Warren, London, Penguin Books, 1990, pp. 140-163.

class women were produced by these discourses even as they reproduced them to consolidate middle-class control'. What Langland terms 'the complexities of social change and human agency'[21] ought not to be overlooked, and yet a careful consideration of the birth and evolution of the modern cookbook as a cultural phenomenon suggests that those editorial endeavours were capable of giving women a chance to appropriate a dedicated space within the private sphere, where the creative self could express itself and coexist alongside the domestic self. The deliberate 'split'[22] from the predominantly masculine and unwelcoming public sphere proved ideal for women who wanted to write but wished to avoid the level of exposure of most professional female writers (e.g. George Eliot, Harriet Martineau, Elizabeth Gaskell, the Bröntes). Indeed, as Langland concludes, they actually 'performed a more significant and extensive economic and political function than is usually perceived [… by] administering the funds to acquire or maintain social and political status[23]

In those terms collecting, recording, compiling and realising recipes represents a political act proper, one that engaged with current gender discourse and probed the ideological limits of accepted roles. As noted, one area where women's agency was evident was the nutrition-and-health combination required of qualitative food preparations; there was then the transition to the so-called 'science of cookery' which women mastered thus demonstrating their flexibility and ability to schematise recipes, quantify ingredients, calculate times and portions. Equally, women's agency is evident in the introduction of modern styles of recipe writing as well as in aspects of domestic economics and household management, and it is further demonstrated by their interest in exotic food and food ways. Expected to become 'universal' cooks, to recall the title of Francis Collingwood's book[24], Victorian women excelled in the art of foreign cuisine and gained for themselves a leading role as much as, if not more than, their male counterparts. During the nineteenth century women tended to explore and write about exotic culinary traditions, they experimented with diverse ingredients and cooking methods which gradually entered and merged with the local tradition, enriching it in an enduring way as testified today in British culinary heritage and food culture and in the gastronomy lexicon of the English language.

---

[21]   Elizabeth Langland, 'Nobody's Angels: Domestic Ideology and Middle-Class Women in the Victorian Novel', *PMLA*, 107 (2), 1992, pp. 290-304, p. 291.

[22]   Catherin Judd, 'Male Pseudonyms and Female Authority in Victorian England', in John O. Jordan and Robert L. Patten eds, *Literature in the Marketplace. Nineteenth-century British Publishing and Reading Practices*, Cambridge: CUP, 1995, pp. 250-264.

[23]   Langland, p. 291.

[24]   The author of a popular gastronomy book entitled *The Universal Cook* published in 1792.

Foreign influences in Britain's cooking tradition predate Collingwood's manual of 1792, owing partly to political reasons and especially imperialism[25], partly to geographical reasons, as was the case with neighbouring France, considered to be gastronomically the 'most advanced nation in the world', and therefore widely imitated by British cooks[26]. Historical and economic motives were also decisive: wars, poverty, and epidemics caused large waves of immigration to England, a wealthier and more peaceful country by contrast with the rest of the Continent. Migrants, including seasonal and economic travellers, traded food from their native lands and left a permanent trace of their presence in their host countries. The development of a travel culture in the modern age and, later, the emergence of the middle class enabled the English to come into contact with different food cultures that they brought home, perhaps nostalgically, as if they were souvenirs. Some recipes replicated the French, the Italian, the German, the Japanese or Chinese 'manner' of cooking[27]; some were translations or even 'thefts', from earlier writers[28]; others were recorded as a traveller's first-hand experiences[29] or else they had been donated to the author by foreign friends and acquaintances (cf. Preface, Mrs Beeton). More flavours and combinations of food entered the British kitchen by way of recipes reported directly from the Grand Tour such as letters, diaries and professional writings, thereby becoming assimilated into the national cuisine[30]. As women specialised

---

[25] As Alan Davidson maintains in this respect, 'the existence and global extent of the British Empire began [...] to exert important influences on British cookery and cookery writing'. Cf. 'The Natural History of British Cookery Books', p. 105.

[26] Davidson, p. 104.

[27] Mrs Beeton prepares 'Italian', 'Japanese' and 'Polish' salads (pp. 1102-1103), dedicating careful attention to the origins and uses of food types she introduces regularly in her recipes, especially herbs.

[28] A manual from 1574, was 'written in Latin by Gulielmus Gratarolus, and Englished by T. N.'; in 1598, 'Epulario', was a translation of a book by Giovanne de Rosselli; in 1745 a manual was based on translation from the Italian of Antonio Cocchi of Mugello by R. Dodsley. Cf. Whitaker Oxford, *English*.

[29] For instance, 'A Lady' refers to how travelling experiences led to the publication of oriental food recipes in her *Domestic Economy and Cookery* (1827).

[30] In his history of British cookery books, Davidson refers to the way in which foreign recipes were traded into the country, usually through foreign cookbooks, letters exchanged with authors, and as travelling abroad became easier for women too by way of individual experiences. The anonymous Lady authoring *Domestic Economy and Cookery* (1827) could publish exotic recipes following 'a long residence abroad [which] had made her familiar with European cooking'. Cf. Davidson, p. 105. Curious references to food and the English travellers of the Grand Tour are found also in Attilio Brilli, *Un paese di romantici briganti. Gli Italiani nell'immaginario del Grand Tour,* Parma, Il Mulino, 2003.

in the art of cooking and in the creative art of writing recipes, their role as mediators between foreign food cultures and their national readers gained further
strength. In transcribing, personalising and following those cooking instructions
women *de facto* facilitated a process of cultural encounter; they adapted to consumers' demands but also shaped their tastes, ultimately asserting their female
expertise and authorial power. A good example of their role is found among the
pages of *The Handbook of Household Management*. Mrs Beeton presents her
reader with a 'Soup à la Solferino' which she describes as 'Sardinian Recipe [...]
inherited from an English gentleman who '*Anglicised* it and somewhat, *he thinks,*
improved it' (*emphasis mine*)[31]. The wording betrays the communicative strategy and narrative ability of a skilled woman who shares a rare recipe and lets
readers know that a) it is *not her* make, and b) that in its present ('Anglicised')
form this foreign soup is an improvement according to the English donor (*he
thinks*, but does she?), to whom she is openly grateful and deliberately gives full
credit.

The circulation of foreign recipes at home facilitated cultural encounters, it
has been noted, and it also helped open gastronomic frontiers. These processes
were reflected at the linguistic level by the introduction of a new *ad hoc* vocabulary: as with recipes, foreign words were assimilated into the national idiom in
order to articulate the constantly changing food landscape. In this respect, the
permanence of foreign food types and terms of the English language as spoken
today (*zucchini, broccoli, aubergine, pomegranate, macaroons, etc...*), is a remarkable legacy of nineteenth-century female writing and its place within the
cultural history of their country. On the one hand, the incidence of original food
names testifies the fascinating otherness of the foods prepared; on the other,
linguistic faithfulness contributed to enrich the English vocabulary with new gastronomic words whose translation was and remains unnecessary. There appears
to be a will to preserve the 'exotic aura'[32] surrounding ingredients and recipes,
and to value the vitality and creative force of food preparations that are distinc-
tively experimental, and at times bizarre, both linguistically and gastronomically.
Fidelity to tradition was never of the essence, it seems, nor did the question of

---

[31] Mrs Beeton, p. 159. The Englishman, recounts Mrs Beeton, 'was present at the battle of Solferino, on June 24, 1859, and was requested by some of Victor Emmanuel's troops, on the day
before the battle, to partake of a portion of their *potage*. He willingly enough consented and
found that these clever campaigners had made a most palatable dish from very easily-pro-
cured materials'.

[32] Laura Pinnavia, *The Italian borrowings in the Oxford English Dictionary. A lexicographical, linguistic and cultural analysis*, Roma, Bulzoni, 2001, p. 100. An analysis of borrowings found in
the OED is also included.

authenticity appear to pose obstacles to new culinary trends that nonetheless guaranteed the provision of healthy and tasty meals. Viewed in this light, the art of cooking became the art of mediating between cultures, languages, tastes, geographies, between past and present, between one's tradition and traditions of the mind, both exotic and invented. This brings us back to the role of women who, in the nineteenth century, inherited, copied, plagiarised, adapted, collected and transmitted the several recipes we still use. And it is perhaps not fortuitous if the Latin term *recipere*, from which the English 'recipe' is coined, means *to exchange*[33], *to give and take* some precious *exchange* goods. Recipes, in other words, reflect the kind of cultural exchange that the Grand Tour was meant to promote.

To conclude, there is more to gastronomic manuals than ordinary cooking instructions, and where the history of English cookery books is concerned there is also a fascinating world of stories about food and the people who dealt with it. In the nineteenth century, the development of a popular and successful literary genre owes to the efforts of a host of talented women whose voices emerged from the domestic sphere to become agents of cultural encounters and claim for themselves a space wherein to nourish and liberate their culinary imagination. The art of writing and realising food recipes, a form of expression in which these women became proficient, bears a broader significance as an art of mediation between different and distant cultures. In these terms, recipes by nineteenth-century professional female were narratives capable of exerting a socially normative function, sites where different languages, cultures, and customs, both local and foreign, meet and mix, like the ingredients of a new and promising recipe, waiting to be sampled and exchanged.

---

[33] Cf. Susan Leonardi, 'Recipes for Reading: Summer Pasta, Lobster à La Riseholme, and Key Lime Pie', *PMLA*, vol. 104, no. 3, 1989, pp. 340–347, p. 345, www.jstor.org/stable/462443 (accessed 20 September 2019), cited in Theophano, p. 41.

Bolg an tSolair, or: A Gaelic Miscellany

Mary Delargy

The 1790s were a decade of great turmoil in Ireland. The Society of United Irishmen, founded in 1791, initially sought parliamentary reform but, inspired by events in France and America, gradually became more radical, eventually resulting in the rebellion of 1798. Nor was the Ireland of this time free from sectarian strife. One of the most bitter incidents of the conflict was the Battle of the Diamond of September 1795: 'Protestants occupying a strong hilltop position fought off a large crowd of Defenders from surrounding counties, killing thirty or more' (Connolly 2002: 154). This incident led to the formation of the Orange Order dedicated to 'sustaining the glorious and immortal memory of King William and his followers at the Battle of the Boyne' (Connolly 2002: 434), in which the Catholic King James was defeated, and the Protestant monarchy restored.

Against this political strife was a contrasting and growing interest among members of the Protestant community in various aspects of Irish culture. One of these was in archaeology, another was the Harp Festival of 1792 which took place in the Assembly Rooms in Belfast. Its aim was to preserve and record the music of the last harpers, with Edward Bunting, then assistant organist to Sir William Ware, charged with recording the music. Ten Irish harpers and one Welsh took part in the event, with the oldest being ninety-six years of age, and many of the participants being blind. Several of the tunes which Bunting collected at this time were later included in his Ancient Music of Ireland.

The first magazine in the Irish language was published in the same year. The title *Bolg an tSolair* literally translates as 'the stomach of the work', or, more poetically, as 'a miscellany'. Three people were associated with the magazine, all of very differing backgrounds. The three were Charlotte Brooke, Thomas Russell and Patrick Lynch (or Padraig Ó Loinsigh).

At this time, three main languages were used in Ireland; English among the aristocracy and those in positions of authority; Latin as a written means of communication and in the church and Irish, which as the language of the native was considered the language of the poor and the peasant; few of the better off would have considered learning anything about it. Charlotte Brooke, however, stood in stark contrast to this prevailing attitude. Born in County Cavan in 1743, she was one of twenty-two children of Henry Brooke. A playwright and author, Henry Brooke was the son of a Church of Ireland minister. Charlotte was the only one of the children to reach adulthood and had a close relationship with her father from whom she got her love of literature. It is said that she spent a lot of her early years with her father's servants and those from the neighbouring estates. And it was from them that she learned the Irish language. She took an interest not only in the language itself but in the poetry and stories associated with it. In 1789, the year of the French Revolution, Brooke published her own revolutionary work, *Reliques of Irish Poetry* which was reprinted in 1816. The collection was seen as revolutionary in two different ways; firstly it was a bilingual collection, with the English translation on the facing page to that in Irish but also it was seen as one of the works challenging McPherson's assertion that his Ossianic poems were his own creation rather than derived from an Irish source. The preface to the book sets out her views on the importance and significance of Irish literature (Brooke 1816: cxxxii):

> It is really astonishing of what various and comprehensive powers this neglected language is possessed. In the pathetic, it breathes the most beautiful and affecting simplicity; and in the bolder species of composition it is distinguished by a force of expression, a sublime dignity and rapid energy, which it is scarcely possible for any translation fully to convey; as it sometimes fills the mind with ideas altogether new, and which, perhaps, no modern language is entirely prepared to express.

Later in the introduction she turns her attention to the relationship between Ireland and Britain telling us (Brooke 1816: cxxxiii):

> As yet, we are too little known to our noble neighbour of Britain; were we better acquainted, we should be better friends. The British muse is not yet informed that she has an elder sister in this isle, let us then introduce them to each other!

As a woman, Brooke was not eligible to become a member of the recently established Royal Irish Academy; however, she applied for a position as a cleaner there, stating that in her favour she was the daughter of a great man!

Charlotte Brooke died in 1793, because of the uncertainty surrounding the year of her birth, we know only that she was under fifty years old at the time. Such was the significance of her poetry anthology, however, that it was decided to include some of these poems in *Bolg an Tsolair* in order to introduce them to a wider audience.

The growing interest of the Hiberno-Irish as they self-described at the time was also reflected in Joseph Cooper Walker's *Historical Memoirs of the Irish*

Bards, published in 1786, again reflecting a growing interest in things Irish. Both Lesa Ni Mhunghaile in her thesis on Cooper and Eileen Battersby in her review of the new edition of Brooke's poems suggest that this is due to an increased self confidence among the Hiberno-Irish coupled with a growing realisation of their distinctiveness from their English counterparts.

The second person associated with this publication was Thomas Russell, immortalised in Florence Mary Wilson's poem 'The Man from God Knows Where'. Russell was born in Cork in 1767. As a member of a military family, he joined the army and was posted to India. He was subsequently posted to Belfast where he made the acquaintance of many of the important families in the town such as the McCrackens – where Mary Ann fell deeply in love with him, describing him as 'a model of manly beauty' – the Neilsons, and the Drennans. He was one of the leaders at the foundation of the United Irishmen, having already resigned his army commission. Among his later posts was librarian at the recently formed Linen Hall Library to which he was appointed in 1794. From there, he was able to continue his activities with the United Irishmen, becoming the commander in county Down in 1796. He was arrested in the same year and imprisoned although he was never formally charged. In the aftermath of his time in jail, he became acquainted with Robert Emmett whose rebellion of 1803 was a total failure and saw both Emmett and Russell hanged for their part in it.

Prior to this, Russell had expressed an interest in learning the Irish language and found an enthusiastic and skilled teacher in Patrick Lynch from Loughinisland in County Down. While he did not reach a level of fluency which allowed him to make a contribution in Irish to the magazine, he was responsible for writing the introduction, which echoes in part the sentiments expressed by Charlotte Brooke in her earlier volume (Brooke 1795: iv):

> The Irish shall be found to the unprejudiced ear, to excel in the harmony of its cadence; nor was ever any language fitter to express the feelings of the heart; nor need it be wondered at, when we consider that their country was the seat of the muses , from times of the remotest antiquity, and that no nation ever encouraged poets and musicians, more than the ancient Irish. ….It is chiefly with a view to prevent in some measure the total neglect, and to diffuse the beauties of this ancient and once admired language that the following compilation is offered to the public hoping to afford a pleasing retrospect to every Irishman who respects the traditions or considers the language and compositions of our early ancestors as a matter of curiosity or importance.

The final and arguably the main contributor, was Patrick Lynch, or Padraig O Loinsigh, from the village of Loughinisland in county Down. The family were known in the locality as scribes and hedge school masters, versed both in Irish and the Classics. Patrick is recorded in 1794 as teaching Irish at Belfast Royal Academy, a progressive school founded in 1785. In addition to his teaching, Lynch was also employed to accompany Edward Bunting on his travels through Connacht in 1802. His role was to record the words of the songs collected as Bunting was not familiar with the Irish language, these numbered around three hundred in total. The following year, Lynch returned to Belfast where he testified at the trial of his former pupil and friend, Thomas Russell. Although it is known that he was forced to give this evidence, his friends found it difficult to forgive him and Bunting excluded all of Lynch's work from the second edition of his Ancient Music of Ireland. Nothing is known of his life after this time although he is believed to be buried in Loughinisland.

The magazine itself contains one hundred and twenty pages and is divided into sections. The first of these deals with various aspects of the grammar, such as the letters used in the alphabet, the division of nouns into masculine and feminine and their declension. The materials then progress to suggested dialogues, such as one between a merchant and a farmer and another between a merchant, a famer and a priest. Religion is not overlooked as there are several short passages from scripture along with The Lord's Prayer and the Apostles' Creed. The final section of the publication contains the words of songs in Irish with English translations. These are by well-known writers such as Patrick Linden's Maid of the Valley and McCabe's Sgaradh na gCompanach or the Elegy on the death of Carolan.

Also included is a Fenian poem 'Laoi na Sealga' or The Chase, translated by Charlotte Brooke. The poem consists of more than one hundred and thirty-four-line stanzas and takes the form of a debate between St Patrick and Oisin, the member of the Fianna left behind after the death of his companions and who is eventually baptised into the Christian church. These debates are a common motif in literature in Irish, used to illustrate that there is a continuous link between the heroes of pre-Christian Ireland and the saints who bring the Christian faith. Laoi na Sealga is also known under the title Toraiocht Shliabh gCuilinn or the Chase on Slieve Gullion , a mountain in South Armagh, with a mysterious lake at the top whose magical properties included turning the hair grey on any man who attempted to search for the beautiful maiden believed to live there. As with many similar stories, the 'beautiful maiden' becomes a wizened hag just as the men catch up with her.

Bolg an tSolair was published at the press of the Belfast newspaper the Northern Star. Founded in 1792, it was the voice of the United Irishmen, reflecting their radical views in addition to keeping the citizens of Belfast informed of developments in France following the revolution. The press also printed books such as *A Letter to the People of Ireland on the Present State of the Country*, an essay by Thomas Russell. Its editor Samuel Neilson was tried for sedition on several occasions before the presses were eventually destroyed by the Belfast militia in 1797.

Its publishers intended to produce a periodical magazine for they asked their readers to send them articles for inclusion in the next edition: 'Any communications suitable to the design either in prose or verse shall be received with gratitude by the compilers of the GAELIC MAGAZINE' (Brooke 1795: 10). As we have seen, however, circumstances conspired to ensure that there would only ever be one edition of *Bolg an tSolair*.

An examination of the catalogue of Belfast Printed books in the Linen Hall Library gives us an insight into the type of material being published in the town at that period. Titles include *Five Sermons on the Fundamental Companion* and *Sacramental Meditations* as well as *Paddy's Resource*, 'a collection of original and modern patriotic songs compiled for the use of the people of Ireland'. These were originally published in the Northern Star before being collected in a single edition. They were composed by the Reverend James Porter of Greyabbey, who was eventually tried and hanged for treason in sight of his own church in 1798.

Two other books from the same year deal with the French Revolution: *A Discourse on the Rise and Fall of the Antichrist*, wherein the revolution in France is distinctly pointed out, and another, entitled *Prophetical Extracts Particularly such as Relate to the Revolution in France*. This second title was one of the first printed in Strabane.

In 1995, to commemorate the bicentenary of its publication, the Linen Hall Library decided to reprint *Bolg an tSolair*. The continuing interest in this work is reflected in the fact that all one hundred copies of the limited edition of the magazine sold out on the day of its publication. However, even today, the influence of *Bolg an tSolair* cannot be underestimated. Firstly, it appeals to those wishing to learn the Irish language as well as those already well versed in it; secondly, its contributors are from various strata of society as well as differing political and religious beliefs, something still reflected in the Irish speaking community today.

References

Brooke, C (1795), *Bolg an tSolair* (Belfast).

Brooke, C (1816), *Reliques of Irish poetry: Consisting of Heroic Poems, Odes, Elegies and Songs* (Dublin: Christie).

Connolly, S (2002) *Oxford Companion to Irish History* (Oxford: Oxford University Press).

Why Irish?
The Use of Irish in the Oeuvre of Éilís Ní Dhuibhne

Helena Wulff

Inspired by Máiréad Nic Craith's influential work on language, culture and power, especially the role of minority languages and questions of bilingualism, this short essay discusses the use of the Irish language in fiction and short stories by the writer Éilís Ní Dhuibhne. Why, when and how has Éilís, who has a reputation as a writer in both languages, chosen to write in Irish (Gaelic)—which has a relatively small readership as this is a small language—rather than in English with a considerably larger readership?

Éilís Ní Dhuibhne was born in 1954 and grew up in Dublin, where she went to Irish language schools and then to University College Dublin for a PhD in Irish Folklore. She took up a job as a librarian in the National Library of Ireland and eventually got a position as a teaching fellow at the MA in creative writing at University College Dublin. I included Éilís's work in both my anthropological studies in Ireland: the first one considered the social role of dance, memory and tradition (Wulff 2007), while the second study focussed on writing as craft and career: the social world of Irish literature (Wulff 2017). In the latter study, I discuss the small scale of Irish language publishing in Ireland in terms of a 'literary world-within-the-Irish literary world' (Wulff 2017: 22). Éilís Ní Dhuibhne first told me about this momentous literary world as I did not have Irish, and thus could not read its literature. Still, for me, the Irish language literary world remains alluring and largely unavailable. Among the writers I researched such as John Banville, Colm Tóibín, Anne Enright and Deirdre Madden, most published in Ireland as well as internationally, although to different extent. Éilís publishes in three language markets: the Irish and English markets in Ireland, and the English in Britain, the United States and Australia. In addition, her fiction has been translated into Bulgarian, Czech, German, Italian and Japanese. Some of Éilís' stories have been included in international anthologies published, for instance, by Faber in Britain. However, there is one hurdle for Éilís Ní Dhuibhne to publish on a large scale internationally, and thus acquire a major international reputation. She is aware that her Irish name cannot be pronounced by non-Irish speakers (it is 'Alish Ne Gwivne') and thus they will not remember it. This is occasionally an issue even in Ireland. Nonetheless, she is since long a prominent writer in Ireland. She is a member of *Aosdána* (meaning 'people of the arts'), an academy of writers and artists, and serves on juries for literary prizes and scholarships. Still, her career trajectory has been more fragmented than for most other Irish writers (or most other writers, probably) as she has published under all of three names, some of which are pseudonyms. Her full English name is Elizabeth Deeney but she used the name Elizabeth Dean when she began publishing at age 18. She preferred a pseudonym because not only was she timid about being a writer, but also one who wrote about sexual feelings in Catholic Ireland. When she eventually started writing children's books, she wanted to use a different name than the one she used for adult books. Then it became important to use a name that many people would be able to pronounce so she chose Elizabeth O'Hara, which was her grandmother's family name. Yet, for most of her publications both in Irish and in English, she has used Éilís Ní Dhuibhne, the Irish version of her name (Wulff 2017: 22-23)

For this essay, I asked Éilís on email why and when she prefers to write in the Irish language.[1] Here is her reply:

Although I am a fluent Irish speaker/writer when I started writing stories and poems I wrote only in English. In 1995, a theatre director asked me to workshop some of my English short stories with an Irish theatre company. I did this and as a result of the project wrote a play in Irish—Dún na mBan Trí Thine (1994). It was produced in the Peacock Theatre and was a success. I felt at home writing in Irish and for an Irish speaking audience—it was like a sort of homecoming. I wrote a second play and then an Irish language publisher asked me to consider writing a novel. I did so and it went on from there. Since c. 1996 I have written five novels in Irish, two radio plays, two stage plays, and I have also written TV scripts for an Irish language drama series.

Éilís went on to tell me that her father was a native Irish speaker, which means that he was born and grew up in an Irish speaking region of Ireland, in Donegal, and 'I was given the Irish language as a gift from him and my mother'—she never had to learn it systematically, but picked it up. So her first language is English and it is her strongest, which she suggests would be the case for any person, that one language is the strongest. Writing in Irish was a revelation and a significant political statement, one of national identity:

---

[1]   The date of the email from Éilís Ní Dhuibhne where she replied to my questions was 23 May 2019. I am grateful for her comments on the essay.

> Once I began to write in Irish I realized I could do it. I also felt that this was the one thing I could do to keep the Irish language alive. I didn't want to be the generation in my family to break our language chain—presumably my family has been speaking Irish for hundreds of years.

To my question if there are topics that she 'saves' for Irish language publications, topics that she does not write about in English, she explained that she has usually written quite differently in Irish from the way she writes in English. Her first Irish text was a play, and she has never written a play in English. Her first Irish novel was a detective novel. She had never written in that genre in English, but was in fact inspired by reading Henning Mankell's novels in Swedish. She had noticed that it was easy for her to read his novels in the original Swedish, for various reasons: '1.) the vocabulary was simple (even if it includes a lot of words relating to crime), 2.) The sentences were short, and 3.) the story was so gripping that I had to keep on reading once I got into it.' So she thought that a crime novel in Irish might work in the same way, for readers who might not be accustomed to reading Irish language books. And it turned out that she was right: 'The novel—although not as good as anything by Mankell!—was a best seller, by Irish language standards!'

A note of clarification is in place in passing here: the reason that Éilís reads and speaks Swedish is that she was married to the leading Swedish folklorist, Bo Almqvist, for over thirty years, until his death in 2013 (see her memoir, Dhuibhne 2018). She continues:

> In English I usually write literary fiction—short stories and novels. In Irish, I have broken into other genres. I have written one 'literary fiction' novel, Cailíní Beaga Ghleann na mBláth (2003). Otherwise novels for teenagers, and two detective novels.

> I don't think there are topics that I write about in Irish that I would not write about in English. My last novel in Irish, however, dealt with the issue of abortion in the context of Ireland—I wrote it in the year or two before the 8th amendment was repealed and abortion finally legalised in Ireland. I don't think I would have shied away from this topic in English, but the fact is that I chose to write about it in Irish.

Before wrapping up, let us juxtapose Éilís Ní Dhuibhne's relationship to the Irish language with that of Máiréad Nic Craith. The first thing to note is that Máiréad's name is easier to pronounce for a non-Irish speaker. Just like Éilís, she had a bilingual upbringing, but in the south of Ireland (Nic Craith 2012: ix):

> The language of my childhood home was primarily English but my mother would frequently engage with me in Irish. At the time I perceived this as primarily an effort to improve my linguistic skills in a language which was important for stable employment in the state sector. With hindsight, I also appreciate it as an expression of my mother's love for the language in which she was educated and in which she communicates very successfully—probably more effectively than in English. My sister and three brothers frequently and affectionately teased us about speaking Irish—a banter which served to encourage rather than discourage our 'private' conversations.

Combining her own experience of growing up speaking two languages with her research, Máiréad states that bilingualism within households is quite common in Ireland also historically (Nic Craith 2012: ix). Contrary to Éilís, Máiréad has done almost all her academic writings in English: 'Although my first two books were written in Irish Gaelic, all subsequent volumes have been written in English. This was a deliberate decision based not just on the limited numbers of readers of Irish Gaelic, but also on the marketability of such work outside of Ireland' (Nic Craith 2009: 205). Her 2020 book, *The Vanishing World of The Islandman*, explores the life story, in Irish, of a fisherman, Tomás Ó Criomhthain, who a century ago lived on the Great Blasket Island, just off the west coast of Ireland. Although Máiréad Nic Craith stopped writing in Irish herself, her expert knowledge of the language and its culture has been very useful for her career, as she has been able to include it in her research. She has written extensively about the Irish language making it one characteristic of her distinguished career.

References

Nic Craith, M. (2009), 'Writing Europe: a Dialogue of Liminal Europeans', *Social Anthropology* 17(2): 198-208.

Nic Craith, M. (2012), *Narratives of Place, Belonging and Language: An Intercultural Perspective* (New York: Palgrave).

Nic Craith, M. (2020), *The Vanishing World of The Islandman: Narrative and Nostalgia* (New York: Palgrave).

Ní Dhuibhne, É. (1994), *Dún na mBan trí Thine*. Play performed by Amharclann de Hide, at the Peacock Theatre, Dublin, November.

Ní Dhuibhne, É. (2003), *Cailíní Beaga Ghleann na mBláth* (Dublin: Cois Life).

Ní Dhuibhne, É. (2018), *Twelve Thousand Days: A Memoir of Love and Loss* (Belfast: Blackstaff).

Wulff, H. (2007), *Dancing at the Crossroads: Memory and Mobility in Ireland* (Oxford: Berghahn).

Wulff, H. (2017), *Rhythms of Writing: An Anthropology of Irish Literature* (London: Bloomsbury).

On Potatoes
The Many Powers of a Popular Tuber

Michaela Fenske and Ulrich Marzolph

From Ireland to the European Continent: Potatoes as Actants

Potatoes for breakfast, potatoes for lunch, potatoes for dinner (if you were lucky enough to have three meals a day): In a casual and matter-of-fact way, Irish author Tomás Ó Criomhthain's (Thomas O'Crohan's) autobiography *An tOileánach* (The Islandman, 1929), one of the most important works of modern Gaelic literature, makes readers aware of the tremendous relevance of potatoes in the diet of Irish people at the beginning of the twentieth century (and beyond).[1] After potatoes had been introduced to Europe in the context of the sixteenth-century Spanish expeditions to South America, farmers were at first slow to adopt the previously unknown tuber. Although it is not known exactly how potatoes reached the British Isles, at the end of the sixteenth century they were apparently grown in English gardens as ornamental plants. Sir Walter Raleigh (d. 1618) is credited with a key role in bringing the potato to Ireland (Salaman 1949: 148) that subsequently became one of the first European countries where farmers cultivated the tuber for its nutritional value in large quantities in the fields. From Ireland, potatoes started their triumphal procession through Europe, enriching Europe's cultural heritage (Krug-Richter 2019, Heidrich and Kohlberger 2004). Even if general assessments of European history do not specifically emphasise the point, there is little doubt that potatoes stimulated unity in Europe in terms of everyday essentials. As a powerful actant (Latour 2010) in European history, potatoes had a lasting impact on European societies and played a major role in the history of modernity, especially the nineteenth-century population boom and the industrialisation in Europe. The present essay is a modest contribution towards highlighting narratives and popular writing on the tuber whose forceful effects on humans not only, but especially in European societies, can hardly be overestimated. Particular attention will be devoted to the popular writing of women, who were responsible for preparing the family meals and whose daily routine was shaped by potatoes.

---

[1] We used the German translation prepared by German author Heinrich Böll and his wife Annemarie, published in one of Máiréad's favorite German towns, entitled *Die Boote fahren nicht mehr aus: Bericht eines irischen Fischers* (Göttingen: Steidl, [8]1999); potatoes are mentioned, e. g., pp. 15, 24, 26, 37, 39, 41, 42, 48. The book's international impact has been studied in great detail in Nic Craith (2020).

As a plant, potatoes are humble and productive, as a diet they are at the same time nourishing as well as tasty and healthy, including the positive effects of carbohydrates for the human production of Serotonin, a neurotransmitter that is popularly regarded as contributing to happiness. Simple to prepare as a meal, potatoes also offer a large variety of possible preparations, and they are affordable at relatively low price. No vegetable was as influential in times of increasing populations as potatoes. Once accepted by the people, potatoes became the food staple in many European societies. Potatoes were one of the important motors of modernity in Europe, supplying energy to people to work for many hours as fishermen, farmers, and increasingly as workers in factories. Particularly people from the working classes profited considerably from the new food, and potatoes soon became an effective instrument to stave off the hunger of the many. Consequently, if potatoes were not available or if the crop failed, particularly the poor suffered, as dramatically evidenced by the Great Irish famine 1845–1852. Against the backdrop of the historical experience, potatoes have become a symbol of the working class in art and literature. Rather than being celebrated as a monumental contribution to nutrition, it is precisely the casual appearance of potatoes as a factor of daily life that marks their supreme relevance for European cultures since early modern times.

Potatoes Narrating Everyday Lives

If one considers the whole universe of practices of narrating—oral, written, and visual narratives alike, explicitly performed as well as implied ones (Marzolph and Bendix 2014)—there are numerous stories about the role of potatoes in everyday life. For instance, in Dutch artist Vincent van Gogh's impressive painting *De Aardappeleters* (The Potato Eaters, 1885), a peasant family shares a meal of potatoes. Illuminated by the warm light of a little lamp dangling from the ceiling, five persons gather in a paltry chamber around a bowl of steaming potatoes. With this painting, van Gogh mainly intended to communicate the harsh reality of peasant life and the peasants enjoying the fruit of their strenuous physical labour. Even so, the steaming potatoes in the painting's centre tell an additional story. They communicate how a meal of potatoes brings people together, allowing them to share not only a simple meal, but also the basics of a good life with people eating their fill. One might mention in passing that the Dutch peasant family also enjoys a hot beverage, most likely coffee, but the beneficial and consolatory effects of hot (and sweet) coffee is another story that will have to be discussed elsewhere. If the social institution of the meal brings people together (e.g. Barlösius [3]2016: 179-217), it is the potatoes that makes them full and satisfied.

Potatoes also make an appearance in popular narratives or folktales about clever people such as peasants or workers for whom being tricky, resilient and resourceful was a way to counterbalance their underprivileged position. Variants of the tale of 'The Crop Division,' a tale that is widely documented from nineteenth- and twentieth-century European tradition as tale type 1030 (Köhler 1984), tell about a peasant who outsmarts the devil: When the devil demands half of the year's crop, the peasant readily offers to let the devil have everything growing above the ground. When harvest comes, the devil learns that the peasant has grown potatoes. Therefore, although the peasant performed the contract as agreed, there is no crop for the devil.

Until today potatoes constitute an important element in narrating social and cultural history in popular culture. Probably the single internationally most popular potato is the one Leopold Bloom, the fictional protagonist of Irish author James Joyce's novel *Ulysses* (1922), makes sure is in his pocket before heading out for the day. The initially cryptic reasons why Bloom carries the tuber on him are gradually revealed, and finally it becomes clear that for Bloom, the potato is a talisman, a home remedy that his mother had given to him: 'Poor Mama's panacea' (Merritt 1990; Chou 2019). Bloom's initially enigmatic habit thus mirrors popular belief in Ireland (and other countries) holding that a dried potato carried in the pocket protects against rheumatism (Marzell 1931/32: col. 1025; Salaman 1949: 118). Another random example of the potato's prominent role in popular culture is encountered in an episode of *Outlander* (2014), a TV-serial based on the original series of novels written by US-American author Diana Gabaldon (see 'List of *Outlander* Episodes'). The story focusses on the adventures of Claire Randall, an Englishwoman visiting Scotland in the 1940s who is involuntarily transported two hundred years back in time by the magical power of a mythical stone circle. Arriving at the very same location in 1743, Claire not only finds romance and adventure with Scotsman James Frazer, but also experiences traditional highland life at the time when the Scottish Jacobites aim to restore the House of Stuart to the thrones of England, Scotland, and Ireland. Knowing what is to happen in the future, Claire attempts in vain to prevent the disasters recorded in history books, particularly the battle of Culloden in 1746 with its dramatic loss of human life and its devastating effects for traditional Scottish highland culture. In one episode (season 2, episode 8), Claire suggests cultivating potatoes to protect the members of her new family from a forthcoming famine. They escape starvation, and the whole family celebrates the previously unknown tuber, gathering around the table happily discussing new potato recipes. As in van Gogh's painting, the potato here again communicates the vegetable's power, which lies not only in supplying food but also in its social power to bring families and friends together. In addition, the final scene also demonstrates the high esteem potatoes were awarded by people from different social milieus. This esteem is equally evident in the popular writings of nineteenth- and early twentieth-century middle-class women in Europe.[2]

Women Writing Potatoes

Researchers studying the autobiographical writing of less privileged people often focus on genres like diaries or other explicitly autobiographical reports. Until the beginning of the twentieth century, the majority of these sources were produced by men, such as the autobiographical report written by the Irish fisherman Tomás Ó Criomhthain, mentioned above. The numerous autobiographical texts written by women have so far not received the attention they deserve. As a rare exception to the rule, American folklorist Janet Theophano convincingly argued that handwritten cookbooks produced by women from early modern times until today may potentially also be read as autobiographical texts. By taking down and exchanging cooking recipes, young women were integrated into the social meshwork constituted by those of different generations in their neighbourhoods, families and friendships. By writing about cooking, the young women were also gradually introduced into their social roles as prospective housewives and heads of household. Historically, the individual writing of a cookbook was primarily an informal practice of female education in upper middle-class families that also served to improve female literacy. In Germany, the practice increasingly became part of the formal education of young women in institutions teaching household management, so-called *Haushaltungsschulen*.

From the perspective of an anthropology of writing (Barton and Pape 2010), handwritten cookbooks offer fascinating insights into the culture of the middle classes of the late nineteenth and early twentieth centuries (Fenske 2017). It is probably not surprising to discover that Irish fishermen and German middle class people shared a similar delight in potatoes. The pivotal message concerning potatoes documented in the handwritten cookbooks is that one can prepare potatoes for any meal at any season. Potatoes could serve as essential ingredients in almost every daily dish. Why should cooking potatoes in the kitchen be a boring task? To the contrary! Women knew so many varieties of cooking potatoes, whether boiled, fried, or roasted. Potatoes could be prepared as soup, casserole, salad, dumpling or whatever else. If a vegetable had such a

---

[2]   The following recipes are taken from the authors' private collection of handwritten German cookbooks dating to the late nineteenth and early twentieth centuries.

large potential, no wonder that potatoes also offered themselves to demonstrate refined culinary education. Writing potatoes allowed women to mark their social status.

The cookbook of Theresa H., undoubtedly a lower middle-class woman, states that no meal should be served without (boiled) potatoes. Potato dishes recorded in other cookbooks are more sophisticated. In the cookbook that Sofie H. began and that was continued by another woman of her family, there are different potato dishes for each day of the week: potatoes boiled in meat stock on Monday, potato in béchamel sauce on Tuesday, raw fried potatoes on Wednesday, potato in their skin on Thursday, followed by roasted potatoes, potato salad with sausage in it, dumplings, mashed potatoes etc. (Sophie H., 1924). Variety and diversity serve as a possibility to demonstrate a sophisticated potato kitchen. One could cook potatoes à la French, as recorded in Emilie L.'s cookbook: pommes soufflé, pommes lyonnaise, pommes croquets, potatoes à la maître, pommes dauphin, espagnole-potatoes, pommes frites, pommes chateau (Emilie L., 1902, 1906).

If a woman was very fond of potatoes, the cooking knowledge of her time allowed a variety of three courses menus to make the cook and her family or guests at the same time full and happy.

How to Become Full and Happy: Conviviality with Potatoes

The best way to start a meal with potatoes was to cook a soup. A popular recipe at the beginning of the twentieth century goes: 'one kilo of potatoes, 20 grams of flour, 1.5 litres of water, greens, 10 grams of salt, 30 grams of fat such as bacon. Wash and peel the potatoes, boil them together with the washed, polished and cut up greens in the water and add salt. Mash the potatoes and add the flour, mixed with cold water. Boil the soup once again. Now you add the roasted bacon and probably some salt.' (Anonymus, ca. 1920) There are also recipes without bacon, and that might be a good choice in case an extensive second course follows.

For second course, potatoes were an essential side dish for meat or fish, and most often some other vegetables were added: 'roast mutton, red cabbage and potatoes', 'beef and dumplings', 'roulades, potatoes and carrots', 'meat burgers, mashed potatoes and lettuce' or 'fish, mustard sauce and potatoes' were popular combinations (Sofia H. 1929; Else K. 1931). If potatoes should constitute the menu's main ingredient and not only an aside, one might follow the recipe of that woman whose handwritten cookbook has more than 500 pages, many of them filled with potato recipes. Her proposal for a convenient second course named 'potato chops' (probably corresponding to today's potato cro-quettes): 'good mealy potatoes are boiled in their skin, then peeled; after they are totally cold they are mashed; 220 grams of them are mixed with 70 grams of foamy butter, three egg yolks, a little bit of salt and rubbed nutmeg. This dough is formed into finger thick chops. Turn them in a battered egg and bread-crumbs, bake them on each side brown and serve them with carved meatballs.' (Anonyma, about 1900).

At the end of a menu, there are several possibilities to serve sweet pota-toes. Potato macaroons, potato doughnuts, sweet potato pudding, potato pie, sweet potato dish with raspberries are listed as the most popular recipes. But why not prepare a tarte of potatoes? The following recipe, recorded by Louise H., was popular in the upper middle class households at the beginning of the twentieth century: 'Potato tarte: 12 eggs, ¾ pounds of sugar, 1.5 pound of (boiled) potatoes, the peel of a lemon, 60 grams of farina, 30 grams of bitter almonds, three spoons of starch flour (some recipes also add rum). Egg yolks, sugar and lemon must be beaten until they are foamy. Add the dry mashed po-tatoes and the peeled crumbled almonds and at last the beaten egg whites. The tarte has to be baked more than one hour.' (Louise H., about 1904).

Having enjoyed such a sumptuous menu it is hard to imagine that potatoes may ever lose their importance in the German kitchen. Nevertheless, a century later there are some decisive changes concerning the power of the potato.

Potatoes in Danger?

Since the end of the twentieth century due to a fundamental change of food culture, the consumption of potatoes has dwindled in Germany and other Euro-pean countries, especially in Northern Central Europe, where most potatoes are grown (Müller and Bergmann 2019). For example, in 2016 the consumption of potatoes per year in Germany was up to 60 kilograms per person; Irish people ate about 90 kilograms, with Latvians at the top of the list consuming 117 kilo-grams (Henrich 2019). Instead of cooking fresh potatoes, Germans increasingly prefer convenient food, dried potatoes as potato chips or instant meals. If today potatoes still constitute the fourth most important staple food worldwide (after rice, corn, and wheat), this largely results from the growing interest in potatoes in regions other than Europe. Especially in countries that are on their way to industrialisation such as China or India, people discover the potato's power (Müller and Bergmann 2019).

In the future, climate change constitutes a severe threat for potatoes in Germany and elsewhere. Especially in northern Lower Saxony, the main potato-growing region of Germany, the crop yield is below average because of lacking precipitation. Since potatoes need constant and regular water supply, farmers begin to develop ways of irrigating their fields.[3] Since the moderate climate potato plants prefer is changing, researchers develop new brands of plants that will be able to cope with the new climate conditions.[4] Ecological potato production at present is marginal in Germany. Gardeners recommend this method because they regard organically grown potatoes as tastier (Kreuter [27]2016). In addition, they hold that ecological farming is going to be more effective against the negative effects of climate change.

In sum, popular narratives and writing communicate the message that caring for potatoes is tantamount to caring for humans; because a meal of potatoes brings people together, they make friends. Is there any other food can be served in such a great variation, as an hors d'oeuvre, a main course, and even as a dessert?

References

Barlösius, E. (2016), *Soziologie des Essens: Eine sozial- und kulturwissenschaftliche Einführung in die Ernährungsforschung* (Weinheim/Basel: Bentz Juventa).

Barton, D., and U. Papen eds (2010), *The Anthropology of Writing: Understanding Textually Mediated Worlds* (London: Bloomsbury).

Chou, H.-C. (2019), '"Poor Mamma's Panacea"—The Potato in Ulysses', *EuroAmerica* 49(1): 1–43.

Fenske, M. (2017), '… nachhaltige Praktiken: Kochen im Fokus einer Anthropologie des Schreibens', in M. Tauschek (ed.), *Historizität und die Zirkulation von Wissen: Potenziale kulturwissenschaftlichen Denkens* (Münster: Waxmann), pp. 101-116.

Heidrich, H., and A. Kohlberger (2004), *Kartoffel in der Früh: Ein kulturgeschichtliches Koch- und Lesebuch* (Bad Windsheim: Fränkisches Freilandmuseum).

Henrich, P. (2019), 'Pro-Kopf-Konsum von Kartoffeln in Deutschland in den Jahren 1950/51 bis 2017/18', *statista*. Available at: https://de.statista.com/statistik/daten/studie/175422/umfrage/pro-kopf-verbrauch-von-kartoffeln-in-deutschland/ (accessed 2 September 2019).

Joyce Project, The (n.d.), 'Potato'. Available at http://m.joyceproject.com/notes/040047potato.html (accessed 28 August 2019).

---

3 See, e.g., https://www.syngenta.de/news/aktuelles-kartoffeln/klimawandel-veraendert-er-unseren-kartoffelanbau (accessed 30 August 2019).

4 See, e.g., https://www.agrarheute.com/pflanze/kartoffeln/forscher-entwickeln-duerretol-erante-kartoffel-553850 (accessed 30 August 2019).

Köhler, I. (1984), 'Ernteteilung,' in *Enzyklopädie des Märchens* vol. 4 (Berlin: De Gruyter), cols. 225–234.

Kreuter, M.-L. (2016), *Der Biogarten: Das Original* (München: BLV).

Krug-Richter, B. (2019), *Von Tomaten, Kartoffeln, Kaffee und Tee: Neue Nahrungsmittel verändern die europäische Esskultur*. Presentation at the University of Würzburg, 22 May.

Latour, B. (2010), *Eine neue Soziologie für eine neue Gesellschaft: Einführung in die Akteur-Netzwerk-Theorie* (Frankfurt a.M.: Suhrkamp).

List of Outlander Episodes. Available at https://en.wikipedia.org/wiki/List_of_Outlander_episodes#Season_2_(2016) (accessed 2 September 2019)

Marzell, H. (1931/32), 'Kartoffel,' in *Handwörterbuch des Deutschen Aberglaubens* vol. 4 (Berlin: De Gruyter), col. 1023–1026.

Marzolph, U. and R. Bendix (2014), 'Introduction: Narrative Culture: A Concept and its Scope', *Narrative Culture* 1: 1–8.

Merritt, R. (1990), 'Faith and Betrayal: The Potato in "Ulysses"', *James Joyce Quarterly* 28(1): 269–276.

Müller, M., and B.-D. Bergmann (2019), *Bericht zur Markt- und Versorgungslage: Kartoffeln, 2019* (Bonn: Bundesanstalt für Landwirtschaft und Ernährung).

Nic Craith, M. (2020), *The Vanishing World of The Islandman: Narrative and Nostalgia* (New York: Palgrave).

Salaman, R (1949), *The History and Social Influence of the Potato* (Cambridge: Cambridge University Press).

Theophano, J. (2002), *Eat My Words: Reading Women's Lives through the Cookbooks They Wrote* (New York: Palgrave).

From Print Media to Blogs:
A Note on Rewriting Heritage

Christian S. Ritter

After returning a book to the library on Magee campus, I strolled over to the Aberfoyle House. A short footpath connected the two buildings. The sky was filled with dark grey clouds, and a further heavy rainfall was imminent. I walked through the main entrance and took the first door on the right-hand side. A small Christmas gathering was about to begin. My doctoral supervisor Máiréad Nic Craith had organised the get-together. It was easy to talk to everyone, and the hierarchical distance, which often shapes relationships in academia, was completely gone. Tea, coffee, and chocolate cake were consumed. Many personal stories and gossip were shared. During the gathering, Máiréad told me for the first time about the memoir *The Speckled People* (2003) by Hugo Hamilton, which deeply inspired my interest in Irish literature and heritage. Only a few weeks earlier—in late September 2009 –, I had moved to Derry and enrolled in a PhD programme at Ulster University. The informal event prior to Christmas set the tone for my doctorate and epitomised the collegial atmosphere of which my doctoral research benefitted in the following years.

Reflecting on two cases from my ethnographic research, I query how the rise of digital media in everyday life transformed ordinary writing about heritage. Digital media are understood as communication channels for text, audio, and video content that can be reduced to binary code and transmitted over the internet. The smallest units of digital media are bits, generating unprecedented possibilities of convergence between previously separated media technologies and content. Ordinary writing can be seen as an everyday communicative practice (Barton and Papen 2010). In contrast to more conventional forms of the written language, ordinary writing refers to all forms of everyday writing, regardless of the educational background and social status of their authors (Gillen and Hall 2010). Traditionally, ordinary writing encompassed among other things diaries, postcards, letters, notebooks, minutes, instruction manuals, leaflets, flyers and booklets. With the omnipresence of digital media in everyday life, new mundane writing practices proliferated, including interactive feeds on social media, websites of organisations and personal blogs. In this essay, I trace the transformation process from print-based ordinary writing to digital mundane writing. The first section addresses the changes ordinary writing underwent within the internal public of the Lutheran church in Ireland. Drawing on ethnographic examples from my fieldwork in Tallinn, I proceed with a brief assessment of heritage restoration in the Estonian capital. Finally, I describe how travel blogs were established as a form of ordinary writing in global tourism.

Ordinary Writing within a Lutheran Church

During my doctoral research, I carried out an ethnographic study of the Lutheran Church in Ireland. I mainly conducted fieldwork in the Lutheran congregations in Belfast and Dublin (Ritter 2015; Ritter and Kmec 2017). To keep the dispersed membership informed on the latest developments in the congregations, the Lutheran community established a set of internal media practices. The quarterly newsletter or community letter (Gemeindebrief), which was posted to all paying members, was the main form of internal ordinary writing. The pastors regularly suggested religious interpretations of local events in its greeting section (Grußwort), which was printed on the back of the title page. The newsletter also contained remembrances of deceased church members and presentations of newly arriving interns. In addition, the church council reported on its annual meetings in the newsletter, and members were informed about upcoming events. By sharing stories from within the congregation, the newsletter constituted a stable layer of the church's internal public. The ordinary writing practice was furthermore a vehicle for maintaining a sense of German identity among its members. Their linguistic heritage could be conserved in the newsletter, which was mainly written in the German language. The pieces printed in the newsletter also expressed experiences from the profane selves of congregation members. Their socio-cultural status was mediated by the written language, conveying a sense of both belonging and place (Nic Craith 2012: 6).

A new ordinary writing practice was integrated into the internal public of the Lutheran church in Ireland with the arrival of a new pastor in 2015. He brought his passion for blogging to the small congregation, using a WordPress website to post personal and religious messages at regular intervals. The lively, collage-like blogging style combined pictorial and textual elements while juxtaposing religious and everyday writings. The blog has been a form of ordinary writing which escaped the constraints of print-based publishing and became a new vessel for the word of the Lord within the Lutheran Church.

Figure 1: Newsletter of the Lutheran Church in Ireland

The blog posts entailed stories about the inner life of the faith-based community. For instance, reports on youth group outings or concerts in St. Finian Church in Dublin were posted. The blog also announced the annual Christmas Bazar taking place in the St. Killian's German School in Dublin. Another blog post shared experiences from an outing on Ascension Day. A small group of about 30 Lutheran believers participated in a hike to Dalkey Hill near Dublin. A service was held on top of the hill during sunset. The blog post displayed a photograph of the hikers. The pastor shared the religious messages of the Ascension sermon, comparing the ascension of Jesus to heaven with the story of the tower of Babel from the Biblical book Genesis 11. By posting ephemeral impressions from internal events, the pastor could strengthen the sense of community among church members and provide a symbolic container where their linguistic heritage could be stored.

UNESCO World Heritage and Tourism in Estonia

While the dissemination of newsletters and blog posts is part of the expertise of a myriad of religious communities around the world, digital forms of ordinary writings also proliferate in the global tourism industry. To set the analysis of travel blogs in Estonia in its local context, I will briefly describe the heritage objects that are exposed in the tourist sites of Tallinn. The city was founded in 1219. One of the first records that mentions Tallinn dates back to the 13th century, describing the construction of a castle. Tallinn was strategically built on the coast of the Baltic Sea and established itself as an important trade centre of the Hanseatic League in the following three centuries. Numerous buildings from this prosperous era have been restored in the modern-day Old Town of Tallinn. In the medieval period, gentry and merchants resided in the fortified settlement of the then city centre. The built environment of the historic centre was divided into two distinct areas. The upper town area, which was initially built on a limestone hill, is home to the majestic Toompea Castle, the Lutheran St. Mary Church and the Alexander Nevsky Cathedral. The lower area of the historic centre includes the Town Hall Square, the Town Hall Pharmacy, various monasteries, remains of medieval city walls and towers. Visitors can also explore the homes of merchants and guild houses, which were built within the narrow windings of cobblestone roads. Significant religious buildings, such as St. Olaf's church and St. Nicholas' church, have also been preserved in the lower town. The upper town of Tallinn has remained the administrative centre of Estonia, hosting for instance its present-day parliament. In 1997, the collection of medieval buildings scattered over Tallinn's Old Town was declared UNESCO World Cultural Heritage.

Since Estonia regained its independence in 1991, tourism has been considered as an opportunity for economic growth and a means for solidifying the identity of the Baltic nation. The Estonian state has digitised numerous public services. Estonia was for instance the first country to offer its citizens the opportunity to vote online during the general elections of 2005. Simultaneously, services in the global tourism industry have been increasingly mediated by digital media in the last decade. Both developments reinforced the role of the digital within the heritage sites of Tallinn's Old Town. The National Heritage Board and the Tallinn City Government oversee the preservation of cultural heritage sites in Tallinn. A group of curators administer the architectural treasures and document the cultural inward meanings local experts attach to the restored buildings. Many tour guides are well-trained in local history and retell authentic stories about the cultural heritage. However, the rise of digital media in tourism and the increased use of mobile phones by tourists have dramatically disrupted the host-guest relationship in present-day tourism. The conditions under which stories about Estonian cultural heritage are shared have been shifted. Numerous travel bloggers come to Tallinn and other popular tourist destinations to write about their own impressions of tourist attractions. They share visual and textual content about heritage objects with their followers. In the context of heritage tourism, the act of assigning cultural outward meanings to heritage objects is not completely controlled by the local tour guide. Such negotiations of cultural meanings are increasingly played out on digital media. A heritage building in Tallinn's Old Town undergoes multiple processes in which meanings are assigned to its various components. Since sites of heritage tourism compete with other tourist attractions, many tourist boards create their own digital media profiles and develop strategies for promoting their heritage sites online. Influential travel bloggers, who manage to attract large audiences on multiple platforms, often receive invitations from local tourist boards or hotels to write about their touristic experiences.

Blogging Heritage

Accounts of travel experiences can be traced back to the era of the Ancient Greeks. The Greek geographer Pausanias wrote the Description of Greece in the 2nd century, which is widely considered one of the very first contributions to the genre of travel literature. Travel stories also enjoyed great popularity in the Song Dynasty of medieval China. In the 14th century, a further influential account about the inspiration that can be drawn from travelling was written by Francesco Petrarca. The Italian Renaissance scholar and poet reflected on the experiences he made during a climb to the top of Mont Ventoux during a journey to France. Stories of Grand Tours, which were undertaken by clergy, aristocrats and other affluent people in the 17th and 18th century, renewed the tradition of travel literature with the travelogue. The Grand Tour was an educational rite of passage, exposing the travelling people to the legacies of classic antiquity and Renaissance. Travel literature has been traditionally classified into outdoor literature, nature writing, guidebooks, and travel memoirs (Cuddon 1999). Guidebooks or travel guides are a genre of travel literature that includes detailed descriptions of travel destinations for a specific readership. The authors provided precise information about places that were considered attractive for early modern tourists. In contrast to travelogues, travel guides were more impersonal and emphasised the properties of the described places. The travel journal is a further genre that evolved between the 18th and 19th century. This form of travel writing, which was often written as a diary, reaccentuated the personal voice of the travelling authors and their experiences. Travel journals were often based on first-hand drafts, which were written during the journey. Guidebooks and travel journals are forms of ordinary writing within the genre of travel literature.

In the early 21st century, the possibilities of posting user-generated content on digital media significantly changed the ways in which tourists acquire information about their travel destinations. Hence, a new form of ordinary travel writing began to evolve: the travel blog. The expression blog was initially used as a shortening of the word weblog. The first travel blogs were published in the mid-1990s. The reach of such travel accounts has been enhanced by sharing hyperlinks to the blog posts on popular digital media, such as Facebook, Twitter, Pinterest, and Instagram. The administering of personal accounts on multiple platforms in combination with a content management system, such as WordPress and Weebly, quickly became the preferred publishing style of many travel bloggers. In the last decade, travel bloggers have disseminated accounts about millions of travel destinations around the globe. Travel blogs give their readers access to places that they have never physically visited, shaping their experience of the world (Nic Craith et al. 2016: 439).

Many travel bloggers seek to turn their passion for travelling into a solid source of income and travel to 'blogworthy' destinations almost throughout the year. The vast majority of travel blogs give fellow tourists advice on where to stay and what to do in the travel destination. Committed to an authentic writing style, travel bloggers portray tourist attractions based on their personal experiences and encounters. I make a case for understanding travel blogs not only as a new global trend, but also as a newly established form of ordinary writing.

Travel bloggers engage in complex digital storytelling and playfully combine image and word on webpages. In doing so, they inscribe themselves into the tradition of travel writing. The historic centre of Tallinn's Old Town has been portrayed in countless travel blogs. A thorough travel blog was, for instance, dedicated to a trip to the Estonian capital in the winter season, portraying the author's experiences in the Old Town as a walk into a wintry fairy tale (OTL 2019).

Figure 2: Travel Blog: Tallinn in Winter: The Magic of Tallinn in the Snow

The blog post began with a comprehensive overview of Tallinn's history. After sharing tips about the winter weather in Tallinn, the author listed a series of tourist attractions located in the Old Town. A long narrative described the medieval walls. The author recounted her experiences of the walls during a stroll on a wooden walkway. The blog post also explained that the medieval walls were originally 2.4 kilometres long and that the restored walls are 1.9 kilometres long. By providing her readership with such detailed information, the blogger reassigned meanings to the architectural structure. The negotiation of cultural outward meanings about heritage sites increasingly occurs on the internet. The rise of digital media has multiplied the sense-making processes inherent in heritage sites. Digital media complicate the circulation of symbolic meanings attached to heritage objects, such as handicraft and architectural structures. The ontological status of heritage objects is grounded in the unity of their material qualities (Zemach 1966). Travel blogging practices generate surrogates of heritage objects. Words and things that circulate on digital media take on new lives as digital surrogates, copies, and remixes (Hennessy 2008: 346). Digital surrogates exist outside of the materiality of heritage objects but play a crucial part in the sense-making process of the represented objects. The traditional triad of heritage curator, tour guide and spectator has been complemented by the blogger whose accounts assign meaning to heritage objects on digital media. Heritage objects that are showcased as tourist attractions have turned into palimpsests on which numerous actors leave their interpretations.

The two ethnographic cases discussed above demonstrated how forms of ordinary writing were transformed by the advent of digital media. The Lutheran case indicated that the linguistic heritage of the religious community has been conserved through ordinary writing practices. Blog posts attributed meanings to internal events, adding a new communication channel to the congregational life. The internal public of the Lutheran church in Ireland has been strengthened by digital layers, such as the pastor's blog and the church's Facebook page. The case of travel bloggers in Estonia showed how the meanings attached to heritage objects were constituted in highly frequented tourism sites. Digital technologies have democratised cultural expressivity and multiplied media voices. Travel bloggers became a new voice in popular heritage sites. Heritage objects are not solely filled with the expert meanings of curators and tour guides but are increasingly mediated by the ordinary writing of travel bloggers. Based on ethnographic evidence from two cases of ordinary writing, I argue that blogs nest symbolic containers where digital surrogates of heritage items can flourish. Digital surrogates of buildings, sermons and other heritage items circulate within communities of spectators on the internet. Heritage objects and practices do not only exist in the physical environments, but their symbolic meanings increasingly flow through a physical-digital continuum. The inscription of symbolic meanings in heritage items involves complex figurations of actors, digital technologies and media expertise. The sharply increased uses of digital media in heritage tourism and religious communities challenge traditional ethnographic methodologies and makes the integration of digital methods into ethnographic investigations necessary. The diversity of heritage practices also requires a bolstering of transdisciplinary perspectives of media scholars, anthropologists, and heritage scholars to unravel the multiple representations of heritage on digital media. The manifold digital records of heritage items necessitate new forms of archiving to document physical heritage in combination with their digital surrogates. In addition to the textual and pictorial materials of travel blogs, travel influencers increasingly share audio-visual content on digital media and further in-depth investigations into travel vlogging are much needed. In order to influence the streams of meaning about heritage on digital media, heritage institutions ought to increase their online presence by creating comprehensive websites and digital labels for authentic content about heritage. Blogs have transformed forms of cultural expressivity in multiple contexts, which might be only one stage in a larger wave of disruptions.

References

Barton, D. and U. Papen (2010), 'What is the Anthropology of Writing?', in: D. Barton and U. Papen (eds), *The Anthropology of Writing: Understanding Textually Mediated Worlds* (London: Continuum), 3-33.

Cuddon, J. (1999), *The Penguin Dictionary of Literary Terms and Literary Theory* (London: Penguin).

Dodsworth, L. (2019), 'Tallinn in Winter: The Magic of Tallinn in the Snow', *On the Luce, Travel Blog*. Available at: https://www.ontheluce.com/tallinn-estonia-in-the-snow (accessed 08 November 2019).

Gillen, J. and N. Hall (2010), 'Edwardian Postcards: Illuminating Ordinary Writing', in: D. Barton and U. Papen (eds), *The Anthropology of Writing: Understanding Textually Mediated Worlds* (London: Continuum), 169-189.

Hennessy, K. (2012), 'Cultural Heritage on the Web: Applied Digital Visual Anthropology and Local Cultural Property Rights Discourse', *International Journal of Cultural Property* 19(3): 345-369.

Nic Craith, M. (2012), *Narratives of Place, Belonging and Language: An Intercultural Perspective* (Basingstoke: Palgrave), 1-25.

Nic Craith, M., U. Boser and A. Devasundaram (2016) 'Giving Voice to Heritage: A Virtual Case Study', *Social Anthropology* 24(4): 433-445.

Ritter, C. (2015), 'Unveiling the Unspoken in Life Story Interviews: The Dynamics of Storytelling in the Lutheran Congregation in Belfast', *Civilisations* 64(1&2): 103-113.

Ritter, C. and V. Kmec (2017), 'Religious Practices and Networks of Belonging in an Immigrant Congregation: the German-speaking Lutheran Congregation in Dublin', *Journal of Contemporary Religion* 32(2): 269-281.

Zemach, E. (1966), 'The Ontological Status of Art Objects', *The Journal of Aesthetics and Art Criticism* 25(2): 145-153.

Admiring Athens

Angelika Dietz

Culture contact was a theme that I had pursued mostly theoretically[1] until my encounter with Mairead, Ulli and the Academy for Irish Cultural Heritages. In Derry we were a colorful bunch of PhD students from different countries, religions and backgrounds, and had plentiful opportunity to make contact in the study room we shared (and beyond). But even after I left the Academy, life continued to be culturally colorful. Not only did (and do) I, a German, have an Italian partner, but he went to Athens for further studies, and I was happy to go with him. I would like to dedicate this experience to Mairead with her interest in cultural contact and her love for gyros.

In Greece, I was particularly fascinated by culinary matters. When we arrived in Athens, we first had to stock up on provisions, and so stopped at the greengrocer next to the police station—an Albanian who had been living in Greece for twenty years, and who seemed to be delighted with my rudimentary Greek. We bought fruit and vegetables, including some very, very tasty spinach. Then we went to the butcher shop where we took advice from the owner, a former teacher of English, who told us in excellent English about different types of sheep's cheese. There is a kind of 'ricotta salata', made from sheep's milk, and a cheese that sounds like 'Gruyière'. Both taste very good. After the bakery, where we, of course, bought bread as well as samples of the various puff pastries, we quickly returned to the supermarket near us and then trotted home.

In the following days we roamed through Athens. On the one hand we were exploring, but on the other hand we also, initially, sought to escape our cool and until then still musty, chaotic apartment. Once we ended up in a lively and cheerful tavern. Nino's love for tzatziki and Greek salad was awakened, and I was able finally to enjoy a real Greek grill platter with chips and eggplant salad. This pleasure was only clouded by the many smokers, who were not bothered at all by the public ban on smoking. As I had imagined it would be with the smoking ban in Italy, so it was in Greece. And according to Italian sayings, the Greeks smoke like the Turks. Lived Mediterranean culture!

Oriental resonances met us as we stepped into the beautiful Byzantine church next door. A service was taking place, and the priest started an oriental-

---

[1] Apart from studying a year abroad in Perugia, Italy, but that is another story to be told.

sounding litany in Greek. However, the letters did not appear to be 100% Greek, and in fact we might have caught the Russian Orthodox Church in Athens. It was full of gold ornaments and paintings on golden background, icons and elaborate carvings, and the floor was covered with colourful carpets. We listened to the unfamiliar sounds for a while, but then a woman rustled so loudly with her bags that we were torn from our rapture.

The greengrocer in Efroniou had been all over the world. Fortunately, he could speak English. He had travelled by boat and had visited Germany, Denmark, Switzerland (via inland navigation on the Rhine?), Russia, Finland and Poland. I no longer remember how we got on to politics. But politics is an issue that one will inevitably come to, sooner or later. The politicians are the problem. They would always make promises and would not implement the reforms, and they would be corrupt. Napolitano, he is good, and a technocratic government like in Italy—perhaps this will be introduced in Greece, too? The greengrocer would be happy with that.

In the meantime, everyday life had caught up with us, because by now we had made our apartment very habitable, and had successfully settled into it (Vilem Flusser 1992; cited in Theater in Heilbronn 2011):

> People think of *Heimat* as a relatively permanent location, their residence as an interchangeable, relocatable location. The opposite is true: you can change your *Heimat* or have none, but you always have to live somewhere, wherever that may be. Without a residence, without protecting the ordinary and the usual, everything that arrives is noise, nothing is information, and in an informationless world, in chaos, you can neither feel nor think nor act.[2]

And so we had settled into the daily rhythm of the ordinary and the usual—a good reason to get out and about, and to explore our new place of residence and its cultural offerings. When I go to the cinema in other countries, I often have to think of Heinrich Böll's *Irish Journal* and his description of a visit to the cinema in Ireland. Our first visit to Pallas was probably equally memorable. To the sound of a blaring Adriano Celentano, and supplied with all sorts of delicious Greek pastries, we entered the theatre. Like the lobby, this was kept strictly in the 1930s style and decorated in shades of light blue, yellow and old rose. There was a gallery, but it was so far at the back that we gratefully declined and took

---

[2] The German term *Heimat*, used in the original text, is difficult to render into English, and has therefore been retained here, and italicised.

our seats in the first row of a slight elevation in the main auditorium. The cinema seats were also relics from the past and accordingly a little uncomfortable. However, we forgot about that, enchanted by the story of *Poulet aux Prunes*, and perhaps also because of our efforts to follow the somewhat difficult to understand French. This was only partly due to a lack of knowledge of French on our part, but rather because the original sound had been turned down as the Greeks were reading the subtitles. If at home the film music is often a tad too uncomfortably loud, it is regulated quite comfortably here in Greece—that's as long as you don't want to follow the dialogue.

There were many other exciting discoveries and when my partner's four-month course was completed, we left 'our Athens' with a heavy heart, but each with a kilo or two extra on the ribs as a souvenir.

References

Flusser, V. (1992), *Bodenlos. Eine philosophische Autobiographie* (Düsseldorf: Bollmann).

Theater in Heilbronn (2011), *Wohnzeit*. Available at http://wohnzeit.wordpress. com/projekt/ (accessed 3 February 2020).

Regaining ethnic ancestry and heritage
'Roots' identity as cultural citizenship of Lithuanian immigrant descendants in Texas

Vytis Čiubrinskas and Jolanta Kuznecovienė

According to David Hollinger (2005), who conducted research on American cultural diversity from the perspective of a 'post-ethnic America' condition, efforts should be made to understand and articulate 'cosmopolitan instincts' within this new ethnic connectedness that appeared after the melting pot metaphor of a homogenising 'American culture' in the late 1960s. Hollinger describes the current processes of identity in America as post-ethnic but characterised by increased sensitivity to roots. 'Sensitivity to roots' initiatives can become examples of identity politics when 'ethnic roots' grow into an insistent attempt to take back one's own culture, one's own cultural heritage in relation to other ethnic groups and cultures that had become rooted earlier.

However, one can also observe opposite processes that are ethnically levelling and supporting ethnic blending through assimilation to mainstream society by adopting 'cosmopolitan skills' (Hall and Werbner 2008). Stuart Hall calls the intermediate version of cosmopolitanism—a 'cosmopolitanism from below' (Hall and Werbner 2008: 348), and other authors (e.g., Hollinger 1995) call it a 'rooted cosmopolitanism'. In this sense, 'post-ethnicity' is the critical renewal of cosmopolitanism in the context of today's greater sensitivity to roots and (re)territorialisation of places.

Actually, it is not cosmopolitanism but (trans-)nationalism here that serves as a platform of understanding how identity politics is mobilised and manifested through the empowerment of places, both as imagined and constructed as places of 'origin', of 'shared memory', of 'our heritage', of 'mutual home' etc. Transnationalism is visible in the politics of diasporic-homeland nationalism (or long-distance nationalism, according to Glick-Schiller), or in cultural citizenship of empowerment of 'roots' and cultural 'difference'. Another resource of such empowerment of places and 'roots' stems from American multiculturalism that, partly due to ethnopolitics and a highly popular quest for roots (inspired by the highly popular 1980s American TV series 'Roots'), stimulated initiatives of recognition of ethnic ancestries, heritages and 'roots'. The compilation of family genealogies, indigenous story writing, as well as preservation and commemoration of ethnic heritage sites and objects, provided a key starting point in this process.

At the same time, memories of places where the pioneer immigrants came into the New World as well as notions of family histories of migrant descendants circulated in public discourse. Therefore, these memories of places (not only those of transatlantic homelands) could serve as examples of transnational expansion of space and production of locality. Production of locality, which, in Friedman's terms opposes globalisation, becomes part of fragmentation as the structures that bind space, time and memory also become fragmented. In his view, globalisation, as the decentralisation of capital accumulation and decline of modernity, produces fragmentation. 'In this decline, there is a turn to roots ... [and] ... to ethnicity... [that provides] the basis for cultural politics and political fragmentation' (Friedman 2002: 295). According to Friedman, 'cultural politics in general is a politics of difference, a transformation of difference into claims on the public sphere, for recognition, for funds, for land'; it appears as 'a question of the practice of a particular kind of identity, an identity of rootedness, of genealogy as it relates to territory' (Friedman 2004: 69).

Territorialisation of migrants and, in particular, their descendants is tightly related to their family memories of 'putting roots in American soil' as well as heritages. If memories of homelands and birthplaces, real or imagined, become symbolic connections for diasporas, similar symbolic resources, although traced from local (American) histories, are relevant to the descendants of migrants who are assimilated to mainstream society. Thus it is not only a quest for 'production of locality' as reterritorialisation of 'uprooted' immigrants (Malkki 1992), but also the quest for a common ancestry and common historico-cultural roots that occupy an important place in the expression of ethnic identity, and even more so in making it prominent vis-à-vis other groups' ancestries, memories and heritages. It is actually becoming a motion towards 'culture' as territory, history and generational memory, establishing distinct groups' 'right to be different', in terms of empowerment of belonging and cultural citizenship.

Cultural citizenship refers to a 'right to be different' (Rosaldo and Flores 1997; Bretell 2008) in terms of ethnicity, native language, religion and other resources (Nic Craith 2004). International labour migrants and refugees usually care for their cultural distinctiveness to be recognised and valorised, and easily become motivated to claim ownership of their cultural heritage practices and identity by constructing histories about their roots and by shaping their public and political practices of homeland (Malkki 1992, Olwig 2004, Appadurai 1996, Krohn-Hansen 2003). Thus, immigrant ethnification becomes one of the countervailing strategies against uncertainty and challenges of migrant livelihoods as well as their lifestyles, often categorized as 'strange cultures'. Responses to that are often essentialist, pointing to the exclusiveness of cultural resources and cultural embedded-ness of immigrants. Such cultural embedded-ness could be seen as a model of cultural citizenship.

From another, less essentialist and more constructivist point of view, the approach to citizenship as a prime expression of loyalty is altered by the concern with the moral and performative dimensions of membership beyond the domain of legal rights (Glick-Schiller and Çağlar 2008: 207). Similarly, Máiréad Nic Craith defines cultural citizenship as 'simply a system of "group rights" that supports the majority's language, history, culture and calendar' (Nic Craith 2004: 291). According to Will Kymlicka, cultural citizenship, like ethnic nationalism, is securing a right to be different, and its management does not mean assimilating to common culture and language (Kymlicka 1995: 24, cited in Nic Craith 2004: 291). But management of both 'non-assimilation' and 'assimilation' cannot be politically neutral and 'culture blind', because 'citizenship is not culture blind' (Nic Craith 2004: 292). This applies in particular to assimilation into mainstream society of migrant groups where 'ethnic identity ...has shrunk to the symbolic form of individual heritage/ancestry in the self-perception of the group' and 'ethnicity is reduced to ancestry' (Doane 1997: 385, cited in Berking 2004: 114) and this becomes a major point of departure for the family history activism of Lithuanian descendants in Texas.

A long and diverse history of the waves and generations of the Lithuanian migration to the USA provides numerous examples of how the politics of identity works – not only among those who move, but also for subsequent generations who choose to integrate 'with a difference', following a cultural citizenship path, and conversely for those who choose to assimilate into mainstream American culture.

Our case study of the application of identity empowerment and cultural citizenship by descendants of nineteenth century Lithuanian immigrants to Texas aims, first, to point out the issue of ethnic ancestry related to the group identity of the mainstream American population. In order to show the patterns of how cultural descent or ethnic background is perceived, felt and handled, the ways of Lithuanian ancestry and the enactment of 'roots' in Texas are considered. A further focus is on the activities of the Lithuanian descendants reclaiming local heritage associated with the 'pioneers of Texas prairies', who fought on both sides of the American Civil War and, over the generations and through intermarriage, almost merged, first into hyphenated German-American, and later into mainstream American society. Nevertheless, the fourth generation of descendants challenged assimilation by opening their interest to 'difference' and launching a greater focus on heritage and 'roots', thus reclaiming identity politics. Such processes began in the form of genealogies and pioneer family histories, family relics, letters, photos, or simply materials inherited from relatives.

This became a focus of our anthropological fieldwork, conducted in 2002, 2004 and 2012 with Americans of Lithuanian background in the south-eastern part of Texas, in areas in the city of Victoria and the vicinity of Yorktown in DeWitt County.

Lithuanian immigration and 'roots' identity of descendants

Lithuanian immigrants came to Texas in the 1850s-1870s from Western Lithuania, also called Lithuania Minor, the region that was at that time the Lithuanian part of East Prussia. The first Lithuanians (about a hundred) came to Texas through the ports of Indianola, near Victoria, as gateways for European, mainly German immigration, as well as through Galveston and New Orleans. They made their cross-Atlantic journeys with a German wave of early migration to Texas mainly from the port of Bremen, settling about one hundred miles from the coast, in the counties of DeWitt and Goliad.

They were supposed to be coming to the 'land of opportunity' with no shortage of land, safety from military obligation, and freedom of religion. However, as Kerlick Bruns (1980:8) noted, they found that

> in this period of Texas history temper and turmoil prevailed throughout. It had only been some 10-20 years since Texas became an independent nation [independent Republic of Texas existed in 1840-1860], then the Civil War, and finally a war with Mexico ended.

All those hardships the immigrants had to face meant their livelihoods and identity were framed as a particular ethnic history (cf. Cidzikaitė 2006) in a certain period of American (and Texas) history, which since has been assumed into a history of the people 'overlooked for generations'.

This nineteenth century Lithuanian immigration to Texas lasted only for about twenty years and consisted of no more than two hundred immigrants who eventually assimilated to mainstream American society. Despite the rather short period and small number of immigrants, it became a point of departure for quite a remarkable pattern of 'roots' identity empowerment. It started with the fourth generation of descendants 'discovering' their belonging as 'sort of Lithuanians', as generation after generation the stories, records, letters and pictures from that period were passed on and material heritage (graveyards, churches, historical sites, historical objects and artefacts) along with collective memory became the focus of those searching for their genealogical roots and ancestry. It resulted in the reclaiming of Lithuanian heritage through genealogy. At first, the focus was on family histories and genealogy in general, with a closer look at individuals' personal family history and family relics, letters, photos, or simply 'stuff' inherited from relatives. Family histories of local Texans with a Lithuanian background led to the awareness of a particular heritage, first approached as 'overlooked', and eventually, along with objects of the ethnic legacy, put forward to be reclaimed. The most notable example of such interest is the local ethnographic and genealogical research of Patricia Hand, a Texan of Lithuanian descent.

Indianola Lady and the Rise of the Lithuanian Heritage in Texas

It all began with Patsy Hand's interest, in her words, 'in the most popular pursuit in the United States after gardening—genealogy.' In 1968, while exploring her family history she learned from her grandmother, that her great grandfather George Lundschen settled in Texas after moving from Lithuania (Hand 2009: 20). The fact that besides her German origin, she has a Lithuanian one has focused her attention not just on genealogy but also on the history of the local area. In 'discovering' her Lithuanian ethnic origin, in her birth city of Victoria in southeast Texas, Hand founded and became president of the state Historical Society, a popular network of societies interested in U.S. local histories.

In 1990, she took the initiative to establish the Victoria County Historical Commission to store the historical database of the Indianola Port (one of the largest American seaports of the nineteenth century, located south of Houston, which was swept away by a hurricane in 1886 and was never rebuilt). By focusing on the creation of a passenger database for all the ships moored in the Indianola Port during its lifetime, 1846-1886, Hand made such a significant contribution to the project that she was nicknamed the Indianola Lady.

She initiated research on the first Lithuanian immigrants in Texas by studying documents and passenger lists of transatlantic ships that came to Indianola port from 1846 to 1874 by initiating the project called 'The First Lithuanian Immigrants in De Witt and Goliad Counties,' that lists Lithuanians who arrived in Texas through the ports of Indianola, Galveston, and New Orleans with their families, and traced those who travelled over a hundred miles to settle in De Witt and Goliad Counties, Texas.

Through her research Hand became a leader in the community of Lithuanian descendants 'searching for their roots', and her reputation attracted many more enthusiasts in search of their Lithuanian ancestry. One such enthusiast was Beverly Kerlick Bruns, who currently runs the local history museum in York-town (De Witt County), where part of the exhibition is dedicated to the heritage of the Lithuanian immigrants. Since 1988, in collaboration with the Balzekas Museum of Lithuanian Culture in Chicago, P. Hand has created a separate collection called 'Lithuanians in Texas.' It is comprised of manuscripts, letters, and documents that belonged to the Lithuanian pioneers in Texas. In 1991, she handed the collection to the museum (Balzekas Museum Manuscript Department, 12/17/91; 1991. 489 Dupl. B.). However, Hand's most significant contribution was the erection of the 'Lithuanians in Texas' historical marker on the road near by the Lithuanian cemetery in 1994. Her idea was that Lithuanians are a small but important body of Texan immigrants and should be formally recognised as one more ethnic group in multicultural Texas that has contributed to the development of the state. The pride in the Lithuanian pioneers, who contributed to the development of the country by their hard work and moral values in the post-Indian period of Texas, became an important and powerful tool for re-creating ethnic identity.

Hand, along with an interest group of descendants of early Lithuanian immigrants, thus provided the necessary historical documents needed to put together a memorial plaque of these Lithuanian settlers. The historical marker 'Lithuanians in Texas' includes an inscription about Lithuanian immigration and was eventually erected on the road crossing the main area of the former Lithuanian colony in DeWitt County.

This plaque and the inscribed text demonstrated that not only the descendants of the most populous ethnic groups in the area–i.e., the Germans, Czechs, and Poles 'can memorialize themselves.' Not only are their 'ethnic roots' transformed into 'rooted Texan-ness', but so too can the Texans of Lithuanian descent take back their culture and distinguish their cultural heritage from the common Euro-American, and especially from the German, cultural heritage. Such memorialisation helps the Lithuanians present themselves as a culturally important historical group in the history of Texas and contrast their contributions with that of other immigrant groups.

Quest for roots: documentary reclaims of heritage and local history
Genealogical and Historical Societies as well as Commissions in Texas are the most important institutions in documenting multicultural history in the area. Local historians and members of those societies are most instrumental in compiling Lithuanian pioneer history and family histories-genealogies and creating new topic-oriented databases. For example, in the 1980s and early 1990s, 'Lithuanian Family Genealogies and Directories' were prepared by the Houston

branch of the Texas Historical Commission; their authors were local historians and Commission members of Lithuanian descent. It is noteworthy that the data collected in these books clearly reflects the common family histories of Lithuanian and German immigrants and the assimilation of Lithuanians with Germans.

In the 1980s, those genealogists and local historians (some of Lithuanian descent) were joined by local immigrant descendants and formed an interest group that actually united 're-creators of Lithuanian-ness' in Texas. One the goals of this group was to create a network that could help groups to 'recover' their own family histories and ethnic heritages.

It was also a means of regaining 'the past' via 'concrete' documentary proof. This was important for those eager to learn about their family's ethnic background 'by discovering' it. Therefore, their own family histories are of particular interest to them, especially after they 'discover' themselves having not only German but Lithuanian backgrounds. These groups are instrumental by taking the initiative in retaining material heritage of the migrant past such as lobbying for the designation of official status to Lithuanian heritage sites by the Texas State.

This interest group (network) of descendants, along with the genealogical and historical societies as well as local historians (mainly of the Lithuanian ancestry), does enact heritage reclamation. They frequently present at heritage-related public events and work to maintain ethnic sites, for example the Lithuanian graveyard in the former immigrant colony.

Another popular initiative relates to family reunions that are directly connected to the descendants' own interest in their ancestries and genealogies. Family reunions started in the area of the former Lithuanian colony in the late 1970s, and annual meetings are extremely popular among the families of Lithuanian descendants. For example, family reunions of the Kirlick family are held every summer near Yorktown and in 1994 numbered over 100 members (Wolf 2002).

Such family gatherings serve to create new genealogical circles as well as ethnic and local heritage interest groups similar to those of Hand and Kerlick Bruns. Initiatives tend to rise and interest in one's own family history is generated when it is found out that, besides German ancestry (which is very common in Texas), there was also Lithuanian ancestry. This is followed by compiling a list of ancestors, drawing a genealogical tree, and putting efforts into recording a detailed family history. Often help is asked from a more experienced ethnographer or family historian, such as members of the aforementioned history and genealogy commissions. Engagement in genealogy and local history thus helps to constantly uphold a Lithuanian-Texan identity in relation to other Texas-based ethnic groups and cultures that had been rooted there earlier, for example the vibrant German community.

This renewable engagement is characterised not only by fostering, memorializing and granting heritage status to the immigrant past, but also by seeking knowledge of historical (especially Lithuania Minor) and present-day Lithuania. Thus, it leads to planning ethnic tourism-type trips to Lithuania and so forth.

Evaluation

Transnationalism as a resource and mobilisation of identity politics is manifested through the empowerment of places via diasporic nationalism but also through (re-)construction of 'roots', places of memory and heritage. Our research shows that in multicultural America today, partly due to the ethnopolitics of the USA, which in the second half of the twentieth century turned from assimilation to multiculturalism, there exists a highly popular quest for 'roots' and ethnic origins, stimulated by public and individual initiatives of recognition and heritage: compiling family genealogies, indigenous story writing, preservation or commemoration of ethnic heritage sites and objects, as well as family gatherings and similar activities related to ethnic backgrounds.

Modern (post-)ethnic identity is characterised by pride in the narratives of ethnic heritage, which are constantly circulating in public discourse. In today's diverse American society, such ethnifying manifestations of identity (i.e., pride in the past as well as moral values of older immigrants) can be interpreted as a social desire to express the power of ethnic identity, but it also serves as a plausible instrumental paradigm for exploring fragmented migrant identities.

In the case of migrant descendants (assimilated mainstreamers), cultural citizenship as a claim for cultural difference can be traced in, and could be proven by, the historically documented ('reified') ethnic Lithuanian enrootedness in local Texas soil as different from, say, local ethnic German, Polish or Bohemian heritage. Such a claim rests on territorially and historically documented genealogies and local histories compiled, at least partly, by descendants themselves. Claims for cultural distinctiveness also focus on the Lithuanian language, which survived up to the third generation. Values 'transplanted' from Eastern Europe, such as diligence, as well as Lutheran pietism became a source of 'ethnic pride' for descendants. This 'ethnic pride' at least was fixed, and later evoked, in the social memory of our informants, and thus became a platform for their identity search and eventually the empowerment of a 'rooted' identity. This serves as a good example of the 'moral and performative dimension' (Glick-

Schiller and Çağlar 2008) of citizenship based on group's heritage engaged loyalty which in Nic Craith's terms perfectly proves her idea about how citizenship is never culture blind even among long assimilated migrant descendants.

References

Appadurai, A. (1996), *Modernity at Large. Cultural Dimensions of Globalization* (Minneapolis: Minnesota University Press).

Berking, H. (2004), '"Dwelling in Displacement": On Diasporization and the Production of National Subjects', in J. Friedman and S. Randeria (eds), *Worlds on the Move. Globalization, Migration, and Cultural Security* (London: Tauris), 103-115.

Bretell, C. (2008), *Migration Theory: Talking Across Disciplines* (New York: Routledge).

Cidzikaitė, D. (2006), 'Pirmieji lietuviai Amerikoje kūrėsi kaubojų žemeje. Pokalbis su asoc. prof. Vyčiu Čiubrinsku', *Amerikos Lietuvis* 15 April 2006, pp. 1 & 35.

Doane, A. (1997), 'Dominant Group Ethnic Identity in the United States.' *Sociological Quarterly* 38: 375-397.

Friedman, J. (1996), *Cultural Identity and Global Process* (London: Sage).

Friedman, J. (2002), 'Transnationalization, Socio-political Disorder, and Ethnification as Expressions of Declining Global Hegemony', in J. Vincent (ed.), *The Anthropology of Politics* (Oxford: Blackwell), 285-300.

Friedman, J. (2004), 'Globalization, Transnationalization, and Migration: Ideologies and Realities of Global Transformation', in J. Friedman and S. Randeria (eds) *Worlds on the Move. Globalization, Migration, and Cultural Security* (London: Tauris), 65-88.

Glick-Schiller, N. and G. Fouron (2001), *Georges Woke up Laughing. Long Distance Nationalism and the Search for Home* (Durham/NC: Duke University Press).

Glick-Schiller, N. and A. Çağlar (2008), *Migrant Incorporation and City Scale: Towards a Theory of Locality in Migration Theories*. Willy Brandt Series of Working Papers in International Migration and Ethnic Relations, Malmö University, Sweden.

Hall, S. and P. Werbner (2008), 'Cosmopolitanism, Globalisation and Diaspora', in P, Werbner ed., *Anthropology and the New Cosmopolitanism* (Oxford: Berg), 345–60.

Hand, P. (1993), *Lithuanians in Texas* (Chicago: Balzekas Museum of Lithuanian Culture).

Hand, P. (2009), 'The Lithuanian Presence in Texas: the Early Background', in V. Čiubrinskas and J. Genys (eds), *The First Lithuanians in Texas*. Exhibition Catalogue, Lithuania Minor History Museum (Klaipėda: Jokuzys), 23–27.

Hollinger, D. (1995), *Post-ethnic America: Beyond Multiculturalism* (New York: Basic).

Kerlick Bruns, B. (1980), *The Kerlick Family. 1800-1979*. Manuscript (Chicago: Lithuanian Research and Studies Centre).

Krohn-Hansen, C. (2003), 'Into Our Time: The Anthropology of Political Life in the Era of Globalization', in T. Eriksen (ed.), *Globalization. Studies in Anthropology* (London: Pluto), 78–98.

Kymlicka, W. (1995), *Multicultural Citizenship* (Oxford: Oxford University Press).

Malkki, L. (1992), 'National Geographic: The Rooting of Peoples and the Territorialization of National Identity among Scholars and Refugees', *Cultural Anthropology* 7(1): 24–44.

Nic Craith, M. (2004), 'Culture and Citizenship in Europe. Questions for Anthropologists', *Social Anthropology* 12(3): 289-300.

Olwig, K. (2004), 'Place, Movement and Identity: Processes of Inclusion and Exclusion', in W. Kokot, K. Tololyan and C. Alfonso (eds), *Diaspora, Identity and Religion. New Directions in Theory and Research* (London: Routledge), 53–71.

Rosaldo, R. and W. Flores (1997), 'Identity, Conflict, and Evolving Latino Communities: Cultural Citizenship in San Jose', in W. Flores and R. Benmayor eds, *Latino Cultural Citizenship: Claiming Identity, Space, and Rights* (Boston: Beacon), 57-96.

Wolf, H. (2002), 'Many in De-Witt have Lithuanian Roots', *Victoria Advocate,* 29 May, p.3.

Autoethnography from the Island
Thoughts on Memory and Connection

Liam Campbell

I can think of no better element of the natural world than the allure of the islands to describe both the person and her work. In previous eras the sea was a highway and islands ports of call on that route. The sea is the great connector not a divider and we on this western fringe of Europe are at the centre of a maritime world not on periphery. Since the Mesolithic hunter-gatherers in their skin-covered boats came to the shores of Ireland some 10,000 years ago, people have lived, worked, travelled and buried their dead in these coastal places. Community was built in these places.

Máiréad has the immense ability to make connections and ensure that the lore of these people and places is not forgotten. She has been a light and beacon for many of us over the years. A bridge on the pilgrimage of life between the tangible and intangible, between land and water, past and present, this world and Otherworld. As the ring of lighthouses around Ireland connect with each other (you can always see the light of another lighthouse from each one no matter where it is) this a quality that has epitomised the life and work of Máiréad.

Rathlin Island -'the plucky, persevering, self-reliant ... little kingdom between the Gael of Eire and the Gael of Alba' (Bigger 1908)—is Northern Ireland's only permanently inhabited offshore island, sitting twixt Scotland and Ireland in the turbulent eco and mythology rich Sea of Moyle straddling habitats, cultures and peoples. Ballycastle on the mainland is some 6 miles away and its nearest Scottish neighbours are the Mull of Kintyre some 13 miles away and the islands of Islay and Jura.

Like the energetic and boiling sea, the island is a busy, vibrant and beautiful place with a steady population of around 100 (down from 1,200 in the 1780s) that swells in the summer with visitors both human and seabirds. Even the direct translation of the name Rathlin into Gaelic means 'uncertain'; and indeed, the 'disputed island', as it was once known, is full of an uncertain past, with histories of shipwreck, drowning, massacre of islanders by Vikings, Scottish clans and English forces, and more recent memories of famine and emigration.

Despite all this, it is a place that I have been going to regularly, on 'pilgrimage' a place where the ambience is so conducive to bringing me face-to-face with myself, where there is no possibility of escaping that meeting. I go especially to the lighthouses of which Rathlin has no less than three. In Virginia

Woolf's novel, *To the Lighthouse*, I often feel like James when he looks at the lighthouse and says, 'It satisfied him. It confirmed some obscure feeling about his own character'. There has always been something of the monastic about lighthouses for me and indeed from the 11th to the 15th centuries monks and hermits were amongst the most diligent of keepers of beacons in Europe. In those post Dark Ages when Europe was literally 'coming into the light' again these monks and hermits were the first keepers of these primitive and tentative beacons. I have always been intrigued by the power and wisdom of place to influence our lives and how a landscape, seascape, its people and the story can affect our whole lives and our view of the world—tangible and intangible.

I first saw Rathin some forty years ago and the three lighthouses have been my references ever since. My exploration and pilgrimage was just beginning. Lopez (1986: 29), the Arctic explorer and naturalist reflecting on the way we set on an exploration of a fresh landscape writes:

> When exploration is viewed as a process rather than as a series of distinct events, its major components are seen to be clearly related to the imagination. No exploratory adventure begins without objectives based on the imagined nature and content of the lands to be explored.

In a sense, the visits to Rathlin were and are a pilgrimage, a *peregrinatio,* a seeking, quest adventure or wandering in faith and hope. The pilgrimage phenomenon has been an important part of Irish spirituality since the early Middle Ages and especially connected to our islands. I became a *peregrine*. To De Waal (1996: 21), 'this journey is only possible because I am finding my roots'. This *peregrinatio* involves a journey through both space and time. It both necessitates 'a sense of connectedness to the earth itself' and 'finding my roots takes me back to the part of myself that is more ancient than I am' (Lopez 1986: 21).

Lane's Dictionary at the turn of the last century translated *Dinnesheanchas* as the 'naming of high or holy places ' or more recently topography, but in a world that has fallen to the all-consuming vice of empiricism that allows that if you cannot measure it in any way, then it doesn't exist. *Dinnsheanchas* for me is the result of our emotion-imaginative involvement with the physical features and landscape of this island that I call home. We are always involved with the landscape, projecting outwards onto our inner landscapes, the *'payasge interieur'* which is the landscape of our souls.

When is an island an island or not? There are many places with the word 'island' in the placenames of Ireland. Míchael Ó Mainnín examined the occurrence of the word 'island' in eastern Ulster (1990: 200) and concluded that in many instances these places were not a true island but a place that in the past had been marshy land or a flood plain of a river surrounding a hill or piece of higher ground. Therefore, the temporary situation could apply a permanent one in the name. What makes me think of Rathlin, and indeed all our islands and coasts? What is fixed in this Anthropocene era of rising tides? Transformation is possible—inevitable? The land becomes sea and the sea becomes land depending where you are.

This area off the north coast is also the legendary burial place of the Celtic sea god Manannán Mac Lír (McKay 2007), in early Irish mythology the chief god associated with the sea, an Irish (not necessarily Celtic) equivalent of the Roman Neptune and the Greek Poseidon. Manannán was a Dé Danann prince who was killed when fighting the invading Milesians. He then became a water creature reincarnated as Manannán Mac Lír—son of Lear—the sea. Known as the chief pagan Irish god of the underworld, of water and of crops, he is supposed to have possessed a huge cauldron (Green 1986). Manannán is said to be buried in the Tonn Banks at the entrance to Lough Foyle off the coast of Inishowen Head. Shipwrecks have occurred here and the spirit of Manannán is supposed to ride at intervals on the storm. Darcy Magee describes him in a poem: 'Their ocean— god was Manannán Mac Lír / Whose angry lips / In their white foam full often would inter / Whole fleets of ships' (cited in Mac Cana 1985: 74).

There is evidence of a belief in more recent times that fairies still lived in the flooded region beneath this area and there are other indications that the happy antediluvian realms of the distant past were equated with the blissful Otherworld thought to exist in the present (Carey 1987). Carey (1999: 33) contends that, 'we can posit a threefold symbolic parallelism: land: water / past: present / Otherworld: this world'. A striking example of this chain of analogies is provided by the well-known poem recited by Manannán in *Immram Brain*; here the contrast between the fertile plain and the barren sea, reflected in the temporal hiatus in the 'Dialogue' becomes merely a matter of perception:

> For Bran it is a wondrous delight / To go across the sea in his little boat; / For me, in my chariot from afar, it is a flowery plain which he traverses. / What is clear sea / To the beaked ship in which Bran is Mag Mell abounding in flowers / To me in my two-wheeled chariot / Bran beholds / Many laughing waves across the clear sea. / As for me, I behold on Mag Mon / Flawless red-topped flowers.

As Carey (1999: 33) says, 'The radiant land of the immortals, and the water traversed by human voyages, are simultaneously real; but only the eyes of the god can discern their coexistence'. This mysterious poem gives the impression of belonging to the pagan past, but it was composed in the seventh or eighth century and is according to Carney: 'from beginning to end a thoroughly Christian poem. It seems in fact, to be an allegory showing Man setting out on a voyage to Paradise' (Carney, cited in Murray, 1986: 10). Moriarty has called this *Voyage of Bran* 'Ireland's Bhagavad Gita or Ireland's Song of God'. He says: 'Manannán is telling us that there is literally a world of difference between how he sees things and how we see them. Bran's was a voyage to where we are. And that's it. That's the story of original perception, of silver branch perception, to Ireland' (Moriarty 2007: 112). Moriarty (2007: 112) tellingly asks:

> Our Song of God sung to us at sea by the god of the sea, how come that every child in the land doesn't know it by heart? For the sole reason that he sang this one song to us, how come Manannán isn't as well known across the world as the God of Christians or Muslims? How come Bran mac Feabhail isn't as well known across the world as Moses is, as Mohammed is?

Lopez (1986) contends that human stories originate in the difference between the inner landscape and the outer one. I wanted to look at this. My journey of enquiry arose out of a chance to return to the island for some work a few years ago. My mother was 90 that year and I was 50. It had not been the easiest of years. As my mother slipped quietly into the mysterious world of dementia and the specific country of Alzheimer's disease. I had been on sick leave for a few months and a few friends had passed away. But then something happened—call it coincidence, chance, accident or serendipity or whatever, I am not so sure. She had always talked about her sister Bid (a pet-name for Brid or Bridget) who had died at the age of six from tuberculosis on Rathlin Island. Consumption was the common name in usage at the time, ironically due to weight loss. It was rife in Ireland in the 1920s and most families had some connection to this horrible infectious disease of the lungs, now mostly confined to the bovine type but on the rise in places with the impact of poverty again.

My mother was living on Rathlin because her father was stationed there as a lighthouse keeper on the East Tower. They loved our most northerly island and had great times there she used to say. But it was not all romantic as you could be, and often were, moved at very short notice to another station anywhere on the island of Ireland at three days instruction. How did that effect ones idea of home and place?

Little Bid died shortly before the entire family were moved to Blacksod in Co Mayo on the other side of the county. I can only begin to think what it must have been like for my grandparents to have to leave their child who died so young, in a grave that in all probability they would never see again.

Some time ago, I discovered the only known photograph of Bid in classic sepia tones. The hair stood on the back of my neck—Bid was, as they say a 'ringer' for my daughter Gráinne, who was then about the same age as Bid when she died. Her poise, her hair, her size and indeed her whole demeanour in that photograph—she was the image of Gráinne. I spoke to my mother and expressed a deep desire to visit the grave. My mother as far as her failing memory could remember said that she was buried in some other family grave as the family would not have had a grave of their own. They would not have opened a grave especially for a family that had no roots there. Lighthouse keepers were rather rootless in many ways. It is the way of the sea, I suppose. One lovey thing on Rathlin is that 'Catholics, Protestants and Dissenters' are buried in the one graveyard at the Church of Ireland in Church Bay. I spent much time and effort trying to locate the grave mulling over church and state records and even contacting old lighthouse keeping families. Always turning up a blank. It was almost 100 years ago after all—people forgot, I supposed.

My family and I went to that wonderful island many times, often birdwatching, but always stopping to say a prayer and have a thought at the wall of the graveyard, that was the resting place of little Bid. Yet, we had no grave to visit. Then I had, in the course of my work, to bring some archaeologists over to the island for two days. However, I had to leave early on the first ferry on the second day, as I had to do best-man duties at a friend's wedding in Derry. I brought a flask of coffee with me on the boat to keep me going as I was rather tired after the island's hospitality. There was nobody on board except the pilot and a young woman who was collecting the fares. Marianne was a marine biologist from the island who had recently moved back into the island to start a new life market gardening and was working on the ferry part-time. We talked about my reasons for being on the island, marine biology and the puffins etc. Then I told her about my aunt Bid and my search for her grave over the past few years especially since we discovered her photograph and her likeness to our own daughter.

Immediately she beckoned me to stop talking and went on to say that, how just on the previous night at home with her mother, Angela, they were discussing their own family grave and how it was full and how they may have to look at getting another plot. Marianne then said that her mother recalled how there was a little girl buried in their grave—the daughter of a lighthouse keeper who had died of TB and how they were the nearest neighbours to the lighthouse and how they had offered their family grave.

I went on to the wedding much distracted and travelled immediately back to the island the next day to meet Marianne's mother, Angela. She recalled, that as children, when they would say their prayers at night and remember dead relatives, they were told to remember the wee girl buried in their grave.

Bid was not forgotten and I was able to tell my mother this before she slipped away. It was a great comfort and I can now visit the grave, pray and think there. Coincidence, chance, serendipity or the spirt of God—whatever you want to call it. One of my favourite lines in the whole bible comes from Hebrews 'and remember always to welcome strangers, for by doing this, some have entertained angels without knowing it'.

It is strange that some outside pressure was needed for me to see that the obvious point to begin when trying to link the inner and outer worlds is where you can look in both directions: with oneself (Hägerstrand cited in Buttimer 1993: 256). This re-exploration has its own difficulties. Where does prayer, soul and memory come in culture? Intangible yet tangible in some ways. The island took on a new and deeper meaning for me. The silence of landscape conceals vast presence. Place is not simply location. A place is a profound individuality— its surface, texture of grass and stone is blessed by rain, wind and light. With complete attention, landscapes celebrate a liturgy of the seasons, giving itself unreservedly to the passion of the goddess. The shape of the landscape is an ancient and silent form of consciousness. Mountains are huge contemplatives. Rivers and streams offer voice; they are tears of the earth's joy and despair. The earth is full of soul (O' Donohue 1997: 115).

References

Bigger, F. (1908), 'On Rachrai's Rocks', *Irish News*, 19 August.

Buttimer, A. (1993), *Geography and the Human Spirit* (Baltimore: Johns Hopkins University Press).

Carey, J. (1987), 'Time, Space and the Otherworld', *Proceedings of the Harvard Celtic Colloquim* 1: 8-10.

Carey, J. (1999), 'Transmutations of Immortality in the "Lament of the Old Woman of Beare"', *Celticia* 23: 29-37.

De Waal, E. (1996), *The Celtic Way of Prayer* (London: Hodder and Staughton).

Green, M. (1986), *The Gods of the Celts* (Godalming: Bramley).

Lopez, B. (1986), *Arctic Dreams: Imagination and Desire in a Northern Landscape* (London: Harvill).

Mac Cana, P. (1985), *Celtic Mythology* (New York: Hamlyn).

McKay, P. (2007), *A Dictionary of Ulster Place-Names* (Belfast: Institute of Irish Studies).

Morriarty, J. (2007), *What the Curlew Said: Nostos Continued* (Dublin: Lilliput).

O'Donohue, J. (1997), *Anam Cara* (London: Bantam).

Ó Mainnín, M. (1990),'The element ISLAND in Ulster Place-Names', *Anim: A Journal of Name Studies* IV: 200-210.

Go to Your Grandfather's House

Iain MacKinnon

Yes.
Here you are
Standing in front of the house at 22,
Shirt tied to the neck, sleeves rolled up,
And dark grey trousers braced.
Black shoes,
The ground beneath them mown and bare
And life past and life future raised
into one mountain of a *cochd* by the long fork you have now pushed into the
ground

A memory of you
Making hay
Facing the bay,
The Sound of Sleat,
with Knoydart over by.

Give some bearings, then, to the boy, lost by your side. Give the places that you
knew.

'Sgeir a Chàraidh
then
Sgeir nan Gillean,
Sgeir an Fhaing Bheag
and then
Sgeir an Fhaing Mhòr
and that's where the
Faiche
is'

Why even speak this old half-forgotten stuff?

...because those names are good to say...

A small cloud moves in over the running sound
And then, without movement, you are fifteen yards
And fifteen years away
Dying on your bed in the front room,
Behind you the window and the bay
And the silent rocks,
The little boy still by your side.

I watch your chest grow and fall back, and picture your lungs,
serrated, holed and blotched like the old shed's corrugated roof.
There pitchfork, peg-rake and mower lie in still, cool, air.
Growing useless, slowly, coming to their end.
It is summer. Time to make hay.
But we are inside, falling and rising, passing away.
The rasp and crackle of a half century of tobacco fills the room.
Painfully regular, the sound of dying is everywhere,
and the world outside is silent; not present.
The end of life is breathing; its absence begins to fill the world.
And when it seems the world can hold no more of it,
sounds more terrible emerge:

'I wish I was dead
 then
All my friends are gone
 and then
There's nothing here for me now'

We are in the shade now. Us two
The little boy is held, wrapped in a soft and ancient hand,
Made strange by a force that clouds memory, demanding to forget
(the tide ebbing far from the rocks)
Made feeble by time seeping through aspiration's little stackyard
(turning life into black sludge).

But not today.
Today you are among your own,
Making hay.
Pitchfork held firm in one hand,
a cigarette cocked in the other.

Looking over the newly bare croft,
Fresh blue waves coming in rows toward you,
Sun easy on your back,
And the rocks and hills of Camuscross, of Sleat,
The island itself unfolding around you

In the summer of 2009, I was moving towards the third year of my PhD at the University of Ulster's Derry campus with Máiréad and Ulli as supervisors. My research had developed into a project in which I was trying to understand the historical colonisation of Scotland's Gaels, and, relatedly, how my own self-understanding, as part of the collective being of my people, had been radically interrupted and reformed under the force of Scottish and British imperialism.

That summer I was visited by my grandfather in the house where I was living in Donegal. I was sitting on the sill of an internal window between the living room and kitchen when he appeared behind me and said to me, in Gaelic, two words: *Chan eil*. This translates into English as 'is not'. It is perhaps the main phrase of negation in the language and I took him to mean that I should cease what I was trying to do with my work.

There followed a period of around eighteen months of ontological doubt and emotional distress, at times acute, as I went against my grandfather's wishes to finish the work. Ulli and Máiréad had some inkling of the process that was unfolding in me and showed considerable tact and understanding in supporting me to finish. I should say that my fellow student and close friend (and co-editor of this book) Liam Campbell, was a lifeline during the rest of my time in Ireland, as was Seamus Canavan of Gulladuff House in Moville, and Caroline McDaid.

The poem first emerged in the summer of 2013, four years after my grandfather's visit, and began with an affirmation. It was my first attempt to begin to reconcile with him. It speaks, I think, to some of the themes—of creativity, memory, language—which Máiréad follows in her work, and it features a short quote from the work of a favourite author of Ulli's, Keith Basso.

Most of the Gaelic words are the names of *sgeirean* or large rock outcrops in the horseshoe bay of Camuscross that has cradled the being of my family for generations. My grandfather used to tell me these names as we stood at his living room window overlooking the bay, although otherwise we spoke to each other almost entirely in English.

I have reached an understanding that the decisions taken to keep me—and many in my own and others' generations—from my language and culture in my early life were taken out of a sense of love, however misplaced those decisions might seem to me. They were taken to protect the children from the world that the dear suffering ancestors had faced, so that the children might be less unprepared to face that world than the ancestors were.

On Learning to Say Longing
Drawing on the Power of Fado

Victoria Walters

> *Coimbra é uma lição*
> *De sonho e tradição*
> *O lente é uma canção*
> *E a lua a faculdade*
> *O livro é uma mulher*
> *Só passa quem souber*
> *E aprende-se a dizer saudade*
>
> Coimbra is a lesson
> Of dream and tradition
> The lens is a song
> And the moon the faculty
> The book is a woman
> Only those who know pass
> And learn to say longing[1]

I am honoured to contribute to this publication for Máiréad Nic Craith, whose teaching, scholarship and support I have long valued and admired. I had planned to write about Joseph Beuys, the artist whose work has been the main focus of my research to date, however fate, or fado, if you will allow, had something else in mind. What follows is a set of reflections emerging from a sketchbook drawing I made in response to the song tradition of fado while in Lisbon, Portugal, a drawing I later developed into a larger piece for exhibition. Art is an interest both Máiréad and Professor Ullrich Kockel encouraged me to pursue alongside my PhD, having pursued studies in creative arts before starting a doctorate under their supervision. I had not considered the drawing in research terms until now, but it feels appropriate to reflect on this practice-led journey here, as some of the questions it raises around fado, art and place find a valuable theoretical provocation in Máiréad's work, particularly her writing on intangible heritage. At the same time, to watch fado is to witness a form of utterance, and I was

---

[1] Galhardo, J. and R. Ferrao (1952), *Coimbra* (Rio de Janeiro: Rio Musical). Author's translation. This was the signature song of renowned *fadista* Amália Rodrigues (1939–1999).

intrigued to consider this song tradition in connection with this publication's theme.

In 2011, I attended the International Society for Ethnology and Folklore (SIEF) Congress 'People Make Places: Ways of Feeling the World' in Lisbon with Máiréad, Ullrich and fellow PhD students. The event provided a forum for ethnologists and anthropologists to discuss methods they were using to understand how people shape places in creative ways. The Congress theme focused on how 'the ways in which people construct their views, opinions, values and practices are constantly being re-negotiated and re-interpreted in various creative forms' and asked participants to 'present new perspectives on how people's lives, memories, emotions and values interact with places and localities.' (SIEF Congress outline) During free time, with the rich input from the conference jangling in my mind, I visited art galleries, went to the National Museum of Ethnology and sought out spaces where music played. Like many visitors and tourists, I was captivated by the musical tradition of fado.

Fado usually comprises a mournful-sounding solo singer accompanied by two other musicians, one playing a Portuguese guitar (which, unlike the Spanish classical guitar, has a smaller wooden body shaped into a wider, tear shape) and the other a viola or viola baixa (more recently a double bass has also been used). In Portuguese, the word fado literally means insurmountable fate (from the Latin fatum in the sense of destiny or prophecy), but also utterance, and it is described as evoking saudade, a sense of nostalgia and loss that has no direct translation in English, a longing that relates to the hard realities of daily life and hope for their resolution. As Congress participants, we were treated to a wonderful recital by professional fadistas at our conference dinner, but I was particularly drawn to performances I encountered on the streets and suspected there were other locations where I could find community-based performances of amateur fado, or fado amador.

Lisbon fado appeared in the city in the earlier part of the 1800s and a number of excellent studies have brought into view its compelling power to affect situated, social bodies in place. In her book *Fado Resounding: Affective Politics and Urban Life*, Lila Ellen Gray gives a compelling ethnographic account of the song tradition, considering 'the power of a musical genre to sediment, circulate, and transform affect, sonorously rendering history and place as soulful and feeling as public' (2013: 2). The book reflects Gray's interest in the senses in anthropology and is based on extensive fieldwork, not a fleeting experience like my own. She interviewed key practitioners and took participant observation seriously, learning to sing fado, a challenge for an American with English as her mother tongue. Gray notes the diverse and strongly held feelings about how fado emerged, narratives varying from sailors' songs of the sea to songs once sung only in Lisbon's brothels, but then popularised. She outlines a variety of theories about the origins of the tradition and the dominant academic position that Lisbon fado emerged following the re-situation of the Lisbon court to Brazil (Gray 2013: 12):

> Polemic surrounding origins has been central to published fado discourse at least since the beginning of the twentieth century (Carvalho 1992 [1903]; Pimental 1989 [1904]). While the main strains of this polemic argue for African-influenced derivations via the black slave trade and Lisbon's positioning as port city vis-à-vis colonial contact and expansion, Arab derivations due to the long-standing presence of the Moors in Portugal, or a combination of the two, others link fado to the music of the medieval troubadours, to expressive traditions from rural Portugal, to the Celts, or to the 'gypsies.' The theory of origins granted the most currency by contemporary academics situates fado's 'birth' in the first half of the nineteenth century and locates its primary influences as Afro-Brazilian.

While thoughtfully noting the 'excess' of discourse on origins, Gray focuses on the way fado operates within 'the realm of the emergent that is social life' rather than becoming too embroiled in an essentialist discourse on singular origins.

A second Portuguese fado tradition, Coimbra fado, is connected to the city of Coimbra and its University, as alluded to in the verse opening this chapter. In the English translation of 'Para além da Vista e do Som: Fado de Coimbra, Património Imaterial com Valor Turístico' ('Beyond Sight and Sound: Fado of Coimbra, Intangible Heritage with Touristic Value') Joana Costa and Paulo Nuno Nossa explain (2017: 558) that 'the classic expression of the Fado of Coimbra is the serenade' made by a male suitor to a potential lover at night, wearing the dark clothes and cape students traditionally once wore. They acknowledge that Coimbra fado is understood by the majority of scholars to have emerged from a 'regionalization of the Lisbon fado' and to be 'an urban tradition, of Afro-Brazilian origin' (2017: 558-59), charting the tradition through particular fado composers, singers and historical periods, including its role in student resistance during the Salazar regime, up to the present day. Costa and Nossa echo Gray's observation of the plethora of speculative myths around how Coimbra Fado developed (2017: 566) and express concern at these 'adulterant facts and narratives', arguing that 'cultural identity and the authenticity of the intangible asset in question can only be founded on knowledge of the city of Coimbra and the analysis of various artistic constraints – aesthetic, musical, human and urban – that led to the song.' Costa and Nossa (2017: 565-566) recognise the degree to which tourists admire fado but show concern about the attendant danger of its commercialisation and globalisation, threatening 'the forms of expression and the traditional cultural knowledge surrounding them' which are an expression of particular places and communities.

During my stay in Lisbon I tried to draw every day to 'keep my eye in' and at one point made a sketchbook drawing in charcoal in response to listening to amateur fado. I wanted to capture the soulful feeling of connection I had experienced when I listened, as though something simultaneously intimate, tragic and hopeful about a place and its people and histories were being shared [Figure 1]. Fado is, of course, exactly the kind of sensory cultural tradition through which people co-create and respond to place, but despite the conference I was not thinking in academic terms, rather I was trying to communicate empathy for the human stories of love, marginality and suffering I sensed – but given my lack of language skills in Portuguese could only imagine – I was hearing.

Figure 1: Sketchbook drawing (detail, willow charcoal, 420 x 594mm, ©Walters 2011)

The emotive songs moved me greatly and I felt I was hearing a tradition which was both particular to Lisbon and had a wider reach, connecting to the city's colonial past and the stories of those caught up in its painful and complex transatlantic narratives. The sketch is neither purely figurative nor abstract and only the Portuguese guitar is depicted, presented as both a singing bird and a machine, rather than the two instruments usually supporting a fadista. The vocalist's singing head is also a listening figure holding a hand to their ear, reminding me of Gray's observation (2013: 7) that 'to focus on the voice is to be attuned to the ear, to listening'. The fado is being performed at night and the abstract forms to the left are oblique; perhaps listening humans, a non-human audience or even rocks in the water of the Targus, they are a group presence I felt was needed to complete the sketch.

In spring 2019, eight years after the Congress, an unexpected opportunity arose to revisit my sketchbook drawing. I am a member of the research group Space, Place, Practice – an artists' research collective that comes together to create dialogues and develop projects informed by a shared interest in notions of space, place and creative practice. One of the network members, Dr Michele Whiting, is of Portuguese ancestry and shared an exciting call to artists to show work in an exhibition at Fábrica Braço De Prata (which translates literally as the Silver Arms Factory) in Lisbon. A vibrant arts centre opened semi officially in a former ammunitions factory, Fábrica operates under the Directorship of its Founder, Professor of Philosophy at the University of Lisbon, Nuno Nabais. The show was to be curated by the artist, curator and academic Diana Ali – known by many for her supportive mentorship to participants in BBC's 'Big Painting Challenge' – and had the theme 'Loss & Lucidity: The Lost and Found'. I remembered the sketch and the connection between fado and loss and decided to submit an image of it, proposing to work it up at a larger scale for exhibition.

I was delighted when the proposal was accepted, but not without trepidation. Responding to a cultural tradition in a sketchbook is one thing, producing work for display in the cultural context in which it emerged quite another. When I had first visited Lisbon, I was a researcher in Visual Culture interested in the relationship between anthropology and art, not an anthropologist researching fado in an intensive way through fieldwork, so it was inappropriate to see my response as an etic (outsider) perspective, in anthropological terms. Perhaps I was simply an observing tourist and fledgling artist, experimenting. I was mindful that the history of art is littered with cultural appropriation, some of it very dubious in terms of the power relations involved. If fado was not my cultural tradition, had I any right to try to convey it?

Figure 2: José Malhoa, *O Fado* (1910), oil painting (1500 mm x 1830 mm). Original painting in colour. Collection Museu de Lisboa /Câmara, Municipal Lisboa – EGEAC [public domain]

I looked for depictions of fado in art history. A Portuguese friend interested in my search mentioned José Malhoa's oil painting *O Fado* (Figure 2). The painting, created in 1910, depicts a woman listening, enraptured, to a male fadista playing the guitar and singing. The depiction of both performing and listening is wonderfully conveyed by the facial expression of the fadista and the tilted head of the woman. It is clear from her attire that she is a prostitute, and the wooden bench and broken mirror point to modest circumstances.[2] It is an accomplished work, certainly, reflecting Malhoa's considerable skills as a realist painter, alt-

---

2   Many have suggested, probably erroneously, that Malhoa was depicting renowned fadista Maria Severa Onofriana (1820 – 48), the first fado singer to find fame.

hough within Portugal it received a negative reception from critics initially, gaining acclaim outside the country until it was fêted at the National Society of Fine Arts in Lisbon in 1917. Malhoa came to be known as a painter of the people. In an essay by Rui-Mário Gonçalves (2011) I then learned that futurist artist Amadeo De Souza-Cardoso had created a futurist 'replica' of Malhoa's painting that same year. A homage to both fado and the machine age, De Souza-Cardoso's collage 'represents typewriters, letters, pistons, levers and a metal pole running through a violin that bleeds!' (2011: 103).

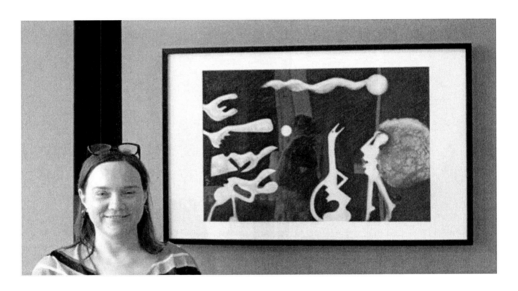

Figure 3: 'On Longing' (willow charcoal drawing on Fabriano paper, 500mm x 705mm; ©Walters 2019). Photographer: Sarah Rhys

The work is a clear critique of the romantic realism of Malhoa's painting and typical of Futurism's emphatic drive to do away with the sentimentality of past aesthetic forms in favour of those deemed more suitable for the machine age. Further, there was the sense of an overlap between listening and performing and human and non-human worlds which felt important to me. I was satisfied that the version I sent to Lisbon was ready for exhibition, but even on the opening night, standing next to it I had doubts about my capacity or right to try to capture the power of fado and whether it responded sufficiently to contemporary contexts or the communities that created it (Figure 3). At the same time, I was excited and grateful to Diana Ali for giving me this wonderful opportunity and fascinated by the Fábrica arts centre and its history, combining generous spaces for all forms of art with a large bookshop full of the work of philosophers, critical thinkers, creative writers and artists.

In the Editorial of the centre's aptly named online magazine 'Desarmada' (Disarmed), I noticed a set of critical questions about appearance and disappearance, the tangible and intangible in art with which Nabais had framed the whole of that season's cultural offerings. He notes that philosophical thought in the West has been characterised by the belief that art, as that which appears, is false, and the real, deemed invisible, is true. Nabais suggests that (Western) art's emphasis on appearance, or more recently disappearance, exists in the ruins of these philosophical underpinnings. He refers to Marcel Duchamp's artwork 'Fountain' of 1917[3] as a means the artist used to convey that art is nothing more than pure appearance and suggests that this emphasis seems to have given way to a contemporary art characterised by disappearance, especially in performance art. 'How does art appear to be what is lost, what happens as a disappearance? Is it lucidity in the face of loss, the acute awareness of a void, that defines artistic creation today?' (Nabais 2019: npn).

I wondered how the notion of art as 'pure appearance' – and what Nabais sees as its contemporary turn to incarnate absence or loss – connected to artists' responses to the broader contexts of the First and Second World War and the Holocaust, pertinent, if broad, questions to consider in a former munitions factory.[4] I also tried to place Nabais' reflections in relation to my own work. I had been trying to evoke a tradition that expresses a sense of loss, but did my own artwork demonstrate a quality of 'lucidity in the face of loss'? If my intuition had led me to any lucidity, I needed to research and reflect further in order to understand what it was trying to tell me.

---

[3] 'Fountain' was one of Duchamp's famous 'readymades', a porcelain urinal he placed on its back rather than upright and signed 'R. Mutt 1917'. The artist submitted the piece for exhibition to the Society of Independent Artists in New York which he had helped found and it was rejected by the Society's board of directors, despite the commitment of its constitution to accept all submissions. However, it came to be seen as a key work of conceptual art, questioning the role of the artist as a maker of original handmade objects and championing art that conveys ideas over visual, purely retinal objects. 1917 was also the year Malhoa's work 'O Fado' found success in Lisbon and De Souza-Cardoso critiqued it.

[4] These reflections reminded me of my studies of Joseph Beuys's work. For Beuys, Duchamp demonstrated that art is not a special category distinct from other forms of human making and is inextricably connected to language. Beuys criticised Duchamp for failing to communicate the broader anthropological implications of this. The Dada artist was responding to the absurdity and darkness of the First World War, Beuys to the horrors of the Second.

Issues around appearance and disappearance have certainly had an impact upon how fado is defined and valued in heritage terms. Lisbon and Coimbra fado have been framed as intangible and ephemeral; they are now protected by UNESCO (2003) as a form of 'intangible cultural heritage' defined as:

> the practices, representations, expressions, knowledge, skills – as well as the instruments, objects, artefacts and cultural spaces associated there-with – that communities, groups and, in some cases, individuals recognize as part of their cultural heritage.

Costa and Nossa (2017: 565) note that UNESCO stress the importance of the intergenerational transmission of Coimbra fado to ensure its protection due to 'the fragility of the relationship between communities and their Intangible cultural heritage.' However, they question the limits of UNESCO's emphasis on the intangible (2017: 564):

> we would question the theoretical and practical utility of the polarised de-bate between tangible and intangible heritage. Heritage exists only when it is recognisable within a certain set of cultural or social values, which are in and of themselves intangible.

In the journal article 'Intangible Cultural Heritages: The Challenges for Europe', Máiréad Nic Craith also takes issue with UNESCO's framework for under-standing heritage, but her sense of what might be obscured by such a dichotomy extends further. She discusses a range of issues that beset Europe in its approach to heritage, including the challenges of commercialisation and argues for 'a holistic approach' (2005: 54). She notes (2008: 54-55) that while most people are familiar with the general concept, heritage has been understood in an uneven manner globally and even in a European context, largely because there are diverse translations and attitudes to the notion in different languages and local-ities. She notes that the English language concept of heritage focuses on the built environment and a sense of tangibility which is not shared in Japan, or even France. Significantly here, Nic Craith acknowledges (2008: 57) that delineating what constitutes tangible and intangible heritage is far from clear cut; the boundary between the two is, at best (to use clumsy artistic metaphor), sketchy. She argues (2008: 57) that

> ultimately it is best to think of heritage in holistic terms, recognising the significance of and interactions between the tangible and intangible, ob-jects as well as cultural spaces, embracing both process and product, and

placing particular emphasis on ordinary people as tradition definers and tradition bearers.

Nic Craith supports the notion of the glocal over the global, asking (2008: 69): 'Can we ignore the fact that the colonisation process was an integral element in the dissemination of European ideas and values on a global scale?'

As mentioned earlier, fado has connections with song traditions that lie beyond the geographical boundaries of Lisbon, Coimbra or Portugal as a whole and these transits and translations are embedded in a colonial past that, in efforts to boost notions of national identity, often remains in the shadows. In 'Fados do fado: plots, chronotopes and cultural transits', Jose Machado Pais documents his experience of travelling to Quissama in Brazil and encountering forms of fado he asserts emerged from 'the time of slaves', forms with characteristics that differ from both Lisbon and Coimbra fado. I will not go into the detail of his ethnographic observations here, although they are fascinating, but rather to his reflections on the obsession with origins where Fado is concerned and the problematic tendency to refer to a singular fado rather than a plurality of fados. Where Gray observes that this origin obsession comes from within the community as well as from visitors, Pais (2018: 2) largely ascribes the tendency to those who are 'foreign':

When our foreign colleagues and friends ask us about the origins of fado, they throw us a banana peel that threatens to slip us into the pursuit of an unlikely primordial identity of fado in its alleged uniqueness and essence. … I do not shy away from giving them clues about possible troubadour, Arab, African and Gypsy influences.

One might conclude that fado's many, variant and sometimes hybrid translations emerge from particular communities and places within and outside Europe. That is not to say that they are not expressions of particular places and communities. In his book Fado and the Place of Longing: Loss, Memory and the City, Richard Elliott (2010: 2) argues that fado enables the construction of a 'mythology of place', noting the myriad references in Lisbon fado to the city itself, particularly areas associated with the song tradition such as Mouraria. However, while these traditions require care and protection and relate to place, they are not confined to Lisbon or Coimbra and do not relay static facts. A myth holds a deeper truth, but is a narrative nonetheless and identifying fado only with two specific Portuguese cities without considering its longer, geographically ex-

tended histories risks inviting a kind of slippage, or 'disappearing' of related traditions, and as a result, the protection of some, but not all, of its variants and
actors. Many examples of 'intangible' heritage, fado included, emerge from oral
traditions and while their various manifestations are rooted in dialogue with
specific places, these may be impossible to grasp as a singularity emerging from
one country of origin.

A 'holistic approach' might enable us to perceive more clearly that framing
heritage is itself a constructive creative process that makes certain claims appear and others disappear, thus rendering more explicit the politics involved in
developing a new model. The colonisation process saw fit to legitimate the 'disappearance' of 'non-European' items from their place of origin against the will
of their makers or caretakers and sanction their 'reappearance' in European museums, framed as property, or ethnographic curiosity. In short, to make some
claims to the ownership and origin of objects magically appear and others disappear. The same may be true of intangible heritage traditions. A more holistic
notion of heritage might serve to protect the fado of Cape Verde as much as
that of Coimbra, and reveal hidden narratives about people and place.

The notion that some forms of heritage are intangible, and the value and
protections that are accorded to them as a result of this framing, is influenced
by Western thought and particularly Western ideas about aesthetics and perception. In a book review published in the journal American Anthropologist in
2015, Nic Craith appraises Professor Sophia Labadi's book *UNESCO, Cultural Heritage, and Outstanding Universal Value: Value-Based Analyses of the World Heritage and Intangible Cultural Heritage Conventions*. The book addresses critical
questions around the basis upon which decisions about what constitutes World
Heritage (and thus worthy of protection) are made, including a discussion of the
influence of the notion of Outstanding Universal Value (OUV). Nic Craith outlines
Labadi's observation that European notions of 'Universal Value' have developed
in association with ideas about art and intrinsic values rooted in European philosophical texts, for example the influence of Kant's argument that 'individual
aesthetic judgments are disinterested' (Nic Craith 2013: 845).

Nic Craith points out Labadi's observation that Kant's claim has been belied
by later scholarship in philosophy (in the work of Pierre Bourdieu), which suggests that aesthetic judgments are, in fact, culturally specific. However, Labadi
argues that despite this, other cultural traditions are able to use frameworks
originating outside their own culture, translating them within their own contexts. Nic Craith praises Labadi's publication but is concerned that the simple
acceptance that a European framework can be adapted and used outside Europe's borders does not go far enough. Drawing from Franz Fanon, Nic Craith

(2013: 845) highlights the negative psychological impact of having to engage with a dominating European discourse and put on 'white masks', effects that include 'feelings of inadequacy and inferiority', and concludes that, 'perhaps, this book is also a call to all of us who are passionate about heritage to reconsider the criteria for World Heritage status and to review the Eurocentric nature of the "international" definition of heritage to achieve a more global consensus'.

Nic Craith's important call to address the deleterious impact of universalist thinking and her argument for a holistic notion of heritage resonates with Nuno Nabais' reflections on art created amongst the ruins of Western thought and its notion of the falsity of the phenomenon that appears and a reality that is hidden. Kant's theories of disinterested aesthetic judgement were connected to a particular notion of perception. The philosopher argued that there is a separation between the 'phenomenon', that which can be perceived by (or appears to) the senses, and the 'noumenon', which he referred to as 'the object of reason', an underlying reality which for Kant is invisible and can only be intuited (Mautner 2005: 431). Nic Craith's argument suggested that notions of heritage, like those of art, exist 'in the ruins of these philosophical underpinnings'.

This led me to reflect on how fados, as creative, artistic performances, function as processes involving people and what they bring into view. Fados express wounded relations and encourage a process of listening that might prompt empathy, self-healing and care of place and people and this seemed far more important to me than any potential the tradition might have as a mouthpiece for national identity. As creative processes, they respond to particular situations in specific places, but, while it is important to ascertain where they are situated, defining them solely in terms of their 'Portuguese-ness' may obscure their importance as a vocalised, curative process available for people to leverage against personal, political, individual or collective woes. In 'The Question of Voice: With What Voice Will I Cry My Sad Fado?', Maria do Rosário Dias, Nadia Pereira Simões, Ana Ferreira and Eva Coelho (2016: 106) consider fado's therapeutic quality. While they recognise that fado can reinforce a sense of national identity – pointing out that certain authors have argued that the word *saudade* is impossible to translate, and therefore 'a genuine verbal symbol of the Portuguese soul' (Dias et al. 2016: 113) – they note that fado seems to provide a means for the sublimation of trauma and a 'restorative bridge for... suffering'.[5]

---

[5] Dias et al. (2016) note the tradition's appearance in Lisbon in the 19th century and opine that it may have developed in communities that were pushed into areas 'left out of the enlightenment urban plans of the Marquis of Pombal' after the Lisbon earthquake of 1755, enabling

The authors argue (2016: 111) that the power of fado is not that of enabling the fadista to return to the past through song, but to recount the past to a receptive and active audience in a way that allows them to rebuild an image of themselves and undertake 'emotional remodelling' (Outeiral and Godoy 2003)'. Framing fado as a strategy for overcoming the helplessness inculcated by trauma, their words (Dias et al. 2016: 110) remind me of Nic Craith's concern, as articulated by Fanon, about the damaging effect of putting on 'masks':

> Victims of a relentless trauma have their creativity stolen and are forced to verbalize an endless repetition of stories about themselves that have been demanded of them. These are actually the stories of the aggressor and the victim gradually becomes the ghost of his own empty body. But these are the stories that one has to pay attention to and honour, so that wounds can heal.

Considering the tradition's sense of saudade, of longing, nostalgia and loss in this context, Dias et al. (2016: 112) suggest that

> [l]onging recollection as internal healing of the mind serves the purpose of protecting the subject's internal confidence, thus making it again viable for that subject to invest in both their internal and external world. This is symbolically connected to the subject as the 'presence of the absence' (Kampff Lages, 2002).

The authors draw from Kampff Lages' psychoanalytical notion of the 'presence of the absence' to consider the cathartic way in which the absent object or person the fadista is expressing the loss of is simultaneously made present again through recollection and sharing with others in song. She or he is thus able to gain distance from and understanding of the wound of loss. There is a sense, here, of the psychic importance of fado in reconnecting the fadista with seen and unseen, inner and outer worlds and members of the audience may feel the cathartic effects of this process too. As Dias et al (2016: 113) explain:

> The singer recreates the universe of song by singing it, in a complete surrender to Fado and to the audience. When traumatized individuals, hear

---

them to share their feelings about their conditions. While Gray and Pais led me to remain cautious about discourses on singular origins, the suggestion that the tradition may have emerged in Lisbon from the predicament of those who did not 'fit into the enlightenment picture' was arresting here.

(embodied in) the Fadista, they find someone to address the representation of their internal worlds and his – his Fado – especially as he begins to take control of his story.

Significantly, the cathartic power of fado is transmitted to the audience by the fadista's gestures as well as their sung words. As fadista Lina Rodrigues explains (Dias et al 2016: 110):

Often foreigners do not understand our language, do not understand what we're saying, but they understand the music and our expression … [They] need not … understand what we are saying because we sing it with our faces … We sing it with our faces, we sing it with our hands … They feel our souls, they feel the music that is most often sad, but also joyful.

I now understood why I had felt like an active participant in the fado performance despite not understanding exactly what was being said. The performance was a 'surrender' to the audience and also a therapeutic demonstration to the audience of a person taking control of their trauma and its narrative through art. It also explained why I had been so dissatisfied with my rendering of the faces of the fadista/listener and guitar/bird in the final drawing, which did not seem as compelling as those I had drawn in the sketch; this was an important element of the wider gestural language of the fado.

Perhaps I had been trying to convey through drawing what the process of fado now suggested to me, a means to apprehend those hidden elements of existence Kant had deemed imperceptible, a way for the self to witness itself emerging through the fado event, not as absolute truth or knowledge, in any Hegelian sense but, as Dias et al put it (2016: 113), as 'what one makes out of it: a despair or a glory, much like a phoenix rising from the ashes'.

My journey leaves me with a number of questions about methodology which in a standard research process should arise earlier on. Had this been an anthropological endeavour or an artistic pursuit? Although I had attended a fado performance in Bairro Alto on my second visit to Lisbon, I had not spoken at length with fadistas or come close enough to the practice of Lisbon fado and its shared transmission in amateur community contexts to constitute the appropriate fieldwork from which to draw anthropological pronouncements. Indeed, I did not even understand the stories fadistas were recounting! On the artistic side, my drawings were part of a developing practice and I was unsure that they were anything more than a step on the long road to professional practice. But in seeking to get close to a cultural tradition through an instinctive drawing process I suspected I was trying to make visible invisible, felt elements of the operation of the fado process, some of which were non-verbal, a form of translation for which words alone may not suffice. As contemporary fadista Ana Moura has put it (Rohter 2011:npn), 'Like the blues, flamenco or tango, fado is a feeling, a sentiment, more than a set of notes. Tears are tears in any language.' However, as an audience member, I sincerely hope that I have not created an interpretation of this remarkable tradition at the expense of the actual voices and lived experiences of its subjects.[6]

In conclusion then, fados are part of lived contemporary experience in the places where these traditions have developed, both within Portugal and beyond. They dramatise the utterance of loss in a therapeutic process of reconnection and self-creation that I attempted to show in my sketch and drawing. Listening to and drawing in response to Lisbon fado contributed to my wellbeing and sense of connection to the city, however fleeting, and I have not forgotten the feeling it engendered. Whilst the trauma of human loss – whether of a person, a past time, a species or even an aspect of oneself – is inevitable, fado can play an important role in individual and community psychic survival from the pain of such loss, at times against bitter odds, enabling the construction of compelling myths of place and hope for the future. I have argued here that although Lisbon and Coimbra fado are now protected as 'intangible heritage', these song traditions would be better served by a holistic model of heritage as proposed by Nic Craith and Costa and Nossa, recognising both product and process. This would encompass fado's em-placement and its sensory operations as vital and moving processes in the now, resisting rigidification of a song tradition that speaks to human fragility and reflecting its cathartic role. Fados may help face the loss of a loved one or the pain of unrequited love, the trauma engendered by the colonial encounter or the sorrow of lost species. Fados have a transformative power and wherever the tradition emerges, the power and the work of its tradition bearers merit protection, to the benefit of all humanity.

References

Brown, J. (2014), Book review of Gray, L., (2013) 'Fado Resounding: Affective Politics and Urban Life. Available at https://www.ethnomusicologyreview.

---

[6]   Perhaps this might be seen as an experiment in 'creative ethnology' as it has been emerging in Scotland, 'an attempt to hold the global and the local, thinking and action, in creative confluence through engaged praxis rooted in place' (Kockel and McFadyen 2019: 205).

ucla.edu/content/fado-resounding-affective-politics-and-urban-life-lila-el-len-gray-durham-nc-duke-university (accessed 27 October 2019)

Costa, J. and P. Nossa (2017), 'Para além da Vista e do Som: Fado de Coimbra, Património Imaterial com Valor Turístico', *Revista Rosa dos Ventos – Turismo e Hospitalidade* 9(4): 557-568.

Dias, M. d R., Simões, N. P., Ferreira, A. and Coelho, E. (2016), 'The Question of a Voice: With What Voice Will I Cry My Sad Fado?', International Journal of Social Science Studies 4(10): 106-115.

Elliott, R. (2016 [2010]), *Fado and the Place of Longing: Loss, Memory and the City* (Abingdon/NY: Routledge).

Gonçalves, R. (2011), 'Amadeo De Souza-Cardoso, A Modernist Painter', in S. Dix and J. Pizzaro (eds), *Portuguese Modernisms: Multiple Perspectives in Literature and the Visual Arts* (Abingdon/NY: Routledge), 90-109.

Gray, L. (2013), *Fado Resounding: Affective Politics and Urban Life* (Durham/ NC: Duke University Press).

Nabais, N. (2019), 'Editorial', *Desarmada*. Available at https://www.bracodeprata.com/desarmada/ (accessed 27 October 2019).

Nic Craith, M. (2008), 'Intangible Cultural Heritages: The Challenges for Europe', *Anthropological Journal of European Cultures* 17(1): 54-73.

Nic Craith, M. (2015), Book review of Labadi, S. (2013), *UNESCO, Cultural Heritage, and Outstanding Universal Value: Value-Based Analyses of the World Heritage and Intangible Cultural Heritage Conventions*' (Lanham: AltaMira), *American Anthropologist* 117 (4) 844-845.

Pais, J. (2018), 'Fados do fado: enredos, cronotopos e trânsitos culturais', *Etnográfica* 22(1): 219-35.

UNESCO (2003) Text of the Convention for the Safeguarding of the Intangible Cultural Heritage. Available at https://ich.unesco.org/en/convention#art2 (accessed 27 October 2019).

Rohter, L. (2011), Carving Out a Bold Destiny for Fado. Available at https://www.nytimes.com/2011/03/27/arts/music/ana-moura-is-among-singers-reinvigorating-fado.html (accessed 05 May 2020).

The Attitude of Education

Alastair McIntosh

Albert Einstein! I always warn students about quoting him in their scholarly work. Many of the attributed folksy sayings, and most of the mystical ones, are fabrications. I suggest to my students that if they are going to quote the genius in the hope of basking in reflected glory, then check and give the original source. If they do not, they are no Einstein.

Mahatma Gandhi! The same goes, but in mitigation of the passage I am about to use, there is a slight difference. Some might make out that Einstein was a mystic, but nobody is trying to make out that Gandhi was a nuclear scientist. As far as I am aware, he confined himself to the morality of such issues. For example (Ghandi in Merton 1965: 32): 'So far as I can see, the atomic bomb has deadened the finest feeling that has sustained mankind for ages ... What has happened to the soul of the destroying nation is yet too early to see.'

With acknowledgement that I have been unable to pin down the original source, if any, allow me then to use one of my favourite quotes attributed to the Mahatma. It certainly fits well with his spirit. Reputedly, and according to many a poster that people used to buy in what were called 'head shops', he said: 'Nothing has saddened me so much in life as the hardness of heart of educated people.'

It is one thing to say what is wrong in the world, but quite another to say or show what can be right. Thinking of Máiréad Nic Craith brought Gandhi's line to mind for me because she embodies the antithesis of the problem that he identified. Máiréad has been a student's professor. Yes, she has ticked all the academic boxes. Her ethnography built itself up from a base amongst the Irish people, reaching out to peoples everywhere, translating between languages and cultures. But what most interests me is teaching. Universities are stuffed full of researchers. But researchers are a bit like angels. God already has plenty of them hanging out in Heaven. It is in more worldly realms, not to mention down in the bowels of Hell, that more are needed.

Academics who put students first have become more and more rare during my lifetime. Time was, thinking back to Aberdeen University in the 1970s, when some professors would even have the first-year students round for cheese and wine. These days, that is a rarity. I vividly recall a more senior colleague giving me a few words of advice when I taught human ecology for a few years in the Faculty of Science and Engineering at Edinburgh University, back in the 1990s.

'Why do you spend so much time with the students, Alastair? It's not going to get you anywhere.'

He was right. It was not going to help with the grant grubbing. At one faculty meeting, we were prodded to fissure into several papers across different journals what could otherwise have been published as a single, well-rounded piece of scholarly work. Giving time to student supervision was not going to help with making time for that counting game. This was the brave new world of laying the public resources built up over generations in our universities on the altar of the private sector. In Islam, it is said that notions of 'intellectual property' are a sin, because all wisdom comes from God. It was not going to stamp ™ ('that's mine') onto anything that could be marketed.

Ethnographers such as Máiréad know the truth of what I once heard said by the transpersonal psychologist and mythologist, Ralph Metzner: 'Stories tell us about our past; visions tell us about our future.'[1] Like at the oars, we row forwards looking backwards. If I might apply that to the academy, at the time when Máiréad's career was rising into its full power, British academia was being thrust down the corporate road. The 1993 science White Paper, *Realising Our Potential*, shook the academy far beyond its science faculties. Shock waves ran through the humanities, too, as it laid out the Conservative government's vision 'to achieve a key cultural change ... between the scientific community, industry and government departments,' including 'spin-in' from the civil to the defence sector, because, 'as the Gulf conflict illustrated, technology can provide the decisive edge in military operations' (cited in McIntosh 1996: 51).

On the one hand, under the wise leadership of the principal, Sir David Smith, and his deputy, Professor Barry Wilson, Edinburgh University, where I was at this time, was pioneering action and teaching to tackle climate change (see, e.g., Loening et al. 1991). On the other hand, the very qualities of empathy, responsiveness and depth that were required were being undermined. As public bodies, universities had to bend with the political wind.

My sense is that for Máiréad and her colleague-husband, Professor Ullrich Kockel, the response was to bend but not break. Both at the Academy of Irish Cultural Heritages at the University of Ulster and at the Intercultural Research

---

[1] Pers. com. at the conference of the International Transpersonal Association, Killarney, Ireland, 25 May 1994. Ralph is of the original 1960s counterculture trio along with the late Timothy Leary (of Irish descent) and Ram Dass, a.k.a. Richard Alpert, a Hindu spiritual teacher from a Jewish family. When Ralph told me that he loves Scotland because his mother came from Ayrshire, I quipped: 'So that explains it: the psychedelic revolution started from a Scotsman, an Irishman and a Jew.'

Centre at Heriot-Watt University in Edinburgh, they have succeeded in positioning their work so that mainstream funds could be accessed—on such themes as
human migration and tourism—but to hold fast to the humanities calling of vi-
sioning the human condition. More than that, in this marriage of scholars they
have lived it.

I set about writing this piece today because on Twitter, one of the IRC's
students, Cait O'Neill McCullagh, had commented that the Heriot-Watt unit 'is
an incredible place to study heritage. As a practicing curator and archaeologist,
I chose [it] for my PhD because of the rich and diverse hands-on experience,
academic expertise and human understanding held in this centre'; to this I responded: 'The reason why it's an incredible place to study is very simple. Its
leadership team give high priority to being there for students. Their research
synergises with that. Oh, and they also pay astute attention not just to thinking,
but to competent admin. You'll know who I mean ;)' (@kittyjmac on Twitter, 4
June 2019, responded to by @alastairmci.).

That wink was intended, as everybody would guess, for its director, Prof.
Máiréad Nic Craith. I had experienced that constellation of care at first hand
when, in 2007-08, I undertook a PhD by published works with Ulli and Máiréad.
Ulli was my supervisor, but the two were inseparable. It was the way that they
held students—all of their students from what I could see—that most impressed
me. Here was the antithesis to which I referred earlier, of the hard-heartedness
of the educated.

It was not that Ulli and Máiréad were academically a soft touch. Máiréad
especially was a stickler for keeping the administration and protocol of things all
present and correct. It was the kindness, often expressed through very practical
hospitality including numerous parties and suppers, with which they hosted us.
To be one of their students felt like being their guests. They had their research
and administration to field, but there was no doubt that student wellbeing and
expansion of mind was their priority.

I do not have a lot more to say about it than that. But what I can do, to close
this short piece, is to reflect on why it matters. The title of this festschrift collection is *Per scribendum, sumus!* 'By writing, we are.' When Máiréad and Ulli put
me up to the idea of undertaking a PhD by published works with them—my book
Soil and Soul and a dozen supporting scholarly articles—they said they were suggesting it because to have a PhD would open doors in my future work, but also,
the opportunity to draw together past publications would give an opportunity
to take stock of what I had done and where I might take it forward. In Ralph
Metzner's terms, to reflect upon the story that I had come from, and vision the
future.

These days, it can be too readily forgotten that a PhD is meant to be about original contributions to knowledge. Writing my thesis pushed me to ask what that had been. I gave it the title, *Some Contributions of Liberation Theology to Community Empowerment in Scottish Land Reform, 1991–2003* (McIntosh 2008). The framework that The Academy of Irish Cultural Heritages provided me with allowed me to see that my work had been about liberation theology (and not to flinch from that), about community empowerment, and focussed on modern Scottish land reform from the genesis of the Isle of Eigg Trust to the passing of the Land Reform (Scotland) Act in the Scottish Parliament.

It was not that Máiréad and Ulli did much. As an already seasoned academic who had second supervised the PhDs of others, I did not need a lot of help. What they did, and what I saw them doing for many others, is that they held the space. The Quaker writer, Parker Palmer, speaks of holding 'spaces that are hospitable to the soul'. That is what I experienced. That is also what I have always tried to do for my own students too. They do not need you to fill their space for them. They do need a container to be held, in which they can explore their ideas and let the brew ferment to completion. They need it to be held firmly but creatively and, if I might say so, with love.

Such is the 'maieutics' that Socrates saw as being the function of the educator. His mother had been a midwife. Education, as he saw it, is the art of giving birth to philosophy as philo-Sophia—the love of the Goddess of Wisdom.

Máiréad, supported by Ulli, has fulfilled that role in furthering the scholarly birth of many of us. She has deepened us on that journey of love. It helps to take away the hard-heartedness of the educated. It expresses Gandhi's *satyagraha*—truth force, soul force or God-force—that is the hope for healing of the world. I can but join with others, saying *thank you*.

References

Loening, U. et al. (1991), *Environmental Education for Adaptation* (Edinburgh: Centre for Human Ecology). Available at http://www.alastairmcintosh.com/articles/1991-Edinburgh-Uni-Env-Edn-for-Adaptation.pdf (accessed 3 February 2020).

McIntosh, A. (2008), *Some Contributions of Liberation Theology to Community Empowerment in Scottish Land Reform, 1991–2003*. PhD thesis, University of Ulster.

McIntosh, A. (1996), 'Taking arms against the mercenaries,' *New Scientist*, 4 May, p. 51.

Merton, T. ed. (1965), *Gandhi on Non-Violence* (New York/NY: New Directions).

Third Expedition: Heriot-Watt

あきらめない
ぜったいにあきらめない
なにがあっても
なにがあってもいきる
いきる
ぜったいにあきらめたらあかん
おもってるほどわるくない
たのしくたのしく

たのしくたのしく
いきる
　　　　夏子
Akagawa Natsuko 2020

Live [いきる＝ikiru]

Never give up
Whatever happens
Whatever happens, live
Live
Never give up
Not as bad as one thinks
Enjoy, enjoy

Natsuko Akagawa

By Any Other Name
Language, Identity, and Attribution in
Robert Flaherty's *Oidhche Sheanchais*

Natasha Sumner

Máiréad Nic Craith's research into issues of language and identity in Ireland and further afield has been revelatory, and I feel privileged to have had the opportunity to get to know her alongside her work. I became aware of her scholarship early in my academic career, having used her 1988 study of Blasket Island autobiographer Tomás Ó Criomhthain, *An tOileánach Léannta*, in my BA thesis. However, our paths did not cross until 2016 when Máiréad reached out to Harvard's Department of Celtic Languages and Literatures about a substantial research project that would take her to the Massachusetts destination of much Blasket Island emigration. She subsequently became a visiting scholar at Harvard while she worked on her latest monograph, *The Vanishing World of the Islandman: Narrative and Nostalgia* (2019).

Máiréad's return to Ó Criomhthain's Blasket Island autobiography followed directly on the heels of a significant project at Harvard concerning another western Irish Gaeltacht island: the restoration of Robert Flaherty's rediscovered Aran Island film *Oidhche Sheanchais* (1935). This ca. ten-minute short—the first film in the Irish language—was shot on a London set in January 1934 during post-production for Flaherty's *Man of Aran* and features members of the cast of that film (Ó Catháin 2004: 152, 172-174). Commissioned by the Irish Department of Education (Ibid. 191-192), it depicts a night of storytelling featuring a traditional song and folktale. Presumed lost for decades, an unopened copy of the film in Harvard's Houghton Library came to light as a result of a 2012 cataloguing project, and its restoration was jointly undertaken by Harvard Libraries, the Department of Celtic Languages and Literatures, and the Harvard Film Archive (Sumner, Hillers, and McKenna 2015: 4-5). My role in the restoration process was the production of subtitles in Irish and English (Ibid. 9-15) and a new list of credits for the attribution of the actors. This essay explores issues inherent in both tasks surrounding the use of personal names as markers of identity.

At the height of the Irish Revival in the late nineteenth and early twentieth centuries, Ireland's western, Irish-speaking islands attained an elevated position in the public consciousness as cultural nationalists looked to far-flung, poverty-stricken, and—most importantly—Irish-speaking regions of the country as beacons of national heritage. Just as the Great Blasket Island was presented as 'a closed community speaking a very pure form of Irish Gaelic with an oral tradition untouched for centuries' (Nic Craith and Hill 2015: 42), the Aran Islands were portrayed as 'an outpost of Irish tradition, a simple, primitive place embodying all that was good of Irish culture and language, a place to be revered and pre-served' (Ó hEithir and Ó hEithir 1991: 61). It was this cultural essentialism that drew John Millington Synge there repeatedly between 1898 and 1902 to enliven his native sensibilities and compose his 'brilliant and yet irritating' account of Aran Island life (Irish Press, 23 May 1934: 8; Kiberd 2009), and Robert Flaherty from 1932 to 1933 to film his exoticising, man-against-nature docudrama *Man of Aran* (1934). (Both works, in turn, contributed to the islands' curated primi-tivist image).

Such notions of cultural isolation and linguistic purity were, of course, as skewed for the Aran Islands as they were for the Blaskets. While access to the mainland was weather-dependent, the Aran Islanders regularly made the cross-ing and were by no means out of contact with the rest of Ireland. Nor were they unfamiliar with the primary language spoken by the majority of their compatri-ots, to the astonishment of some visitors: Synge wrote in 1907 (4), 'I was sur-prised at the abundance and fluency of the foreign [i.e. English] tongue.' He need not have been, however, for although Irish would have been the first and most commonly used language of the islanders he met, English would have been the medium of instruction in the schools they had attended, be they hedge schools[1] or national schools.[2] The trend toward bilingualism in the Gaeltacht was not at all unwelcome to Irish speakers (Doyle 2015: 118), and the English lan-guage undoubtedly proved beneficial in many aspects of life. However, its use entailed a negotiation of identity.

I am specifically interested here in the dual use of Irish- and English-lan-guage personal names. One's name is arguably 'the most central aspect of iden-tity in an individual' (de Varennes and Kuzborska 2015: 980). The members of the *Oidhche Sheanchais* cast were all born at a time when it was standard for first-language Irish speakers who habitually used Irish-language names to be known only by English-language names in official records. That people's names were subject to 'translation' means that language mediated not only how they interacted with the world around them, but also whom they were perceived to be, and—we can posit—who they perceived themselves to be.

---

[1]   Seán Ó Direáin, the storyteller in *Oidhche Sheanchais*, describes the English-medium hedge school he attended in a 2014 folklore interview (NFCS MS 2:13-14).

[2]   This is not to say that everyone who went through English-medium schooling would have been entirely proficient (cf. Nic Craith 1999: 80-81, 95-97), but they would all have had exposure to the language. On the history of schooling on Inis Mór, see Powell 1983: 101-2.

I present below brief biographies of the five cast members, including those officially recorded names I have been able to locate:

Seán Ó Direáin (25 Feb. 1873 – 31 July 1939), the storyteller from An Sruthán, Inis Mór, who starred in *Oidhche Sheanchais*, is listed on his birth record as John son of Thomas and Mary Dirrane (née Millane) (Civil Records). He is said to have spent a brief period in the United States as a young man before returning home, where he married and remained for the rest of his life (Mullen 1935: 241). The record of his marriage on 28 January 1896 to Ceaitín Neilín Ní Chuacach of Bungabhla, Inis Mór lists the couple's names as John Dirrane and Kate Cooke (Civil Records; Ó Catháin 2004: 171; Mná Fiontracha 2003: 25). His surname appears as Dirrane on the 1901 census and Derrane on the 1911 census. Several of his stories were collected for the Irish Folklore Commission in the 1930s, and he recorded two tales for a commercial record while in London filming *Oidhche Sheanchais* (Ó Direáin 1934; Ó hÍde 2019: 83-96). Soon afterward, he and two other men were lost at sea while returning home from the mainland in a currach.

Mairéad Uí Dhioráin (28 Oct. 1899 – 14 Sept. 1995), one of the stars of *Man of Aran* and the traditional singer in *Oidhche Sheanchais*, is listed on her birth record as Margaret daughter of Thomas and Mary Conneely (née Dirrane) of Creig an Chéirín, Inis Mór (Civil Records; Mulqueen 1995; Ní Fhlatharta 1984). The 1901 and 1911 censuses record her as Maggie Conneely. For a few weeks in 1916, she worked in Dublin in the household of Eoin Mac Néill (O'Brien 1984; Mulqueen 1995), returning home and marrying not long thereafter. The record of her marriage on 29 December 1919 to Johnny Shéain Éamoinn Ó Dioráin of Eoghanacht, Inis Mór lists the couple's names as John Dirrane and Maggie Connolly (Civil Records; Mná Fiontracha 2003: 21). She was later an informant for American song collector Sidney Robertson Cowell (Ni Chonghaile 2013: 188-189). The last nine years of her life were spent in hospital in Galway (Mulqueen 1995).

Cóil Mac an Rí (1 Feb. 1900 – 16 Oct. 1976) of Fearann an Choirce, Inis Mór, one of the stars of *Man of Aran* and a member of the storyteller's audience in *Oidhche Sheanchais*, is listed on his birth record as Colman son of Colman and Bridget King (née Hernon) (Civil Records; Mná Fiontracha 2003: 41; Ó hEithir 1977: 39-40; Irish Press, 22 Oct. 1976: 1). He is recorded as Colman King on the 1901 census and Coleman King on the 1911 census. He emigrated to London shortly after the completion of the films, where he was employed as a blacksmith for the London Metropolitan Water Board until his retirement. He never married (Irish Press, 22 April 1976: 9).

Peaits Ó Maoláin of Eoghanacht, Inis Mór was an actor in *Man of Aran* and a member of the storyteller's audience in *Oidhche Sheanchais* (Ó Flannagáin 1985: 216; Mullen 1935: 70). He may have been one of several Pat(rick) Mullin/Mullens listed in census data. His wife's name is given as Nannie in the *Irish Press* (6 May 1936: 1).

Mícheál Ó Dioláin (born c.1920) of Cill Éinne, Inis Mór was one of the stars of *Man of Aran* and a member of the storyteller's audience in *Oidhche Sheanchais* (Ó Flannagáin 1985: 216; Mullen 1935: 66). His birth record is not yet publicly available, but it likely lists his name as Michael Dillane. After filming, the Irish Press reported that he attended boarding school in Tuam (15 Oct. 1937: 1). He is said to have emigrated to England and joined the British army (Ó hEithir and Ó hEithir 1991: 208; O'Brien 1984; Rotha 1983: 139).

The cast of *Oidhche Sheanchais* bore not only Irish-language given names, but also English-language legal names bestowed upon them at birth and utilised in dealings with the state, including schooling, and with the broader English-speaking world (cf. Lele 2009: 106-107).

The use of dual names by Irish speakers has a long history. The legal requisite to use English-language surnames dates back to the fifteenth century, when legislation was passed requiring those living within the Pale to use English-language surnames or forfeit their property (Crowley 2005, 11-12). While that legislation was not particularly successful, over time the British government came to exert increasing control over many aspects of cultural expression in Ireland, including naming practises. Returning to the Revival period, Pádraig Mac Piarais, in his short legal career, famously lost a case in 1905 in which his client was accused of not displaying his name on his cart; the Irish-language name that had been displayed was deemed invalid (Ibid. 129). In response, Mac Piarais denounced 'the ludicrous law which requires Irishmen to describe themselves on their carts by names not their own' and encouraged similar acts of civil disobedience (Mac Piarais 1905: 7).

Personal names thus emerge as a longstanding site of identity negotiation and renegotiation for Irish speakers. To complicate matters, regardless of language, in addition to their given and/or legal names, people generally bear context-specific names that express cultural and social identities. The cast of

Oidhche Sheanchais was typical in this regard: they identified themselves and were identified by multiple additional names within their communities (see, e.g., Ó Flannagáin 1985: 216; also Irish Press, 5 May 1934: 4):

> Seán was known as Seáinín Tom Sheáin.
> Mairéad was known as Maggie Tom.
> Cóil was called Cóilí, Tiger, and Cóilín an Ghabha.
> Peaits was known as Peaits Rua, and he is also said to have been called Peaits Rua na gCleas.
> Mícheál was called Micilín.

Aspects of cultural heritage are encoded in these names. In the case of Seáinín and Maggie, patronymics serve as their local designations. The use of patronymics, which identify people with the names of their parents or ancestors, is a traditional practise among speakers of Gaelic languages. In some cases, many generations are recalled, and additional information may also be encoded: Seáinín Tom's full patronymic, according to his neighbour, was Seáinín Tom Sheáin Phádraic an tSrutháin (Ó Flannagáin 1985: 204), the final element recording not the name of a person, but the place where his family resided.

In addition to functioning as markers of heritage, patronymics serve the practical purpose of differentiating between people with the same given name (Lele 2009: 101, 104). This would have been beneficial, given the rare departure from regularly used family names in local naming practises. Epithets can serve the same function. Peaits Rua was so called due to his red beard; also living in his community was Peaits Bán Ó Maoláin, an old and presumably white-haired man (Mná Fiontracha 2003: 21; Mullen 1935: 254). The additional designation 'na gCleas' [of the tricks] suggests a personality trait, while the name Cóilín an Ghabha [of the smithy] reflects the family trade of blacksmithing. Nicknames also communicate something about a person, and can serve to differentiate. The story behind the nickname 'Tiger' is unknown to me, but there undoubtedly was one. Additionally, we see names bearing diminutive endings (Seáinín, Cóilín, Micilín), suggesting familiarity. Culturally significant, these local names contribute to social identification. As Ashley (1996: 1748) writes, 'the knowledge of [special names or name traditions] bespeaks the full-fledged member' in the collective group.

Beyond the local sphere, the forms of the cast's names displayed on screen took precedence over any names they might have utilised previously in Anglophone contexts. The credits to *Man of Aran* identified them as Maggie Dirrane, Colman ('Tiger') King, Patch Ruadh (Red Beard), and Michael Dillane (Flaherty

1934). While these names were not seen as problematic at the time, a critical re-evaluation raises some issues: first, the inclusion of the nickname 'Tiger' turned an internal marker of social identity into a public stage name (Ashley 1996: 1749), and it is unclear whether the actor's consent was sought for this recontextualisation. Second, Peaits's English-language legal name was not displayed at all, but rather a hybrid, English-Irish form of his local, social moniker that served to exoticise his name; it seems unlikely that Peaits was consulted in the creation of his stage name.

The film generated a lot of press, and these names appeared in newspapers with only a couple variations: Tiger King became standard, and Michaeleen, an Anglicisation of Micilín, was used interchangeably with Michael. Whether all of the cast members were entirely comfortable with their media personas is not now possible to say. In any case, the routine use of English-language names in the papers—even during filming, and even when claiming, inaccurately, that the cast knew no English (e.g. Irish Press, 19 June 1933: 3)—reflects how uncommon the use of Irish speakers' given Irish-language names continued to be in the Anglophone sphere just over a decade after Irish independence, when the use of Irish-language names in all areas of life became permissible.

Press reports pertaining to *Oidhche Sheanchais* continued to refer to members of the *Man of Aran* cast by their established English-language stage names. However, the star of the Irish-language short, who had not appeared in the full-length film, was announced in newspapers by his Irish name (e.g. Irish Press, 3 Feb. 1934: 1). *Oidhche Sheanchais* included no credits for the actors, but Seáinín Tom Ó Dioráin's name appeared on screen in the opening text to the film (Flaherty 1935).

The inconsistent naming practices in *Man of Aran* and *Oidhche Sheanchais* presented problems during the restoration of the Irish-language film. Decisions needed to be made about the representation of the cast's names in the Irish- and English-language subtitles, and in the new credits that were to be included.

In recent decades, considerable attention has been paid to names as expressions of personal and cultural identity. From a legal standpoint, the 1998 Oslo Recommendations Regarding the Linguistic Rights of National Minorities recognised people's right to 'their personal names in their own language according to their own traditions and linguistic systems' (de Varennes and Kuzborska 2015: 982), and the UN Committee on the Elimination of Racial Discrimination stated in 2001 that 'the name of an individual is a fundamental aspect of [their] cultural and ethnic identity' (Ibid. 995). From an anthropological perspective,

Máiréad's (Nic Craith 2012b: 111-117) research clearly demonstrates the importance of personal names in self-perception, with the accounts of some bearers of 'translated' names reflecting a sense of a division of the self.

I therefore suggested that in restoring the film, we might also make an effort to restore an aspect of the Irish-speaking cast's identity through the representation of their names. The idea was not to overwrite their widely recognised stage names or their hybrid, bilingual identities, but rather to give them something *Man of Aran* and the popular press of the day had denied them: their Irish-language names alongside the English ones. My colleagues supported this plan. To avoid confusion, we opted to adhere to the stage names in the English subtitles but use Irish-language names where appropriate in the Irish subtitles. The new credits depict the names of the cast in both languages (Figure 1).[3]

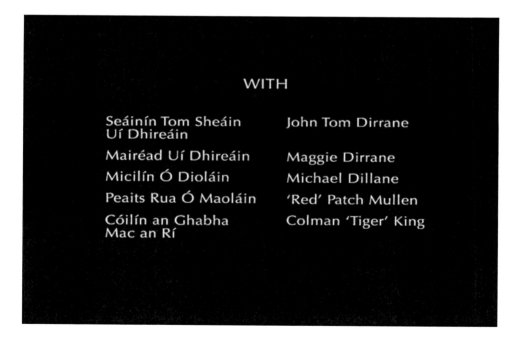

Figure 1: Revised cast names for Robert Flaherty's *Oidhche Sheanchais*

---

[3] Seáinín's surname is generally spelled Ó Direáin in scholarship (e.g. Ó Catháin 2004: 168; O'Leary 2004: 500; cf. Ó hÍde 2019), although it appeared as Ó Dioráin in the film and in contemporary media coverage. Maggie's surname should be Uí Dhioráin; I would hope to be able to correct the spelling if the film were released commercially.

I restored Peaits's surname to his English name and tried to mitigate its exoticisation. I added Cóil's Irish-language epithet, rather than repeat the English nickname. Unfortunately, this attempt to restore the actors' Irish-language names did not reach a widespread audience. The new credits were not shown when the film aired on Irish television (TG4) on 1 November 2016, and only the English subtitles appeared. My credit as translator and subtitler was also cut, and modified text replaced the account of the film's loss and rediscovery that follows the actors' credits in the restored film. The only version of the film publicly available online was recorded from the television broadcast by a viewer and shared on YouTube.[4]

Nonetheless, I cannot help but think the effort was worthwhile. As Máiréad (Nic Craith 2012a: 584) writes, linguistic tradition 'is the mirror in which we look —and see not just ourselves, but our ancestors and their understandings of the world'. Reflected in the Irish-language names of the cast of *Oidhche Sheanchais* is their tongue, their customs, and their ancestral heritage. Regardless of the predominant attitude toward the public use of Irish-language names in early twentieth-century Ireland, these individuals deserve attribution in their own language today.

References

Ashley, L. (1996), 'Internal Names', in: E. Eichler, G. Hilty, H. Löffler, H. Steger, and L. Zgusta eds, *Namenforschung/Name Studies/Les noms propres. Ein internationals Handbuch zur Onomastik/International Handbook of Onomastics/Manuel international d'onomastique* vol. 2 (Berlin: de Gruyter), 1745-1750.

Census of Ireland 1901/1911. Available at http://census.nationalarchives.ie (accessed 30 Sept. 2019).

Civil Records. Available at http://civilrecords.irishgenealogy.ie (accessed 30 Sept. 2019).

Crowley, T. (2005), *Wars of Words: The Politics of Language in Ireland 1537–2004* (Oxford: Oxford University Press).

De Varennes, F. and E. Kuzborska (2015), 'Human Rights and a Person's Name: Legal Trends and Challenges', *Human Rights Quarterly* 37: 977-1023.

Doyle, A. (2015), *A History of the Irish Language from the Norman Invasion to Independence* (Oxford: Oxford University Press).

---

[4]   The complete restored film can be viewed on Harvard Library's online video player, but only by those with Harvard login credentials (https://sds.lib.harvard.edu/sds/video/431967434#). DVD copies are accessible at the Irish National Folklore Collection and the Kilronan Branch of Galway County Library.

Flaherty, R. dir. (1934) *Man of Aran* (London: Gaumont).

Flaherty, R. dir. (1935), *Oidhche Sheanchais* (London: Gaumont; restored Cambridge/MA: Harvard Film Archive, 2015).

Kiberd, D. (2009), 'Synge, (Edmund) John Millington', in J. McGuire and J. Quinn (eds), *Dictionary of Irish Biography* (Cambridge: Cambridge University Press). Available at https://dib.cambridge.org (accessed 4 October 2019).

Lele, V. (2009), '"It's not Really a Nickname, it's a Method": Local Names, State Intimates, and Kinship Register in the Irish *Gaeltacht*', *Journal of Linguistic Anthropology* 19(1): 101-116.

Mac Piarais, P. (1905), 'The Law and the Language', *An Claidheamh Soluis* 7(14): 7.

Mná Fiontracha (2003), *Árainn: Cosáin an tSaoil* (Árainn: Mná Fiontracha).

Mullen, P. (1935), *Man of Aran* (New York: Dutton).

Mulqueen, E. (1995), 'Late Maggie Dirrane—Woman of Aran', *Connacht Tribune*, 14 October, 10.

NFCS: Irish National Folklore Collection, Schools Collection, University College Dublin.

Ní Chonghaile, D. (2013), 'In Search of America: Sidney Robertson Cowell in Ireland in 1955 – 1956', *Journal of American Folklore* 126(500): 174-200.

Nic Craith, M. (2012a), 'Legacy and Loss: The Great Silence and its Aftermath,' in J. Crowley, W.J. Smyth and M. Murphy (eds), *Atlas of the Great Irish Famine* (New York: New York University Press), 580-588.

Nic Craith, M. (2012b), *Narratives of Place, Belonging and Language. An Intercultural Perspective* (Houndmills: Palgrave).

Nic Craith, M. (1999), 'Primary Education on the Great Blasket Island 1864-1940,' *Journal of the Kerry Archaeological and Historical Society* 28: 77-137.

Nic Craith, M. and E. Hill (2015), 'Re-locating the Ethnographic Field: From 'Being *There*' to '*Being* There', *Anthropological Journal of European Cultures* 24(1): 42-62.

Ní Fhlatharta, B. (1984), 'I Was Glad of the Work—'Man of Aran' Leading Lady', *Connacht Tribune*, 12 October, 1.

O'Brien, E. (1984), 'Woman of Aran', Supplement to the *Irish Times*, 18 February.

Ó Catháin, B. (2004), 'Oidhche Sheanchais le Robert J. Flaherty: An Chéad Scannán Gaeilge dá nDearnadh', in R. Ó hUiginn and L. Mac Cóil eds, *Bliainiris 2004* (Ráth Cairn: Carbad), 151-235.

[Ó Direáin, S.] (1934), Record E4075 (London: Parlophone).

Ó Flannagáin, D. (1985), *Ó Thrá Anoir* (Cathair na Mart: Foilseacháin Náisiúnta).

Ó hEithir, B. (1977), *'Willie the Plain Pint' agus an Pápa* (Baile Átha Cliath: Cló Mercier).

Ó hEithir, B. and R. Ó hEithir eds (1991), *An Aran Reader* (Dublin: Lilliput).

Ó hÍde, T. (2019), *Seáinín Tom Sheáin: From Árainn to the Silver Screen* (Dublin: Comhairle Bhéaloideas Éireann).

O'Leary, P. (2004), *Gaelic Prose in the Irish Free State: 1922-1939* (Dublin: University College Dublin Press).

Powell, A. (1983), *Oileáin Árann: Stair na n-Oileán anuas go dtí 1922* (Baile Átha Cliath: Wolfhound).

Rotha, P. (1983), *Robert J. Flaherty: A Biography* (Philadelphia: University of Pennsylvania Press).

Sumner, N., B. Hillers, and C. McKenna (2015), 'A Night of Storytelling and Years on the "Z-Closet": The Re-discovery and Restoration of *Oidhche Sheanchais*, Robert Flaherty's "Lost" Irish Folklore Film', *Folklore* 126(1): 1-19.

Synge, J. M. (1907), *The Aran Islands* (Dublin: Maunsel; reprinted Oxford: Oxford University Press 1979).

Literature and the Common Good

Nigel Rapport

> 'Whoever destroys a single life is considered by
> Scripture to have destroyed the whole world, and
> whoever saves a single life is considered by Scripture
> to have saved the whole world.'
>
> Babylonian Talmud Sanhedrin 37a

Preamble

I have been impressed by the seriousness with which Máiréad Nic Craith takes the literary project, the respect she accords to writers of literature, and the serious relationship she sees between the writing of literature—of fiction in a variety of genres—and questions of belonging to a 'good society'. It is in this Máiréad-Nic-Craithian spirit that the following lines are conceived. In particular, I write as a social anthropologist looking to literary projects for insight into questions of the good society and the 'common good'. I take as my lodestone this sentiment from literary critic F. R. Leavis (1972: 53):

> 'What is the 'social condition' that has nothing to do with the 'individual condition'? What is the 'social hope' that transcends, cancels or makes indifferent the inescapable tragic condition of each individual? (...) Only in living individuals is life there, and individual lives cannot be aggregated or equated or dealt with quantitatively in any way.'

The Talmud

The Hebrew word *talmud* means studying or teaching. 'The Talmud' is considered an authoritative record of rabbinic discussions on Jewish law, Jewish ethics, customs, legends and stories. It consists of the *Mishnah*, a record of oral traditions, and the *Gemara*, which comments upon, interprets and applies these oral traditions (A section of the *Mishnah* is followed by the *Gemara* on that section). Dealing with everything that might have to do with Jewish life and the lives of Jews, an encyclopaedic range of topics are covered: science, ethics, society and folklore. Together with the Old Testament, the Talmud greatly influenced Jewish education and spirituality, and, according to *Vallentine's Jewish Encyclopaedia*, 'in the worst times of persecution and humiliation [the Talmud] has prevented [the Jewish] mind from being blunted and saved them from ruin' (Hyamson and Silbermann 1938).

From the Middle East, study of the Talmud followed the Jewish diaspora, and famous commentaries accompanied the flowering of Jewish communities in eleventh-century Northern France (in particular, the work of Rashi), twelfth-century Iberia (the work of Moses Maimonides), fourteenth-century Poland and Russia, and, especially since the Holocaust, Western Europe and North America. Opposition to the authority of the Talmud has also been present since very early times. The anti-talmudic sect of the Karaites was active in the eighth century AD, while the present-day Reform Movement that would modernise traditional, orthodox precepts has declared against its authority.

I know all this only from reading the entry in *Vallentine's Encyclopaedia*. Even growing up in an Orthodox Jewish family, going to Jewish lessons ('cheder') once a week, and being barmitzvah-ed, has not given me more than a vague acquaintance with the word. I do not know what form the writings take. But I was struck by the above epigraph: 'Whoever saves one life saves the world entire'. On a visit to a Jewish Museum, somewhere, I even bought a poster inscribed with the saying, and decorated with Stars of David, from coloured fabric, such as the Nazis had their Jewish victims sew on their clothes for identification. For a number of years, the poster hung in a frame in my office. I was moved by the insistence on singularity in the saying, the respect for the individual case.

I am largely ignorant of talmudic scholarship, but I do know that my epigraph comes in different versions, because of the different centuries and settings in which the Talmud has been redacted. In some versions, the phrase is not 'Whoever saves one life saves the world entire' but 'Whoever saves one life *in Israel* saves the world entire'. There is the vexed issue of universalism and particularism in the Jewish tradition and of the tension between them. I am sentimentally persuaded, however, by the scholarship that insists that the precept was originally a universalistic one, stressing the unity of the entire human race, and only later narrowed to emphasise Jews (since the Gentiles of the diaspora were outwith Jewish control—another world).

But I am still wary of reading too much of my own interpretation into the epigram. Being an atheist, I feel loath to borrow the authority of religious commentary. Maybe it implies, also, the 'one life' of the Jewish Nation: that single covenant from Jehovah to his Chosen People that makes each of us essentially one descendant. To save the 'one life' of the Jewish Nation is to save the entire world that God's Chosen People represent. Perhaps the talmudic interpretation is that the entire world of Jewish life is reproduced in each family—ultimately in each Jewish individual who communes with, debates with, loves, Jehovah—and that amid pogrom and persecution, to save one Jewish life is to save the way of life because each family, each individual, has within it the seeds to reproduce the whole. In the very entry for 'Talmud' from *Vallentine's Encyclopaedia* cited above, there was reference to 'the Jewish mind' that was educated and saved by the scripture, and filled with spirituality, morals and science. This kind of essentialism I would find 'anathema'.

But the phrase is tantalizing, nonetheless. Each life is a world of its own, a world to itself. Individuality is the nature of existence; the quality of individuality is reproduced from the very smallest things to the very largest; one life and the entire universe share a paradoxical patterning of atomism, of individual uniqueness. Maybe the entire evolution of life—its potential for evolution—can be found reflected in any one life. Perhaps to *save* one life is to engage in the key moral act, to show respect for life per se, on which the entire universe of ethical action can be said to rest.

Studying the Talmud in Eastern Europe, during long centuries of being excluded from wider intellectual life and professions, led to 'dialectics characterized by sometimes exaggerated quibbling and hair-splitting', *Vallentine's Encyclopaedia* informs me, finally, and this 'must be considered to have been unprofitable from a scientific point of view'. There is something tantalizing in the very gnomic nature of this epigraph—whose ambiguity lends itself to becoming a moral flag, emblazoned on a poster. It might be termed 'the mathematics of morality'. How to attach a value to human life, human worth and suffering? How does one balance respect for the individual life with an appreciation of the mass of suffering?

The Common Good

This is not a new debate. It is, indeed, as old as Western philosophy. Should the one be sacrificed for the many? On what basis is one charitably to distribute scarce resources? Can the one be said to have any real or rightful existence independent of the many, the commonweal? The debate is at once a question of ontology: what is naturally prior, the individual or the collectivity? And it is a question of morality: what is of greater or truer worth, the one life or the many? With the coming of modernity and the rise of the nation-state, the moral problem is said to have become more acute. The rationalisation of techniques of governance—our ability to deal bureaucratically, institutionally with greater numbers of people, to oversee their behaviour and chart their education, their health, their sexuality, their religiosity, their lawfulness—means that individuals can more and more be treated in large numbers, as a mass; globalisation now entails not only large nation-states but international and supranational forces of governance. Is there any room, is there any rightful place, for the individual voice in this global cacophony? I hold by this talmudic epigraphy because I wish to insist that there is.

Evelyn Waugh referred to a 'mathematics of war' that insisted on multiplying men (people) together and putting them into droves; he found it 'crazy' and felt that 'by each addition of his fellows you subtract something that is of value, make him so much less a man' (1961: 404). E. M. Forster described 'representative individuals', crowds and 'the people' as something about which 'preachers or scientists' generalised, but he mistrusted such notions; only in the individual proper could he see any value or place any faith (1950). F. R. Leavis, as above, harangued against those who would write and prescribe on the basis of a 'social condition'; life cannot be generalised, individual lives cannot be averaged and only in individual lives does life exist.

Why should it be that these *literary* writers distance themselves alike from what they see as the philistinism or faith of military, scientistic, clerical and political dealings with the individual? Perhaps that, as the poet Joseph Brodsky put it (1988: G2), it is the literary composition that always seeks an 'antidote' to attempts at mass descriptions of humanity and mass solutions to its problems; for Brodsky, literature provides a manifestation of 'the privateness of the human condition', fostering a sense of radical individuality that mitigates against a reduction of human diversity and perversity.

I do not wish to rehearse an argument for 'two cultures': 'literary' as against 'scientific' or bureaucratic perspectivism. (I know, too, the riposte that 'literature' is part of the very same discourse that created 'the individual', with its private, subjective interiority, in Western Europe after the Enlightenment, and so will 'naturally' be attuned to its 'truths'.) Nevertheless, maybe there is something characteristic of the literary approach to the individual and the social that is morally instructive. E. M. Forster provides the clue. He elaborates that even though preachers or scientists may generalise, 'we know that no generality is possible about those whom we love; not one heaven awaits them, not even one oblivion' (1950: 245-6). One life or one death throws no light on others. There is a significant difference, here—whether we call it 'art' versus 'science' or other names—concerning the way in which life is approached; one can approach life from the point of view of the lover or from that of the stranger. Generalisation only makes sense to the stranger. But respect for human life, it seems to me, the proper way to inscribe the value of human life, is in the language of love; in computing the mathematics of human morality, even in an age of global populations, it is important to resist the view from afar that reduces individual details to general outlines.

But what kind of practical advice can this be? And with what moral conse-quence? One approaches the assembly of human lives with an aspiration to love, but how does this give a lead to the computing of the rights of the one as against the many?

Toleration and Love

Forster himself declares that while 'a great force in private life', indeed 'the greatest of all things', loving is hard to effect in public affairs:

> The fact is we can only love what we know personally. And we cannot know much. In public affairs, in the rebuilding of civilisation, something much less dramatic and emotional is needed, namely, tolerance (...). The world is very full of people —appallingly full; it has never been so full before, and they are tumbling over each other. Most of these people one doesn't know and some of them one doesn't like; doesn't like the colour of their skins, say, or the shape of their noses, or the way they blow them or don't blow them.....Don't try to love them: you can't, you'll only strain yourself. But try to tolerate them (...). [Tolerance] is wanted in the street, in the office, at the factory, and it is wanted above all between classes, races, nations. It's dull. And yet it entails imagination. For you have all the time to be putting yourself in someone else's place. Which is a desirable spiritual exercise (1972: 55).

Tolerance, then, becomes the public face of love: the tolerance to put oneself in a stranger's place and feel their worth and their pain as one's own. One refuses the anonymizing generalisation by recognizing the essential equivalency of hu-man life: all life is individual life.

'No cry of torment can be greater than the cry of one man' is something that Ludwig Wittgenstein wrote which seems imbued with the same humanistic and liberal tenor as Forster's belief that to put oneself in another person's place is to refuse to tolerate their pain. And Wittgenstein elaborates: 'Or again, no torment can be greater than what a single human being may suffer' (1980: 45). Torment, pain and suffering do not multiply across human lives; the single hu-man life is the unit, the only unit, in which to measure these. One knows the hurt of another life through the equivalency of the latter to one's own; and to move between hurting human lives is not to find an augmentation but a repli-cation of a quantum amount. Wittgenstein wrote this during the Second World War (as did Forster), when he took time away from Cambridge to assist in field hospitals on the Continent. Both he and Adolf Hitler were born in Lenz, Austria, and in the same year, 1889. It has even been speculated that they were class-mates, and that Hitler took particularly against the idiosyncratic boy of Jewish extraction, beginning a lifetime's antipathy.

Beginning from words of the Talmud and ending with ones of Wittgen-stein's I have wanted to treat issues of number or scale in human life and their moral effects. 'No cry of torment can be greater than the cry of one man', and 'Whoever saves one life saves the world entire'; but through Hitler's policies some six million 'Jews' lost their lives in Continental Europe between 1939 and 1945, some 20 million inhabitants of the Soviet Union, hundreds of thousands from Britain, America, Denmark, Holland, Greece, Canada, Australia, Italy, Bul-garia and elsewhere. Is it a morality of affluence, a bourgeois morality, that has the luxury to worry about individual lives and assert their ultimate value? Is the reality of most people most of the time inevitably one of utilitarian logic where the mathematics of majoritarian conditions command respect? Where six hun-dred or six thousand or six million deaths are precisely that much greater a trag-edy than one, and where morality is ever calculated in terms of bringing the greatest good to the greatest number, and avoiding the greatest harm? Should one feel six million times worse after the Holocaust than when one life is brought cruelly to a premature end? My efforts would be to resist this kind of calculation and calculatedness, for fear of the majoritarian morality of the com-monweal—the so-called 'common good' (Leavis's 'social hope')—to which they accede. I want to place the moral weight on the integrity of the individual life, to begin a moral calculation there and also to end there. I feel that the ethos that I have called 'literary' that attends to this weighting also accords with the social science that I would write—and that Máiréad Nic Craith has written.

After Forster, I have suggested that while one may not literally feel love with all others, one might imagine one's way into the individual life of each and refuse to tolerate the suffering of any; as such, a 'lover' one has no truck with majorities, collectivities or commonweals (Rapport 2019). As a lover, moreover, one approaches all suffering alike: it is all individual human suffering. Whether one person alone is suffering or six million, the suffering is of the same kind and of a quantum amount; as Wittgenstein put it, the quantity of torment that can be suffered is an absolute, a human universal: it is individuals that suffer not crowds. Adapting Wittgenstein, one may also say that the quantity of love that can be felt for the suffering is also an absolute; since it is individuals that love not crowds, 'no love is greater than what a single human being may feel'. One extends one's love alike to the suffering one and the suffering six million. The lover does his or her utmost to alleviate the suffering other but operates accord-ing to the same standards of concern whether the individual sufferer is alone or one of six million sufferers. Where quantity enters the equation in a global milieu is in connectedness. The connections that link the suffering individual to the love of potential caregivers are that much fewer in number than those that link the six million. As those in need increase, so should those able and willing to extend the (quantum of) love of their care. The difference between the one in need and the many in need is the number of others that might necessarily be called upon to alleviate the suffering.

A morality of care that recognises all life as individual life, all need as individual need, all care as individual care, does not fall prey to generalisation or reductionism. 'No cry of torment can be greater than the cry of one man', and 'no act of love can be greater than what one man can extend and be responsible for'. The integrity of individual human life, its value, carries with it the responsibility to love to one's utmost. If the suffering one is met with an equivalency of love and the suffering six million likewise, then it can transpire that 'to save one life has the effect of saving the world entire.'

References

Brodsky, J. (1988), 'The Politics of Poetry', The Sunday Times, January 10: G2.

Forster, E. M. (1950), Howards End (Harmondsworth: Penguin).

Forster, E. M. (1972), Two Cheers for Democracy (Harmondsworth: Penguin).

Hyamson, A. and A. Silbermann eds (1938) *Vallentine's Jewish Encyclopaedia* (London: Shapiro, Vallentine).

Leavis, F. (1972), *Nor Shall My Sword* (London: Chatto & Windus).

Rapport, N. (2019), *Cosmopolitan Love and Individuality: Ethical engagement beyond culture* (Lanham/MD: Rowman and Littlefield).

Waugh, E. (1961), *Scoop, and Put out more Flags* (New York: Dell).

Wittgenstein, L. (1980), *Culture and Value* (Chicago: University of Chicago Press).

Air for Mairead

Commissioned by Margaret A. Mackay
Composed by Katherine Campbell

It was an honour to receive an invitation to contribute to this celebratory volume for Professor Máiréad Nic Craith. She has helped us to expand the discipline of Ethnology here in Scotland through her wealth of experience and understanding in the interconnected disciplines of language and tradition, from Irish and Scottish perspectives and beyond. In her research, teaching and publications as well as in her personal interaction with colleagues from many countries in conferences, symposia and informal gatherings, she has inspired both her contemporaries and the rising band of younger scholars who are taking our subjects forward in local and international contexts and in relevant and creative ways.

I know what a pleasure it is to receive the gift of a specially composed piece of music, and have chosen to commission an air for my friend Máiréad from another friend, Dr Katherine Campbell, who, in addition to being a leading scholar of Scottish ballad and song, is a talented vocal and instrumental performer, arranger and composer. Here she describes the process through which she developed the composition, which is offered to Máiréad with admiration, gratitude and affection:

The presentation of a tune as a gift to mark a special occasion is common in Scottish tradition historically, and typically carries the name of its recipient in the title. AIR FOR MÁIRÉAD aims to give a musical flavour of Máiréad's Irish heritage and of the time she has spent in Scotland.

The air has been developed based on the letters of the name Máiréad and their musical equivalents (see table below). The scale of C is being utilised, beginning on the note C:

Letter of Alphabet	a	b	c	d	e	f	g	h
Musical Equivalent	C	D	E	F	G	A	B	C
Letter of Alphabet	i	j	k	l	m	n	o	p
Musical Equivalent	D	E	F	G	A	B	C	D
Letter of Alphabet	q	r	s	t	u	v	w	x
Musical Equivalent	E	F	G	A	B	C	D	E
Letter of Alphabet	y	z						
Musical Equivalent	F	G						

The letters correspond to the following notes:

M = A   á = C   i = D   r = F   é = G   a = C   d = F

Taken together and in order, these notes suggest a tune that has the note D at its centre, and which can be harmonised in the Aeolian mode. The stresses and rhythms then follow on from the initial selection of notes. An additional note, D, has been added to this opening theme between the two last notes (C, F). No indication of octave register is given in the table above – this is simply decided upon by the composer. The form used is A | Av | B | Bv. A lyrical air has been employed in preference to an instrumental tune type. I was delighted to be commissioned by Dr Margaret A. Mackay to compose this melody.

Words Set in Stone

Donald Smith

Carved inscriptions appear to offer sound evidence for understanding the past, combining a solid artefact with words. Cultural intangibles mediated through language conjoin with tangible substance. A defining example of this might be the extended inscription on the façade of what is now known as John Knox House, within the Scottish Storytelling Centre on Edinburgh's Royal Mile. This is believed to be the oldest surviving stone-carved inscription in the city, in recognition of which Edinburgh City Council's letterhead is based on the same style. It is located within and protected by the UNESCO World Heritage designation covering the Old and New Towns of Scotland's capital.

Figure 1: John Knox House façade by John M. Pearson

Especially interesting is the vigorous Scots vernacular in which the inscription is carved:

LUFE GOD ABUFE AL AND YI NYCHTBOUR AS YI SELF

'Love God above all and your neighbour as yourself' compresses a saying of Christ in the New Testament synoptic Gospels when he is asked which is the greatest commandment in the Jewish Torah. He replies that the greatest commandment is 'You must love the Lord your God with all your heart, all your soul, all your strength, and all your mind', while the second is closely parallel, 'You must love your neighbour as yourself'.

Initials of James Mossman & Mariota Arres

LVFE·GOD·ABVFE·AL·
AND·YI·NYCHTBOVR
AS·YI·SELF

Moses on Sinai

Figure 2: Details from the John Knox House façade by John M Pearson

The existence of this religious inscription may have influenced the later tradition that John Knox, the Protestant reformer, lived in the house. Though there is some contextual evidence that Knox may have lived in the house for the last few months of his life and died there in 1573, he has no connection with this inscription. It dates to 1560-61 when this prominent building beside The Netherbow Port, Edinburgh's principal gateway, was upgraded by the Mosman family, the royal goldsmiths.

This provides a fascinating piece of primary evidence about the return of Mary Queen of Scots in 1561, following the unexpected death of her husband Francois, King of France. Far from presuming that the Protestant coup of 1559-

60 would be sustained, many expected and hoped that the traditional order would be restored. Moreover, they were prepared to invest in that likelihood and display their allegiance prominently. Reconstruction on the site had been intended since the betrothal of James Mosman to the heiress Mariota Arres in 1558, but civil war had intervened. Now, with Mary's return and the re-appointment of the Mosmans to their court offices, the project could be carried through, echoing the French renaissance style of Mary's own improvements at Holyrood Palace, and even using the same sandstone from Craigmillar.

Understanding this context, we can then read the inscription in its intended design setting. The Mossman connection is clearly announced in the heraldic crest surrounded by the initials of the young couple taking up residence in this new high-profile focus for the Mossman family and business. But why Moses? The sundial has the figure of Moses receiving the Jewish Torah on Mount Sinai. The question put to Christ is, 'What is the greatest commandment in the Jewish Law, i.e. the Law of Moses?' The sundial was reconfigured from a very worn original by sculptor James Handyside Ritchie in the nineteenth century, using the French Renaissance models suggested by the overall design of the façade. The Scottish goldsmiths purchased most of their source material in France. There is even a suggestion that given significant Jewish involvement in the continental gold trade, Mosman might correlate with 'Moses Man'.

There is no proof of such an inter-faith dimension, though there is clearly religious significance, and that is where the language question comes into fascinating play. John Knox had a huge influence on language in Scotland because the Scottish Reformation introduced an English bible, not one in Scots. More precisely this was the Geneva Bible translation, which was a development of Tyndall's translation carried through by the English-speaking congregation in the Calvinist city-state of Geneva.

While in exile in mainland Europe in the 1550s, John Knox was actively engaged in this work providing interpretative notes that hammered home his radical interpretations of passages concerning religion and political authority. In addition, Knox brought to Scotland the Calvinist communion liturgy in which all the scriptural passages were from the Geneva version. Both the Bible and the Book of Common Order (service liturgies) were printed in Edinburgh in The Netherbow area opposite John Knox House. It is notable that when Shakespeare quotes the Bible it is the Geneva version, because the King James Bible, later called the Authorised Version, that supplanted it did not appear until his career as an active playwright was at its close.

Of more immediate point, John Knox would not have instructed a Scots Biblical inscription, especially one that was not an exact quotation. The Mosmans did this and their motivations are revealing, throwing in question every popular assumption about the inscription and its significance for John Knox House over four hundred years. The words may be set in stone, but their meaning is anything but obvious.

Protestant reformation was a long drawn out process in Scotland stretching from a failed Lutheran inspired attempt in the early 1540s through to the successful Calvinist revolt of 1559-60. Between these two upsurges, the Scottish Catholic hierarchy instigated their own attempts at reform, encouraged by the Vatican. These Europe-wide efforts were later to be renewed in a major Roman Catholic Reformation movement, often misleadingly called the Counter-Reformation.

In Scotland in 1552, Archbishop Hamilton issued a Catechism in Scotland, still known by his name, which urged the Church at all levels to re-engage with the moral and spiritual teaching of the Church. In this, he had the support of the Universities, of Catholic Humanists and of the orders of preaching friars who had most influence in the towns. Naturally, such a document was crafted in the language understood by most of the Scottish population, not Latin or English, but Scots. In addition, the Catechism urged memorisation of key Biblical sayings in Scots, so reaching out towards the majority of the population whose literacy was oral, not written. At the heart of the Catechism's teaching is

> the command is given by God … first in the law of nature which is prentit in our hartis, second in the law of Moyses written with his awne finger (that is to say be the vertew of the haly spirit) in twa tables of stayne, and last of all our Salviour Chryst, baith God and man, has ratifeit and exponit thame in the new law or Evangel'. We should keep the commands of God 'with ane rycht intention for the luf of God', teaches the Catechism, including 'the second tablet' which is 'the command of lufe qhuilk we aw to our nychbour.

Therefore, the prominent inscription on John Knox House is part of a visual presentation of core medieval Catholic teaching in a renewed, Scottish evangelical form. In case, anyone should characterise this as a general rather than a specific connection, the Catechism goes on to describe the Gospel dialogue in detail with the full question and answer, all in Scots like the inscription. In addition, the Catechism explains how the two commands 'resemble' each other, as the Gospel text suggests. Imagine this as a Catholic homily in the Scots of the time:

Gyf ye merveil how a man luffand his nychbour fulfillis and kepies the hail law, merveil nocht, for the lufe of God is includit in the lufe of our nychbour. For we aw to lufe our nychbour in God, or for God's lufe, and gif we blufe him nocht sincerely and purely as we aucht to do, it follows, thane, that qhasa luffis their nychbour sincerely and purely, thai lufe God.

At the time that the Mosmans raised their inscription in support of this teaching, its content, style and authority were hotly disputed by the Calvinists for whom 'natural law' was a cover for worldly and sinful conduct. Only justification by individual faith in Christ, in Protestant terms, and sanctification by the Holy Spirit could underpin moral rectitude. Yet as supporters of the Stewart Court from James V through Marie de Guise to Mary Queen of Scots, the royal goldsmiths were unafraid to display their religious loyalties, alongside their politics, and their prestigious trading position at the centre of burgh life, on the front of their highly visible house.

It was another twelve conflict ridden years before the Marian project was finally defeated and Protestantism became entrenched in Scottish government, secular and ecclesiastical. In the outcome James Mosman was outlawed, dispossessed and then executed, leaving his magnificent house to become the setting of John Knox's deathbed drama, attended by the great and the good of the new establishment. Yet the words were set in stone and can still be read: 'let those who have eyes to see.'

The stone-carved inscription on John Knox House does not exhaust the Netherbow's store of long enduring words that bridge tangible and intangible meanings. The position of John Knox House itself marks the narrowing of the High Street around the Netherbow Port or gateway. As the principal city gateway, it was subject to many alterations and re-buildings. These were associated with some profound traumas in Scotland's national story including the aftermath of the Battle of Flodden in 1513 and the civil wars of religion, referred to above. Relative stability returned when Mary's son James came into his majority as Scotland's first Protestant monarch in the 1580s, and subsequently from 1603, the first monarch of the united kingdoms of England, Scotland and Ireland.

After James departed to the much richer climes of London, Edinburgh needed ways to remind him that he had another northern capital. One of their favoured ploys was to rebuild and adorn the city gate, appealing to James' love of architecture, drama and language. Here was to be the great ceremonial entry and a constant reminder of the indelible ties between the loyal citizens of Edinburgh and their mainly absent ruler.

The Netherbow Port was demolished in 1764 to widen the road for (horse-drawn) traffic. The capture of the city by Bonnie Prince Charlie through the Netherbow Port, within living memory, may also have played a part. However, two precious artefacts from the gate survived, and in more recent times both have found their way back to The Netherbow where they have been incorporated, like John Knox House itself, in the Scottish Storytelling Centre.

The Port had a number of carved plaques on both facades of the gateway, one of which was erected in 1606, according to the still extant Town Council minutes. It reads clearly: God Save the King IR6 AR 1606 BEATI PACIFICI

Figure 3: Sketch of Plaque by Ian Stewart

This apparently straightforward inscription has puzzled many guides to Edinburgh. 'Blessed are the Peacemakers' was James' personal motto, and the Scots crown is obvious, though it has been replaced at some juncture, probably after Oliver Cromwell had the royal symbols on the Port hacked out to signal his short-lived Commonwealth. However, James VI and his consort Anne of Denmark left Scotland in 1603, and James only revisited once in 1617, with the rather disastrous intention of imposing Anglican structures on the Scots Presbyterians. So why 1606? Was an intended visit cancelled?

The answer lies indirectly in the Town Council records, where loyal notice is made of the attempt on the lives of James and Anne on 5th November 1605. Bells had been rung, and in later years fires were lit 'in remembrance of the Kings Majesties deliverance fra the conspiracie of England.' Clearly, the neighbour kingdom was comparatively deficient in patriotism. A later minute expands this to 'in remembrance of the late delyverie of the Kings Majestie, the Queynes grace, their children and hail estaittis of the realme and parliament of England that day from the cruell and abominabill treasoun and conspiracie intentet be certaine papists of England and by the mercy of God detectit'.

Debate continues about how formidable a conspiracy the Guy Fawkes episode actually was, but undoubtedly, it played on James' own fears of violence and assassination. These had been decisively formed in Scotland. Not only had his own father, Henry Stewart, been brutally murdered, but he himself had been apparently abducted in the still puzzling 'Gowrie Conspiracy' episode.

There is another Shakespeare connection here, as Shakespeare's company toured three times to Scotland under James's patronage, before his move to London. They performed in a specially built temporary theatre in Blackfriars Street, a few hundred yards west of The Netherbow and an equal distance north of where Darnley was assassinated. The visitors were keen to gain intelligence about the likely future king of England and to relay that back to London. The subsequent plots of both 'Hamlet' and 'Macbeth' seem to draw on these circumstances, with Macbeth as the Scottish play and Hamlet relating to Anne's Denmark, specifically Elsinore, where James and Anne had spent their honeymoon in 'Hamlet's Castle'. Both dramas concern the terrible consequences of killing a king.

As James' reign proceeded without further assassination attempts in London, the Town Council in Edinburgh continued to adorn their Netherbow Port. In 1606, they added a lost Latin inscription that was popularly translated as: Watch towers and thundering walls vain fences prove/No guards to monarchs like their people's love. In 1608, the steeple needed repair, the roof was re-leaded, and the tower slated. By this time an extended process had begun to commission an 'effigie or statue' of the king for the gate, along with a representation of his coat of arms. This was to drag on until it had to be completed in a rush, in anticipation of the royal visit in 1617.

Meantime the bell had cracked and a new one was ordered from London. This however proved unsatisfactory. The inadequacies came to the fore in the context of all the 1617 upgrades, and the Council decided in 1621 to order a set of three new city bells to be cast at Middleburg in Holland. The metal for this job was shipped from Leith through the Scottish staple port at Veere, but a hefty sum was then paid to Michael Burgerhuis, the leading Dutch bellmaker, to cast two bells for St Giles Kirk and one for The Netherbow tower. Originally, the smallest one was destined for the Netherbow, but in the event, the middle bell was hung there. In the event, it proved to be the only one to survive the later seventeenth century wars of religion.

Figure 4: Pencil sketches of both sides of the Netherbow bell

We know all this at first hand, because the surviving bell tells its own story in the form of an inscription. The words here are moulded in bronze rather than set in stone, but the durability has been the same if not better. The inscription is cast in Latin round the whole circumference of the bell and translates: 'To God alone be the Glory. Michael Burgerhuis of the sacred convocation of Middleburg made me in the foundry of the Zealanders. The Council and People of Edinburgh arranged to place me at public expense in the topmost tower of St Giles Church, October 1621. Who dares to injure with me will not escape hurt'. The Latin is in an elaborate Renaissance style, exquisitely lettered with a tiny leaping deer to mark the separation of the three lines round the bell:

Soli Dei Gloria. Michael Burgerhuis M(e) F(ecit) SACROS COETUS CON-VOCANDOS MIDDLEBURGH ZEALANDORUM FUSAM PUBLICIS SUMPTIBUS IN SUMMA AEDIS DIVI AEGIDII ARCE LOCANDAM CURARUNT SENATUS POPLUSQUE EDINBURGENSIS CALENDIS OCTOBRIS A DNI 1621 Nemo Me Impune Lacessit

The choice of Latin is interesting in this public setting. It seems that Scots was no longer recognised as a public or official tongue, but Latin was brought in rather than English, not as a medieval fallback but in order to retain civic pride and distinctiveness. This heralds a long rear-guard action in Scotland in favour of Latin verse, which continued into the eighteenth century alongside a closely related revival in literary Scots. The crosscurrents become hyperactive in the final motto, since 'Nemo me impune lacessit' is still popularly current in Scots as 'Wha daur meddle wi me?' But since Mosman's inscription in 1561, the vernacular oral traditions had been downgraded. Yet the bell, in the tradition of camponology, speaks in the first person, telling its own tale.

There are other Burgerhuis bells in Edinburgh at the Magdalen Chapel in the Cowgate and at Cramond Kirk, but none to match the splendour of this one. As in the John Knox House façade, the inscription is part of a wider visual scheme, embracing an early representation of Edinburgh's coat of arms and a stylised Renaissance thistle. The Maiden in the city arms exposes one leg, suggesting that her original was actually the lame St Giles, who had to be 'evolved' after the Protestant Reformation came down hard on saints. The pilgrim token embodying his arm bone relic was similarly changed into the heart shaped Luckenbooth brooch. The stylised thistle was adopted by the Scottish Storytelling Centre as its sign or logo in 2001. The bell itself is now handsomely accommodated in a contemporary bell tower designed by Malcom Fraser Architects and completed in 2006. The bell is once more rung on special civic occasions, sounding a present day note of Scottish renaissance.

These Netherbow inscriptions, all now housed in the Scottish Storytelling Centre, are precious survivals, primary evidence from critical periods of historic change. But the words they embody are only one part of complex stories that they reveal and to an extent conceal, not least because Scotland's place within the European family of nations is still obscured.

Artistic Research
On the Way towards Conceptual Clarity and
Off the Way with the Folkoratorio *Rivers of Our Being*

Rūta Muktupāvela and Valdis Muktupāvels

Theoretical and practical considerations

The theme of this book marks topical transdisciplinarity, transcending bounda-ries of disciplines and research fields, bridging the gap between science and art, between academic and popular discourse. This thematic framework is ex-tremely relevant to the entire European space of higher education, which is con-stantly forced to seek innovative forms and approaches to tackle effectively modern global challenges.

Traditional, pragmatic science alone is not enough in this quest. The abso-lutisation of scientific knowledge that began in the Age of Enlightenment capit-ulates in front of global consumption, enslavement of nature and humanity, mil-itary conflicts, migration and social exclusion. The illusion of objective truth, a social reality based on logical regularities, which scientists hoped to discover solely through knowledge based on empiricism, rationalism and positivism, has not created human society of high ethical standards. Modern technology, even if we attribute to it qualities like 'intelligent' and 'smart', is like the Ice Queen—pretty, self-sufficient, and yet cold, unable to help people in their struggle with their own greed, indifference and craving for power that moves them ever fur-ther away from the fulfilment of a 'bright and happy' future promised by and based on the pragmatic logic of science and technology.

In the period of challenges of information chaos and a levelling of values, Nietzsche's call to observe the development of science with the eyes of art seems to be prophetic, because 'only as an aesthetic phenomenon are existence and the world justified' (Nietzsche 2000: 38). More than that: 'Art approaches as a saving sorceress, expert at healing. She alone knows how to turn these nau-seous thoughts about the horror or absurdity of existence into notions with which one can live' (Nietzsche 1997: 38). Nietzsche's thesis can thus be taken as basis for a mutual ideological rapprochement of science and art.

Both science and art analyse our living reality—science through finding and experimenting, the art through looking for meaning. Moreover, by creating an empathetic state, the artwork enables us to obtain much more than using only facts, as art sparks the emotion that becomes an impulse for a deeper study of certain phenomena of reality. The specific character of art-related research lies in the fact that it invites us to take hold of reality and analyse it, using also non-scientific methods—not only tools of rationality and experimentation, but also those of impulse, emotion, intuition and, above all, of experience.

This conceptual analogy between scientific knowledge and aesthetic experience has been excellently outlined by Nietzsche's contemporary, Wilhelm Dilthey. Both the sciences and the arts are unimaginable without association of a concrete time-space, without association to life or a 'nexus of life'. Researchers and artists are both studying the world around us, only with different tools. Artists are creating added aesthetic value, scientists added scholarly value. The function of science is to explain reality, and therefore empirical data obtained through systematic observations and experiments dominate. Metaphors and symbols, outlining humanly significant matters to be noticed, experienced and conceived, dominate in art. Good scientific research and good art stimulate the imagination, both requiring a high level of preparation and specific knowledge—theoretical and empirical.

These factors and considerations lead to the concept of artistic research that, according to Henk Borgdorff (2012), is different from other kinds of research because of four equally important elements (Wilson 2016):

Firstly, it aims at knowledge and understanding that is embodied and enacted, that is, forms of knowledge about, and understanding of, who we are and how we relate to the world and to other people, which are embodied in practice.

Secondly, its methodology relies not only on reading and writing; its distinctive feature is that it is studio based. Reading, writing, and methods and techniques from sciences, social sciences or humanities might play a role, but central to this research is practice—the practice of both making and playing.

Thirdly, it has to do with the context, as the relevance of such research is assessed in the context of art practice.

Fourthly, It has to do with the outcome, as the outcome of this research is not a book, an article or a report in the first place—it is art works and art practices.

In artistic research, practice is the object, the method and the context of the research, and practice also tends to be the outcome of research.

Understanding or rationalisation of artistic research is especially significant in Latvia at the beginning of 2020s, for two reasons. The first reason is connected to current events in education policy. At present, all three Latvian art academies are developing a model of professional doctoral studies in the arts. The aim is 'to ensure and to develop unity of research and artistic work, to promote excellence and quality, competitiveness and export ability in the student's chosen field of artistic activity' (The Florence Principles 2016). In compliance with the principles, outlined in regulations passed by the Cabinet of Ministers in 2018, the highest professional level in the arts can be reached after the state examination is passed, which includes the elaboration and defence of doctoral level theoretical research and artistic creative work.

Obviously, this model provides for the unity of research and artistic competence, and both parts are treated as equal. In this context, art academies should clearly articulate and define the coexistence of equally significant, but in terms of methodological and theoretical base essentially different kinds of doctoral degrees. To avert misunderstandings among scientists and artists, it should be clear that the Doctor of Arts degree that exists in Latvian scientific nomenclature at present essentially corresponds to the internationally established PhD degree in humanities. It is awarded for scientific research of cultural and artistic phenomena. This is the old model presuming that artists create art, and scholars study it.

The professional degree in arts would provide the possibility not only for scientists, but also for advanced artists to obtain a doctoral degree, if they are able not only to create excellent artworks, but also to communicate the results of their artistic practice to a broader community of researchers, and to society in general. Thus, artists would extend the limits of knowledge, and it would be appropriate to be awarded the Doctor of/in Arts degree. This degree would serve its owner as a licence for pedagogical work in the highest-level academic structures, thus making it possible to hand down one's experience to a younger generation both on a national and on the international level.

This also points to another reason for sharing ideas on artistic research. In particular, it is essential to gather information about the best international practices, and to develop national conceptual and methodological frameworks for artistic research, necessary for the development of artistic discourse on the whole (Kopīgās studiju programmas 2019).

It is important that the task of rationalizing artistic research is not merely simulative, but that it is consistent with the policy makers' view, that all higher education institutions, regardless of their specifics, should be 'academic' and 'based on research'. It is also important not to be among those 'who are afraid of artistic research'—to paraphrase Dieter Lesage's (2009) famous question.

It is also important to rationalize—which means, to identify and explain— the diversity of artistic research at all levels: theoretical, methodological, and, not least, the level of practical utility. Furthermore, It is important to understand the role of artistic research and its communication in respect to three groups: for ourselves—scholars and students—as the actors in the academic environment; for higher education policy makers; and, for the general public.

The communication with all three groups should include explanation of the specifics of artistic research, the necessity of this kind of research, and its perspective in the academic environment, its role and significance for the labour market in the future, creating new knowledge, promoting social self-initiative, analytical and critical thinking, and creativity in general. It is no less important to understand the significance of artistic research in the process of educating future professionals—outstanding charismatic personalities, clever and responsible artists—those who will realize the artistic research themselves.

The realization of artistic research is usually attributed to the reflections of professional artists, fixing and analysing their own practices and experiences, when creating the artwork and communicating the process of creation.

In our experience, while working with students of audio-visual art, contemporary dance, drama and textual studies, and together analysing art in cultural contexts, the emic position—the views and attitudes of artists themselves towards reflecting their own experience on an academic level—turned out to be very important.

While outlining specifics of the discourse of artistic research, Henk Borgdorff (2012) has stressed the necessity of understanding the methods used, as well as the ability to explicate and reflect on the creative process, thus producing new knowledge on an artistic base. As we know, this is not mandatory when art is created beyond the academic milieu. In the case of artistic research, reflexivity can be explained as an artist's cognizance of their artwork's influence on artistic discourse and/or the social environment. As in the case of scientific reflexivity, this can be on two levels:

personal—awareness of one's role, ability to obtain data and objectively interpret personal experience of artwork creation;

epistemological—in respect to contextual aspects (style, succession, influences) of the newly created artwork, and to the theories and methods used.

It is just the element of reflexivity, especially in respect of epistemological aspects, that causes headaches, if not fear, in artists. Our experience participating in the accreditation of professional art doctoral programmes in other countries is that doctoral students mention just this aspect as the most complicated while working on their doctoral thesis projects. One can notice similar attitudes also among students of the Latvian Academy of Culture's Master's programmes, where students in the framework of their studies have to create an artwork as well as communicating the motivation, and contextual, theoretical and methodological aspects of its creation.

The most difficult task, while painting, making design, casting a film or staging a play, is to cope with the creative project's 'written part', or with the dualism between episteme and techne—theoretical and practical knowledge. How can we ensure that know-how or practical knowledge will not be produced simply by chance or accident? Autoethnography, diary, distancing and any other methods suited to Gilbert Ryle's and Clifford Geertz's approach of 'thick description'—everything must be used to help artistic research occupy its place among other activities of research and development, and to stand the novelty test of research and development as they are looking for new expressions (dissemination of research results) rather than for new knowledge.

On the other hand, it is important to realize that the main figure of artistic research is the artist, and he or she might be afraid of artistic research. As we know, even outstanding professionals quite often are not used to articulating their experience. However, this is an essential aspect, making the difference between the discourses of academic and non-academic artistic research. We should find the middle ground, so that the creative impulsivity would not be overshadowed, and artistic research would not become narcissistic, self-aimed activity either. It is important that theories and strict methods should not occupy and exaggerate the theoretical complexity of artistic research, thus alienating and scaring the artists. At this point, we would like to recall a joke about a centipede, who was asked how he knows with which leg to start moving? Trying to answer this question, he realised he simply could not move anymore, anywhere.

A Reflexive Story (not pretending to be artistic research)
Once upon a time there lived a King, and his name was Eucom. He and his people lived happily, until something strange happened. People were so much used to living a calm, satisfied and steady life that they had forgotten who they were. Everyone and everything seemed to be put into boxes, and even songs could not flow freely. All the flavours, tastes and colours started to fade day by day, and grey mist enveloped everyone and everything.

Downcast and desperate, the King spent his days and nights in his castle, until one night a dream came to him: a raven sat in an oak-tree, telling of ancient wisdom that makes living well. It lives in people, in hard times it can hide deeply, but it never disappears. The next day the King woke up, and he knew what to do. He sent messengers to all his kingdom to announce a competition for finding the lost remedy. The message also reached the white-headed Prince of the New Cas-tle, and he was brave enough to take the challenge. The Prince sent heralds to the farthest corners of the country to invite all the wise to arrive. Very soon the council of the wise came together and they made speeches with ever increasing strength and scope. Then stood up the Saxon GUDJA who divulged his wisdom in Edin's burgh at that moment. He said that even the wisest words tell only half of the truth if merely spoken, and that it is only through espousing words with the sound of Muses that they acquire their full power and can reach the depths of the ocean and the highest peaks of the mountain. This wedding of words with the sound of Muses should be stronger than any speech, sermon, contemplation or invocation, it should be a musical prayer—an oratorio.[1]

So, it happened that these words found a fertile soil in the Prince's heart, and he ordered a letter to the King to be scripted and sent that very moment. One thing he did not know was that sixty other Princes had sent their letters to King Eucom, too. And so it happened that the King listened to all the letters and became sadder and sadder. And when it seemed that there was nobody who could put forth the right words, the white-headed Prince of the New Castle stepped up and explained his vision. The King enjoyed this very much and prom-ised him a good reward if the words with the sound of Muses were to make the desired impact.

Upon returning home, the white-headed Prince of the New Castle called the sages together again, and this time he ordered to propose the most effective remedy to be presented for the King and kingdom. Then stood up the Anatolian dervish with his retinue and said: we must go to the main shrine and see if the busts of our ancestors and grands look nice and are properly illuminated. The Masovian ŻERCA nodded with approval and added: we have to put the busts of our saints and martyrs in the foreground there. Then stood up Dansk SKALDS and GUPIS and said: we must collect all our wisdom scrolls and cut them into such small pieces that nobody could cut them any smaller. Then we feed this dust into Yggdrasil's ear, and it will deliver our wisdom to the nine worlds. Some other

---

[1] Oratorio—long musical composition, usually with a text based on Scripture, from Italian *ora-torio* (late 16 c.), from Church Latin *ōrātōrium* 'a place of prayer, an oratory or chapel', from *ōrāre* 'to pray, plead, speak'.

SKALDS, who were good with sibyls from Attica, said: we cannot underestimate the power of repetition. We should put together the nicest words about our kingdom, and then make all inhabitants repeat them together with each breath, so that these words become their breath and seize all their body and thoughts. Then stood up the Emilia-Romagnan AUGURITAS and said: what are your busts, scrolls and words compared to inspiring food! We must take the most delicious fruits, spaghettis, pizzas and wines, and bring them to the King.

And then Saxon GUDJA stood up and said: all these things are so nice and good, but we shall spell ČOJČ-PLOJČ-ZROJČ[2] first, and then we shall make heavenly music. The Prince instantly turned his benevolent cheek towards him, pleading to start immediately. So he looked for a Lettish WAĪDILA whom he knew previously as good with bird songs and cane sounds, and invited him to be good with Muses, too. But before that, his wise companion, the Gaelic druidess, revealed a secret: the sound of Muses will make the necessary impact only if the words are spoken correctly, and when the right spell is pronounced.

The Lettish WAĪDILA secluded himself in ELKS[3], and started to play his KOKLES[4] with copper strings. When he had played for a while, formal spirits crept from near and afar, and started to create the form of the present. Firstly, it took the shape of a body with blood vessels, reminiscent of the kingdom's rivers. The network of rivers changed its configuration from a shell to a cross with its four ends—Northern, Southern, Western, and Eastern. Then a selection of smaller folks gathered around each of them: around the Northern end—Saami, Vadja, Selonians, Nordmen; around the Eastern end—Cossacks, Ashkenazim, Górale; around the Southern end—Sards, Seljuqs, Epirotes; and around the Western end—Bretons, Dutch, Gaels. No more were permitted to gather around, because the bigger a folk, the more noise does it make.

Then Lettish WAĪDILA started to play his KOKLES with silver strings. When he had played for a while, content spirits crept up from near and afar, and started to fill the form of the present. Firstly, they prompted to let rivers make their own language, mingling words and sounds from all folks living on their banks into magnificent streams of conlang. Then a very smart spirit said that the tiniest word from a living language, pronounced with a thought behind it, is a thousand times more beautiful than the most artistic and sophisticated conlang. And then the most advanced spirit said that it is nothing compared to songs that folks have inherited from times immemorial. Such a song has something from every being

---

[2]   *Abracadabra* of Central Eastern Europe.
[3]   Natural sanctuary of ancient Letts, usually a birch or oak grove.
[4]   Eastern Baltic psaltery, the playing of which enables transcendental connection.

who has sung it, and, by travelling from a soul to a soul myriad of times, it has accumulated unseen wisdom and strength. And then the most diligent spirit gathered songs from all possible and impossible moments of life: creation of the world; a heavenly wedding; the sound of a harp overpowering a troll; a girl beneath a tree, weeping for her beloved; happy dancing; a heroic outlaw strolling amidst his native hills and valleys; a baby's future foretold in a lullaby; the rattle of war drums; a prayer to God for protection; a king arriving to fulfil his duty; people enjoying the healing qualities of tobacco; longing for the native country from afar. This very moment, a Dacian VEZINA prompted the oratorio to turn into a folkoratorio.

Then Lettish WAĪDILA started to play his KOKLES with golden strings. When he had played for a while, focal and contextual spirits crept from near and afar, and started to focalise and contextualise the filled form of the present. They said: the human voice is above all, and may you sing these songs. So they gathered a chorus of the most vibrant voices. The others said: the voice is but one of many instruments, so why should we avoid all others? They are so strong and so good to represent something. Brass speaks of vastness and power, brass with drums of heavenly and royal might. Woodwinds speak of birds in the air, of warmth and uplifting. Bagpipe speaks of common joys and dancing. Strings of bowed instruments speak of body and skin, of sad and joyous feelings, of harmony and disharmony. Strings of piano speak of mind, space and its movements. Strings of psaltery speak of deep self, subconsciousness and soul, and of inner peace. Conch shell speaks of all waters—from sea depths to rippling streams. So they added all the instruments to the voices.

Now everything seemed to be up and running, but the Saxon GUDJA puckered his forehead—the garland of songs was still missing something. So he thought: may sages help us!—and added a figurative statement in verse about the same stream of life that runs through all living beings in the world.

Now was the time to take all the wisely prepared presents to the King, and so the white-headed Prince of the New Castle with all his cohorts arrived at the King's palace. The presents were unwrapped and displayed, and all court people were feeling better and better. And then the time came to present the folkoratorio. The chorus of the most vibrant voices sang, the strong and representable instruments played. The white-headed Prince of the New Castle with his companion and the Saxon GUDJA spoke their most secret scientific spells in interplay with the sounds of Muses. It was close to the end, but nothing yet was happening. And then the Gaelic druidess stepped into the very centre and quietly, with all her might, she chanted the words that had lived among the people and were given her by an Alban druid:

> Tomorrow, songs
> Will flow free again, and new voices
> Be borne on the carrying stream.[5]

The chorus instantly picked up the spell and sang out with all their might, and the musical instruments joined. And a miracle happened: all the flavours, tastes and colours became brighter and brighter, the grey mist disappeared, and the light returned to people's eyes. King Eucom was more than happy and gave a good reward to the white-headed Prince of the New Castle and all his wise counsel. The waters as rippling streams were flowing everywhere, and new voices were coming out as if from nowhere. It was life again!

About the Folkoratorio and its Performance

The folkoratorio was crafted as a creative research-by-practice output as part of the European Union Horizon2020-funded CoHERE project, seeking to identify, understand and valorise European heritages, engaging with their socio-political and cultural significance and their potential for developing communitarian identities. It was developed in partnership with Newcastle University, Heriot-Watt University and the Latvian Academy of Culture.

Rivers of our Being proposes a celebration of the diversity of European musical traditions: taking its inspiration from the rivers of Europe, the composition invites audiences to have a unique auditory journey across different European musical traditions. Intertwined with reflexive texts from CoHERE authors' works and other sources, the musical construction provides additional meanings to the established contexts of folk music and initiates reflexion on such topics as culture and identity, identity and performativity, 'others' as a threat to identity, populism and multiculturalism, cultural heritage and local identity.

The folkoratorio music was composed by Valdis Muktupāvels. Song texts are traditional Votic, Latvian, Norwegian, Ukrainian, Polish (Kazimierz Przerwa Tetmajer), Sardinian, Greek, Breton, Dutch and Gaelic (John Campbell) folksongs, as well as poems of Rabindranath Tagore and Hamish Henderson. The authors of the reflexive texts are Philip Bohlman, Johann Gottfried Herder, Máiréad Nic Craith, Kurt Tucholsky, Jack Goody, Patrick Geary, Ayşe Tecmen and Ullrich Kockel.

The first public (preview) performance took place on 1 November 2018 at the King's Hall of Newcastle University, conducted by Simon McKerrell, with a vocal group and instrumental ensemble from students of the University's Music

---

[5]   From Hamish Henderson's poem *Under the Earth I Go* (Henderson 2019: 343f.; here 344).

department augmented by invited musicians, soloists Rūta Muktupāvela and Naomi Harvey, and reciters Christopher Whitehead and Gönül Bozoğlu (CoHERE Folk Oratorio: 2018).

The world premiere was on St Andrew's Day, 30 November 2018, in the Scottish Storytelling Centre in Edinburgh, conducted by Simon McKerrell, with vocal group and instrumental ensemble drawn from students of Newcastle University's music department plus invited musicians, soloists Rūta Muktupāvela and Naomi Harvey, and reciters Ullrich Kockel, Máiréad Nic Craith.

The Latvian premiere was on 29 October 2019 at the Ziedonis hall of the National Library of Latvia in Rīga, conducted by Kaspars Ādamsons, with the choir 'Sōla' of the Latvian Academy of Culture, the instrumental group drawn from students of the Latvian Music Academy plus invited musicians, soloists Rūta Muktupāvela and Laura Štoma, and reciters Christopher Whitehead, Gönül Bozoğlu, Ullrich Kockel and Máiréad Nic Craith. The performance was recorded by video artist Viktors Keino (2019).

References

CoHERE (2018), *Folk Oratorio*. Available at https://vimeo.com/301107016 (accessed 23 February 2020).

Henderson, H. (2019), *Collected Poems*. Ed. C. Gibson (Edinburgh: Polygon).

Keino, V. (2019), *Rivers of Our Being*. Available at https://www.youtube.com/watch?v=-75wVu2dRVI&feature=youtu.be (accessed 23 February 2020).

Kopīgās studiju programmas: Profesionālā doktora studiju programma mākslās 51 21 1/2/3/4. Satura un realizācijas apraksts [Description of the content and implementation of the joint doctoral programme in professional arts]. JVLMA, LKA, LMA, 2019.

Lesage, D. (2009), 'Who's Afraid of Artistic Research? On Measuring Artistic Research Output', *Art and Research* 2(2): 1-10.

Nietzsche, F. (1997), *Philosophical Writings* (New York: Continuum).

Nietzsche, F. (2000), *The Birth of Tragedy* (Oxford: Oxford University Press).

The Florence Principles on the Doctorate in the Arts (2016) (European League of the Institutes of the Arts). Available at https://www.elia-artschools.org/documents/the-florence-principles (accessed 23 January 2020).

Wilson, J. (2016), 'Artistic Research: In Conversation with Henk Borgdorff', *Non Traditional Research Outcomes*. Available at https://nitro.edu.au/articles/edition-2/artistic-research-in-conversation-with-henk-borgdorff (accessed 23 January 2020).

'If I were a Blackbird'
Constellations of Meaning in Birdsong and Folksong

Mairi McFadyen

For Máiréad Nic Craith, with Love

> *Because they have song,*
> *not because they have answers,*
> *is why the birds sing.*[1]

Last April, I attended a rainy-day 'nature awareness' workshop on bird songs and calls in Abriachan, where I now live, in the hills on the north side of Loch Ness.[2] On a verdant walk up through the woods from the loch, we learned together how to pay attention, how to listen, how to begin to recognise each species. This has now become a daily ritual. Pausing to listen to the chorus of the birds draws me out of my conscious mind into the here and now: just for a moment, the mental chatter stops, and I feel overcome with a sense of peace, of belonging, a *sense of being*.

One of the first things I did when moving to our new home was to research how to make a bird-friendly garden, setting up a feeder right next to the kitchen window. As I am writing this, there is a blackbird pecking at the earth, eating the seeds tossed to the ground by the blue tits, great tits and families of finches. Glossy black with its bright yellow bill, I have formed an intimate relationship with this morning blackbird; its daily visit has become intertwined with my breakfast ritual of tea and porridge. The birds and their rhythms have become ecologically bound up with my own experience of and companionship with this new place.

Birds, of course, have captured the collective and poetic imagination throughout the ages. The blackbird is no different. This common and conspicuous species has given rise to a number of literary and cultural references and often appears in folk symbolism. The first part of this essay reflects on how we relate to the sounds of birds, how we 'make sense' of our aesthetic experiences; the second takes the blackbird as a metaphor and motif in folksong, reflecting

---

[1] Haiku poem written by Ian W. McFadyen, inspired by a Chinese proverb.

[2] *Bird Calls and Songs*, a nature awareness workshop run by Dan Puplett (https://www.dan-puplett.net/), Sunday 26th May 2019.

on how, through the process of tradition, our individual experiences can become distilled into a collective and creative 'constellation of meanings'.

A Celebration of Being

Perhaps the most intimate and joyful creative expression of how people relate to the sounds of birds is in their imitation by humans – in speech, whistling, music, and song. In a clip on the online archive *Tobar an Dualchais – Kist O Riches*, recorded on reel-to-reel by Scottish folklorist Hamish Henderson in Fife, 1964, you can hear a selection of whistled bird-call imitations (with impressive technique!) of the cuckoo, curlew, owl and the blackbird.[3] Countless generations of humans before our time had a far more intimate relationship with nature and the ecological rhythms on which our life depends – this is a wonderful example. Another magical clip is of Annie Johnson from Barra, in the Outer Hebrides, sharing the *Cainnt nan Eun* or 'speech of the birds' in Gaelic, recorded by J. L. Campbell on wax cylinder in 1950.[4] Through the creative use of language, she imitates and celebrates the *smeòrach* (thrush), *uiseag* (lark), *feannag* (crow), *faoileag* (seagull) and *calman* (dove). Here, as musicologist John Purser reflects, 'the dividing lines between birdsong, music and speech are impossible to determine.'[5]

Musing upon the questions of singing, presence and being, Irish philosopher William Desmond reflects:

> Compare a singing being with something inanimate. The wind blows around a bush and makes a whirr or a low burr, but neither the wind or bush properly sings. But a bird chirps, a thrush sings out again and again a line of lush notes, and we sense a presence there that was not manifest before.
> Something is coming awake in singing life...Song is a witness of affirming presence...The bird's song is an unselfconscious, effortless, *celebration of being*.[6]

---

[3] To listen to this audio archive clip, visit: http://tobarandualchais.co.uk/en/fullrecord/58034 (accessed 7 July 2020). Sadly for us, the identity of this man has been lost to history.

[4] To listen to this audio archive clip, visit: http://tobarandualchais.co.uk/en/fullrecord/25889 (accessed 7 July 2020).

[5] Purser, J. 2007 (1992). *Scotland's Music: A History of the Traditional and Classical Music of Scotland from Earliest Times to the Present Day*. Edinburgh: Mainstream, pp. 24-25

[6] Desmond, W. 1990. *Philosophy and Its Others: Ways of Being and Mind*. New York: SUNY Press, p. 269

The song of the blackbird is perhaps the most familiar and best-loved song to be heard in any garden, park or woodland. Their call is influenced by the seasons, the weather and changing light. Their stark calls at wintertime roost are very much characteristic of long, dark, cold days; in spring, their spontaneously composed song marks the coming of freshness and new life. The spontaneity of the blackbird's song was once proverbial: 'to whistle like a blackbird' was to do something with ease. Ornithologist William Henry Hudson believed that the 'careless beauty' of the blackbird's song 'comes nearer to human music than any other bird songs,' while the tone was 'even suggestive of the human voice.'[7]

Figure 1: 'In the Garden'; Blackbird print by artist Jenny Sturgeon[8]

7   Cocker, M. & R. Mabey (eds). 2005. *Birds Brittanica*. London: Chatto & Windus.

8   Limited edition 'In the Garden' lino print. Printing ink on somerset paper, by Shetland artist Jenny Sturgeon Ink & Wool. Part of the Ecosystem print series. See: https://www.jennysturgeonmusic .com/art (accessed 7 July 2020). Reproduced with the artist's permission.

Metaphor and Music

At the workshop I attended in Abriachan, we learned how to identify bird sounds by various 'attributes', such as duration, pace, volume, pitch, pattern and rhythm. I found it fascinating how people used language to make sense of these sounds, often using the same kind of language we would use to describe music and song. What is the relationship between our embodied experience and perception, and the language we use to express it? The blackbird's song was described variously as 'rich, fluid and melodious', 'relaxed', 'cheerful and upbeat' and 'fluent and beautifully fluted.' It was suggested that each 'verse' of the blackbird's song ends with 'a twiddle of high squeaky notes, like the opening of a rusty gate.' Some participants even created mnemonics to aid their memory, such as 'rusty rusty hinge squeak!'

This is an example of the creative process of metaphorical thinking, of thinking of one thing in terms of another. Metaphors are so deeply embedded in our consciousness that they often go unnoticed. Ordinary definition describes metaphor as a figure of speech or literary device in which a word or phrase helps make a comparison. There is abundant evidence, however, to suggest that metaphor is not simply a manifestation of literary creativity, but rather a 'fundamental mechanism of mind,' essential to the workings of language and to how humans 'make sense' of the world around them.[9]

We need to make the distinction here between 'conceptual metaphors' which are patterns of thought, and 'linguistic metaphors' which are the expression of thought in language. Philosopher Mark Johnson, drawing on research in cognitive science, makes the case that conceptual metaphors are grounded firstly in our bodily experience, and that it is only through our bodily perceptions, movements, senses and emotions that meaning becomes possible. Shape and colour, taste, movement in time and space – all of these are perceived by the senses, and the signification of these senses through language is the basis upon which conceptions of cultural forms such as music and song are formed.[10]

---

[9]   See Lackoff, G. & M. Johnson. 1981. *The Metaphors We Live By.* Chicago: University of Chicago Press.

[10] Ethnomusicologists such as Steven Feld, Timothy Rice and Lillis Ó Laoire have written about the role of culturally situated metaphors in musical understanding. See Feld, S. 1981. '"Flow Like a Waterfall": The Metaphors of Kaluli Musical Theory.' *Yearbook for Traditional Music* 13: 22–47; Rice, T. 1994. *May it Fill Your Soul: Experiencing Bulgarian Music.* Chicago: University of Chicago Press; Ó Laoire, L. 2005. *On a Rock in the Middle of the Ocean: Songs and Singers in Tory Island, Ireland.* Oxford: Scarecrow.

We talk of music being 'high' or 'low' reflecting our orientation in space; we describe it as dark or light, fast or slow, sharp or sweet. We might say we are 'deeply moved' by a song, which suggests a kind of journey or transformation.

This is all to say, Johnson argues, that *all aspects of meaning-making are fundamentally aesthetic.*[11] The word 'aesthetic' is understood here not in the sense of a matter of beauty, judgement or taste, but rather – as opposed to the *anaesthetic* experience – as one in which our senses are operating at their peak, when we are present in the current moment with heightened awareness, when we are most fully *alive*:

Aesthetic embodiment is being fully present through the distinctive presence of the body with the sensory focus and intensity we associate with the experience of art. It is *being most completely human.*[12]

The Pattern that Connects

Most scientific writing about the sound of the birds attempts to objectify sounds into 'the song' or 'the call', transcribing and categorising various sonic properties and then performing a systematic or comparative analysis. Systematic analysis of an isolated aesthetic object, however, does not explain how or why such sounds become evocative, affecting or meaningful to people.

As part of a research project investigating how people perceive, identify and 'make sense' of bird sounds, anthropologist Andrew Whitehouse suggests that birds, for some people, are not just integral to a 'sense of place' but to a *sense of being.*[13] Birds, he writes, are important to people 'because of their very presence.' The dynamic presence of birds entangles with people's lives and worlds and the changes, constancies and ecological rhythms within it. A sense of being is both aesthetic and affective, and listening to the birds becomes the focal point to a whole bodily experience of the landscape. Meaning emerges in-between our ongoing, multi-sensory experience of the world and the personal or historical narratives that these experiences recall and elicit.

For me, in these late days of spring, the early morning wake-up call at dawn is mixed with the sensation of being awoken by the soft rising sun and the light peeking through the gaps. In the calming chorus at dusk, the spring song of the

---

[11] Johnson, M. 2007. *The Meaning of the Body: Aesthetics of Human Understanding.* Chicago: University of Chicago Press.

[12] Berleant, A. 2004. *Re-thinking Aesthetics: Rogue Essays on Aesthetics and the Arts.* London: Routledge, p. 88.

[13] Whitehouse, A. J. 2017. 'Senses of being: The atmospheres of listening to birds in Britain, Australia and New Zealand' in S Schroer & S Schmitt (eds), *Exploring Atmospheres Ethnographically., 5 Anthropological Studies of Creativity and Perception.* London: Routledge, pp. 61-75.

birds mixes with the scent of damp, freshly-greened branches, wild cherry blossom and the opening buds of the poplar tree, and the sense of the gradual fading of the light. As I come to know this place, high in the hills overlooking the changing textures and colours of the waters of Loch Ness, the sounds of the birds are very much entangled with my experience of this landscape.

I find anthropologist Gregory Bateson's definition of 'aesthetic' useful here. He understands aesthetics as a form of ecological understanding: 'so by *aesthetic* I mean responses to the *pattern which connects.*'[14] He describes aesthetic thinking as a 'sensibility', an 'ability to perceive connections, commonalities, shared properties between different elements of reality and different levels of reality, at different levels of abstraction.' Such a sensibility has to do with conscious awareness and care. To see wholeness – to see the patterns of relatedness and the interconnectedness of things – is a view that goes together with a recognition of the diversity of life and the uniqueness of its individual manifestations, which are each seen to have intrinsic value even in their most insignificant forms.

Aesthetic Encounters

As an ethnologist, I am most fascinated by heightened aesthetic encounters and the emergent and creative processes of meaning-making such encounters elicit. The initial multisensory experience is not the end of the encounter; rather, these 'moments' can inspire further reflection and can hold the potential and possibility for transforming, re-framing or affirming our relationship to the world. For me, these 'moments' most often come in musical experience, although more and more often I find these experiences in the natural world.

One such moment I can recall is the performance of the piece 'Blackbird,' sung by Scots singer Fiona Hunter during the live orchestral performance of musician and composer Martyn Bennett's work GRIT at Glasgow's Celtic Connections festival in 2016.[15] Hunter was singing in tribute to the original recording of the song 'What A Voice (Blackbird)' sung by Traveller singer Lizzie Higgins (1929 - 1993),[16] recorded in 1977 and sampled by Bennett on his original studio album.[17] Here, the free, unmetered voice, intuitive and free-flowing, stood out as starkly elemental against a rigid drum beat, with exquisite strings soaring over

---

[14] Bateson. G. 2002 (1979). *Mind and Nature: a Necessary Unity*. Cresskill (NJ): Hampton Press

[15] Directed by Greg Lawson. A recording is available at https://youtu.be/ol7pQsukzks (accessed 7 July 2020).

[16] This song was released on the album 'What a Voice', released in 1987 by Lismor Recordings

[17] GRIT was released on Real World Records in 2003. See: https://realworldrecords.com/releases/grit/ (accessed 7 July 2020).

the top. The tension between freedom and form made for a powerful emotional release, producing a full visceral response of spine-tingles and chills.

This was a musical event that invoked a context much larger than the immediate performance context itself: it self-consciously embodied and invoked all pre-existing moments in the tradition, giving voice to the those no longer with us. It was a performance that somehow fused the lived present with past, opening up worlds of memory and imagination.

On a very personal level, this is music that has become woven in with my own personal narrative, and the multisensory experience of listening to this music evokes for me multiple layers of meaning and memory. The album GRIT was released in 2003, the year I began my undergraduate degree in Scottish ethnology at the University of Edinburgh. It is the soundtrack to my early twenties, forever bound up with that time, people and place. A friend commented:

> What is the emotion you experience when you listen to Blackbird? I find it so difficult to put the emotion into words. Maybe it doesn't matter that I can't put into words. Maybe that's the beauty, the mystery. But it's the emotion that makes you want to laugh and cry with joy and misery and regret and makes you look back and look forwards all at once.[18]

It is often difficult to express or describe the full meaning or emotion of such significant aesthetic experiences in everyday language. This is why we often reach for *poetic* language, for creative metaphor, to describe or make sense of our lived experience. Metaphor is an abstraction of experience into language: it has poetic power precisely because it reconnects abstract thought with embodied experience.

A wonderfully rich example of creative 'thinking by metaphor' is the idea of the elusive *duende* — an abstract poetic metaphor that reaches to make sense of both the heightened expression of and emotion in response to art, most often associated with traditional song and dance. The Spanish poet Lorca wrote that the *duende* is the 'mysterious force that everyone feels and no philosopher has explained,' that 'draws close to places where forms fuse in a yearning beyond visible expression.'[19] Explanations of the *duende*, of course, appealed to Scottish folklorist Hamish Henderson as an idea that contained all that he found difficult

---

[18] Personal fieldwork, 2016.

[19] For an English translation, see, e.g., Federico García Lorca, *Theory and Play of the Duende*. Available at https://www.poetryintranslation.com/PITBR/Spanish/LorcaDuende.php (accessed 7 July 2020).

to express about the inexpressible and elemental qualities of traditional folk culture.[20] Henderson noted that in Scotland, the Travellers have an expression that
corresponds with the *duende* – the *conyach* – a metaphorical term which attempts to describe the visceral creative power of the unaccompanied human
voice in song.[21]

The quality and materiality of Lizzie Higgin's unaccompanied voice has a
powerful effect on many people. With its particular aesthetic of simplicity and
directness, her voice embodies the elusive quality of being at once ancient and
immediately present, something instantly recognisable yet unrecognisable,
something that most of us are somehow cut off from. On hearing her voice for
the first time, Bennett said this:

> I first heard Lizzie sing when I was about 12 years of age, at a festival in the
> North East of Scotland. She was the only singer that actually made me *stop*,
> and the hairs got me on the back of the neck, you know? There's just some-
> thing about her voice. It's like something wild, something that is not trained
> at all, it's just an instinct. She just sang straight out of her soul.[22]

William Desmond writes that song can sometimes 'rise up' from sources of
being 'where the calculating, controlling will not does not hold sway.' Using similar language to Bennett, he reflects:

> Listening to the old ballads we sometimes hear the elemental – so simple,
> so elegant, so powerful – yet without insistence – as if singers were more
> directly in touch with something irreducible...The elemental is such that its
> expression is just its simple being...as if that song were the most natural
> thing in the world, were the very nature of things. For the elemental is just
> its simple being.'[23]

---

[20] Henderson, H. 2002 (1992). *Alias MacAlias: Writings of Songs, Folk and Literature*. Polygon:
      Edinburgh, pp.288-293.

[21] See: McFadyen, M. 2012. 'Presencing Imagined Worlds': A contemporary ethnomusicological
      enquiry into the embodied ballad singing experience, PhD thesis, University of Edinburgh. See:
      https://era.ed.ac.uk/handle/1842/7948 (accessed 7 July 2020).

[22] See Martyn Bennett's website: http://martynbennett.com/

[23] Desmond, W. 1990. *Philosophy and Its Others: Ways of Being and Mind*. New York: SUNY
      Press, p.272 (my italics).

Constellations of Meaning

The power of folksong lies not just in the materiality of the voice, but in the form's abstract wisdom and style. The use of figurative and formulaic language, imagery and motifs – times of day, seasons of the year, colours, plants, birds – all contribute to what ballad scholar David Atkinson has called the unmistakeable 'ballad world.'[24] In such a highly suggestive narrative setting, the associations of traditional metaphors help establish a deeper recognition of cultural meaning:

> For it to be a story, the song must make you listen; thus it calls upon metaphors from across the land, across hundreds of years and hundreds of generations, to catch your ear. Folk songs are unfathomable and undeniable. The old ballads carry a kind of truth, a collective something that is its own truth.[25]

Through time and through the process of tradition – the process of creating and re-creating meaning – individual creativity can be distilled into a kind of collective memory, into what folksong scholar Toelken calls a 'shared constellation of meanings'.[26] He writes:

> By and large we are not studying the accumulated texts of a few educated poets but the dynamic record of a general dynamic capacity to use the poetic power available in the song traditions and the contexts of everyday life in order to foreground and articulate central features of shared human concern.[27]

Birds feature frequently as motifs in folksong, often signifying sexuality and seduction, as messengers of death or symbolic of romantic dalliances. The blackbird, however, goes against the conventional trend in northern Europe by being a black bird that is not generally associated with evil or bad luck; this said, it is

---

[24] Atkinson, D. 2002. *The English Traditional Ballad: Theory, Method and Practice.* Aldershot: New York.

[25] Wilentz, S. & G. Marcus. 2005. *The Rose and the Briar: Death, Love and Liberty in the American Ballad.* W.W. Norton.

[26] Toelken, B. 1995. *Morning Dew and Roses: Nuance, Metaphor and Meaning in Folksongs.* University of Illinois Press.

[27] Wilgus, D.K. & B. Toelken. 1983. 'The Ballad and the Scholars: Approaches to Ballad Study'. Paper Presented at a Clark Library Seminar.

not entirely free of this taint. In song, blackbirds were especially suspect for young lovers, often suggesting despair, regret or longing for lost love.

The folksong 'If I Were a Blackbird' was well known in the farm districts of the North East of Scotland and in Northern Ireland and even made the crossover into popular music.[28] There are many different versions and variations. The version below, sung by Belle Stewart (1906-1997) was recorded by Hamish Henderson in 1956.[29] In the song, a young girl laments the loss of her young sailor lad who has gone to sea. She wishes she were a blackbird and could follow his ship, or that she could write him a letter to tell of her pain. The blackbird here becomes an abstract motif for the difficult emotional memories we carry with us:

> I am a young maiden and my story is sad
> For years I've been courted by a brave sailor lad.
> He courted me truly by night and by day
> But now he has left me and gone far away.
>
> Now I if was a blackbird, could whistle and sing
> I would follow the ship that my true love sails in
> And on the top rigging I would there build my nest
> And I'd sleep the night long on his lily-white breast.[30]

The song 'What A Voice (Blackbird)' sung by Lizzie Higgins, described above (also known by the title 'I Wish, I Wish' / 'Love Has Brought Me to Despair'), also draws heavily on bird imagery, both the swallow and the blackbird. The singer hears a girl telling of the grief her false love has left her. In this case, the mention of the blackbird has such strong traditional connotations and associations that its very evocation can carry implied meanings not explicit in the text:

> What a voice, what a voice, what a voice I hear
> It's like the voice of my Willy dear
> But if I had wings like that swallow high
> I would clasp in the arms o' my Billy boy.

---

28 'If I Were a Blackbird' was recorded by British music hall singer Ronnie Ronalde (1923-2015) in 1950. The most widely known is a re-working of the song from a male perspective by Andy M. Stewart in 1981, recorded by the band Silly Wizard. It is published in The Andy M. Stewart Songbook, published by Amsco music in 1998.

29 To listen to this audio archive clip, visit: http://tobarandualchais.co.uk/en/fullrecord/32998 (accessed 7 July 2020).

30 Excerpt of song text as sung by Belle Stewart in 1956.

When my apron it hung low
My true love followed through frost and snow
And noo my apron it is tae my chin
He passes me by and he ne'er spiers in.

It is up and doon yon white hoose brae
He called a strange girlie to his knee
And he's telt her a tale that he once told me.

There is a blackbird sits on yon tree
Some says it is blind and it cannae see
Some says it is blind and it cannae see
And so is my true love tae me.

O I wish, I wish oh I wish in vain
I wish I was a maid again
But a maid again I will never be
Till apples grow an orange tree

I wish I wish that my babe was born
And smiling on some nurse's knee
And for myself to be dead and gone
And-a long green grass growing over me.[31]

In Toelken's view, any traditional listening audience does more than just 'hear' a ballad or folksong: they 'glean' it. Songs like this are strange and ambiguous, containing very little explanation or detail. Figurative meaning cannot be said to reside entirely within the text, but somewhere between the text (as it is performed) and that shared constellation of meanings and associative memory that gets triggered when a singer sings a certain song before an audience at a particular time. This is the power of the ballad aesthetic: the story is so distilled that the listener is required to 'fill in the gaps' and so becomes a co-creator in the realisation of the song's meaning.

In embodied aesthetic experience, sensation, memory and imagination coalesce into a pattern that connects different elements and layers of reality. The materiality of the singing voice binds humans to one another in the lived pre-

---

[31]　Full song text as sung by Lizzie Higgins in 1977.

sent. The meanings emerging from the juxtaposition of or tension between personal memories and the abstract meanings in a given song can be understood as a metaphorical process itself, opening up a liminal space for new meanings to be created.

An ethnological sensibility

I was not always so fascinated by the birds; while living in the city I barely noticed them. I was so distracted and disconnected from the world, disconnected even from my own body. It is a marvel what a change in circumstance and attitude can reveal. In our modern world, obsessed with work, productivity and counting things, we have created ways of living that are destroying the natural world that sustains us. When it comes to the environment, the birds are our measure, our meter; they mark the coming and going of the seasons, pollinate plants and disperse seeds, help forests flourish. Their presence – and their absence – is an insight into the health of our world. Through our disconnection and our destruction, we are losing not only the birds, but the very capacity to *notice*, to pay attention. Writer Kathleen Jamie asks: 'Given the state we are in, and the reckless exploitation of the Earth, can a *moment of attending* actually amount to a moment of resistance?' [32]

When we do that – step outdoors, smell Autumn in the wind, *seriously notice* – we are not little cogs, little consumers, in someone else's machine. We are not doing what the forces of destruction and inattention want us to do. It is our way of being, not theirs. It's the simplest act of resistance and renewal.

What we subsequently do with that noticing, whether we transform it into poetry, art, science or activism comes a little later. But first, there must arise that primary act of attending.

Since leaving the city, I have consciously made the effort to resist and renew, to become more attentive and attuned to the world around me. Aesthetic encounters – with the birds, with music and song – gift us a glimmer of a reality that we instantly know for a moment in time: an affirmation of wholeness, of connectedness. Part of my own creative practice is to find ways to cultivate an ethnological, ecological, geopoetic sensibility to this 'pattern that connects' – to find the threads through which life gains meaning.

We all have the power to reclaim where we place our consciousness, of what we attend to, what we attune to. For now, it's me and my garden birds.

---

[32] Jamie, K. (2019). 'Lissen Every Thing Back', on *The Clearing*, https://www.littletoller.co.uk/the-clearing/lissen-by-kathleen-jamie/ (accessed 7 July 2020).

Not Yet Known

Vitalija Stepušaitytė

The shift was going towards the end, only two hours and twelve minutes left.[1] Daiva [da:iva] checks her phone and sees the message from her daughter 'Мама kudutogrisi', she reads 'Mama, kada tu grįši' [ma:ma kada tu gri:ʃi], or in English: 'Mom, when are you coming back?'. Daiva sighs and asks herself whether Joana [Joa:na] not [dʒoa:na], her daughter, will ever learn how to spell. This Anglicised texting is really getting on her nerves recently. She replies 'Grįšiu greit, apie 6 vakaro' ('Soon, around 6pm').

On the way to a ward, Daiva passes an office at the end of the corridor and checks her pigeon hole. She finds a sheet with hours for the next two weeks, with a post note addressed to Diva (which an English=speaker would pronounce [da:iva]). Another quite scream in her head: 'it's D A I V A [da:iva] – can't you spell?'

Daiva gets back to her duties and does not know when she starts lingering on thoughts, which have become rather persistent in the last year:

> If I returned (to Lithuania) that would be right, I know it would be right, would I feel better there? I don't know; should I continue this struggle here? It's probably better here but much more annoying compared to Lithuania, I don't know, I don't know how to stand this noise around me! I am so easily annoyed of phrases that don't mean much to me. They don't care; they just throw at me how are you darling, thanks, cheers, leaving me no space to respond, but I want to respond. I want to be heard! By the time I find the right words, those people are gone; actually, they were never even there for me. Isn't it that a language is only alive amongst people who talk to each other, but we don't share a language in the same way, they use it as if they were playing with Lego, subject verb object, subject verb object. I don't know how to feel the world in English, I can speak it, but I don't feel it, do I?

Daiva concludes that one cannot bring the language in one's luggage; one cannot pack the sounds that one hears on a bus, in a shop, on a street. She cannot hear the language she feels among parents waiting for their kids by the school.

---

[1] Inspired by conversations with Daiva Macko

She remembers her friend who was trying to explain the Russian word *тоскá* in Lithuanian. Her friend was dissatisfied with a descriptive nature of this word in Lithuanian. 'Similar to *ilgesys* or *liūdesys*', she said; in English, that would be longing or sadness. But there was a lack of feeling for her friend when she tried to express what she meant in Lithuanian; those words did not have the right feeling, did not have soul that *тоскá* had. It did not feel right for her. Daiva was wondering if she could ever feel it, experience *тоскá*. Daiva doubted whether she could feel what she cannot describe or grasp in words – could she?

She changed and hurried home. On the bus, Daiva continued dreaming in Lithuanian and felt how her mother tongue calmed her down; it slowed her down. Those persistent thoughts of returning to Lithuania came back to her, as she was missing the feeling of how it used to be. 'What happened to the old 'me'?' she asked herself once again. 'Daiva from the past does not exist anymore, emigration did something to me, I have entered a mental place which cannot be left'. At the same time, she is surprised how this little town in Scotland, how her house in a newly built neighbourhood, her new profession is becoming more and more familiar, and less and less full of otherness. Nevertheless, Daiva finds her new life as an unfolding internal drama, a struggle between the everyday, romanticised past and the search for the life she aspires to.

And it is not that Daiva is not practical about her everyday life, as if there were too much of discomfort, as if her daughter were not happy here, or as if her husband were not trying his best, but she struggles to accept this new life. 'When does all this, ALL of it, become good enough?', she asks herself once again:

> I am afraid to lose the sense of home that I had over there (in Lithuania). Am I replacing it with something that is so unfamiliar to me that I cannot fully grasp and comprehend? How can I know that it is good enough, that it is something that has a prospect of becoming decent, something that you could say 'this is right'? We (Daiva and her husband) were dreaming of different life, and we are here. But why do those dreams do not help me to overcome the annoyance that I feel, why am I so easily irritated?

It would be downplaying the importance of the experience expressed in previous paragraphs if I said that Daiva, as other migrants, is simply experiencing the mismatch of how life should be and how life feels. This feeling of not belonging *here* (Scotland) and not belonging in the same way as it used to be *there* (homeland), and not even knowing if she wants to belong, to imagine her life in Scotland, shows the real complexity of what the idea of home has become. Living what Boccagni (2017) describes as being-away-from-home and searching-for-home-again is an everyday challenging practice for Daiva. Emigration is a thought-provoking experience, as it forces a migrant to discover and expand the notion of home through occurrences of unpredictability, the sense of incompleteness and continuous exercise of placing oneself in a new environment.

Migrants are not only migrants; they are people who are searching for a meaningful life for themselves. And they have reasons to be where they are; there is always a story, a good story. Yet, what is meaningful is changing in time; it could have once been a wish to be paid more, to be treated better, to live further from parents, siblings, wife or husband for a while; to live closer to the beloved one; it could have been a search for a challenge, or being curious to know: 'how is life *there*?' What happens after the initial wish is achieved (or abandoned as not being important any more) is somehow groundwork for how the idea of home is approached by people living abroad.

In my PhD thesis (Stepušaitytė 2017), I was writing about the process of searching for home away from home through leaving places, losing attachments to places and creating places for home-to-become. Once we experience that fixity is not what goes hand in hand with a notion of home, the whole experience of home, which should provide comfort and emotional security, becomes temporary and fragile. The whole business of home becomes an illusion, which is always remembered differently, or imagined, as the journey towards one's dream is usually not as smooth as one wishes. Nevertheless, the dreaming of home becomes the desired proof that one has made the right decision to live far from one's family, friends, and very often mother tongue; it is the state that is driven by the explicit longing that is directed towards this ambiguous something that we call 'home'.

Being one of many to have decided that I want to continue dwelling elsewhere but my homeland, speaking and dreaming in a language which I don't master as my mother tongue, I had to accommodate the idea that I am not 'at home' in the sense as I was 'at home' in Lithuania. I often remind myself that my idea of 'home' is actually my journey home, which I call *Not-Yet Home*. I am getting there. By 'there' I do not mean a particular place, but rather an action of moving towards the state of being when living inside-out and outside-in correlate. This understanding has allowed me to 'live home' in a new light, which is not so much fixed, but rather a mobile experience—not something that becomes associated with the real, but rather the desired, though never complete.

The idea of home has become for me not a given and not a static concept. I am in the midst of being *Not-Yet Home*, which is experienced through reactions, observations, and correspondences with the world, and all of that stimulates my actions and movements towards a new input to my understanding of 'home'. For Daiva, it is the use of language, which exemplifies complex relations to places, memories, daydreams and people. She feels as if she cannot live a life through words she cannot feel as she could in Lithuanian; she is worried that she may struggle to connect to her daughter's worldview, which might be more English than Lithuanian. Our experiences of being *Not-Yet Home* are different, and it would be naïve to believe that there is a single pattern of being a migrant, and all, ALL those variations of experiences are equally important. I cannot conclude this piece with a statement or a tip as to how others should understand 'home', but I can only say that I am extremely curious to know how Daiva will approach her feelings towards life in Scotland, how she will shape her homing, and where that will take her. To be known in the future.

References

Boccagni, P. (2017), *Migration and the Search for Home: Mapping Domestic Space in Migrants' Everyday Lives* (New York: Palgrave).

Stepušaitytė, V. (2017), *Meanings of Home: Lithuanian Women in Scotland*. Unpublished PhD thesis. Heriot-Watt University, Edinburgh, Scotland.

(Re-)Learning to Belong in Europe

Cristina Clopot

My first encounter with Máiréad's work was through one of her earlier publications, *Narratives of Place, Belonging and Language* (Nic Craith 2012). The reading immediately drew me in, as an immigrant going through the process of reconsidering place, identity, and learning to belong in academia. Máiréad's work reflected on belonging and the migrant condition through a literary anthropology focused on the works and lives of several migrant writers. The book touched on topical themes such as the link between language and identity or the creativity drawn from living the liminal life of a migrant. At the time, I lingered more on the lived experiences of the writers that echoed my own circumstances. This intellectual encounter, however, marked the beginning of our academic relationship and set some of the core themes that interest us both today – language, identity, heritage and, of course, belonging.

Studying migration and its intricacies is a rewarding, if not challenging task. There is a marked affective dimension to the immigrant experience. Feelings and experiences of migration and its aftermath stay with the migrant for a long time; sometimes these are transferred to descendants also. It might begin with either the exhilaration or fear of the voyage, and then turn to wander as the migrant begins to explore the new place and begins to find her/his feet. Once settled, however, new affective dimensions become emphasised as the migrant begins to miss people and places.

Once settled into a new society, migrants react in different ways. There is, however, as Nic Craith observes, a commonality of experiences brought by what many 'describe [as] the obsessive desire to belong to the host community' (Nic Craith 2012: 147). Such observations are commonplace in studies of migration that outline the complexities of these aspirations. For example, Cressey's (2006) study of British Pakistani/Kashmiri youngsters shows that their efforts to belong lead to negotiation of what to keep from one's own culture and what to adopt from the host community, with a sense of loss mediating these decisions. 'Migration is both a loss and a gain', wrote Máiréad (Nic Craith 2012: 172), reflecting on her analysis. Migration offered the writers a new set of experiences that they could reflect on in their work. Migration also forced them to build new selves, learn to live and feel in new languages. The experience, as the writers' cases show, presents a source of creative expression that they can draw on in their work. This creativity, although maybe not in the literal sense in which it is the case of writers, is manifested in immigrants' social lives more generally as they find creative ways of solving everyday problems.

Migration, however, also brings negative feelings, especially as one reflects on the point of departure. Antonsich (2010) hyphenates *be–longing* to emphasises the affective dimension. The longing that is experienced has a reference point in a different time (the past) and a different place (departure point), and often manifests itself as nostalgia (May 2017; Clopot 2017; Boym 2001). This nostalgia, enabled in the case of migrants or refugees by a physical departure from home, enables a malaise that some people treat by seeking connections with people from their own background (Fortier 2006), or by engaging with their homeland if possible (Christou 2011).

We have witnessed a marked increase in discussion on migration and its effects across Europe. Intercultural encounters through migration impact both the traveller and the host society, and often lead to clashes and misunderstandings that are part and parcel of the growing concern about migration across Europe and beyond. The migrant, subjected to othering processes, becomes a source of threat for the host society. Media and populist movements across Europe draw on these experiences to spiral inflammatory accusations at national level based on (often) imaginary threats. Meanwhile, in such hostile and challenging conditions, under suspicious eyes from the state, media, neighbours and colleagues, the migrant tries to learn to belong.

Complexities of Belonging in Europe Today

One of the categories of people that have unwillingly contributed to the current state of discontent with migration across Europe is that of refugees and asylum seekers. Fleeing dangerous situations in their homelands, such people leave behind home, earthly possessions and sometimes family. Once arrived in Europe, however, they find an increasingly hostile reception from host countries. The situation is not much different for older migrants who do not yet have a recognised status. It was towards this category that we (Hill, Nic Craith and Clopot 2018) turned our attention a few years back, reflecting on the case of Bajuni Somalis in Glasgow, which shows the dangers of reifying heritage. Belonging, many researchers (e.g. Antonsich 2010) have noted, is a flexible and fluid concept that has both an internal and an external dimension. Refugees are often caught in processes where the 'politics of belonging' (Yuval-Davis 2006) are at play in a brutal manner, where fear leads to value judgements that lead institutions to deny their claims to belong. The 'dirty business of boundary maintenance' (Yuval-Davis 2006: 204) was observed thus in the case of the Glasgow

Bajuni who had arrived in the UK without proof of status documentation, as refugees often do. The Bajuni's applications for asylum seeker status were denied by the Home Office whose evaluation was based on an inflexible testing system that used outdated interpretations of Bajuni heritage to verify the individuals' claims of belonging. The case of the Bajuni points to the difficulties in implementing rights-based approaches to heritage (see, e.g., Logan 2012) in the absence of legislative frameworks that recognise a wider definition of heritage. There has been a marked critique of the UK's use of heritage to refer to the monumental remains of the past and the decision that it would not ratify the 2003 UNESCO Convention for Intangible Cultural Heritage (Nic Craith, Kockel and Lloyd 2018). This restricted notion of heritage has hard consequences for the Bajuni claims to belong, as the unwillingness of officials to recognise that heritage changes and evolves leads to tragic consequences for these people, who are found in a vulnerable situation. The case also points to the fragility of belonging – claims that seem clear-cut for the individual can be easily denied by official institutions. It also shows the tragic consequences of the misguided uses bureaucratic systems can develop, based on a static interpretation of heritage. In an anthology focused on refugee writers' experiences, Chris Abani (2018) reflects on his experience fleeing Nigeria: 'in the body of the refugee we come to terms with the fragility of nationhood and stability'. His comment also perfectly encapsulates the fears driving negative receptions from the host country.

While the example presented above represented a rather grim reality of the UK refugee and asylum seeker system, there are also studies that present more hopeful conclusions. Such studies emphasise how, once given a chance, even those in the most fragile situations can initiate processes of healing and connecting with place. One such case is the study by Wernesjö (2015), focused on young unaccompanied refugees in Barnsele village in Sweden. These young people, who had often lost connections with other family members and their homes, illustrate ongoing processes of learning to belong. Against scarcities of housing and rejections, they formed new relationships and place-attachments. The case also emphasises the external aspect of belonging, that while one might feel one belongs somewhere, one's claim needs to be confirmed by externals, who might decide to reject that claim of belonging. Unlike the Bajuni case, in the small Swedish village claims for belonging are not enacted by an institution, but rather by the youngsters in the village, who often refuse to acknowledge the refugees as part of the community. Racialised immigrant discourses in the village influence their perception and attitudes, but all is not lost. Some of the participants to the study present experiences where they had formed relationships with members of the majority population, or hope to do so in the future. Hope is an important feeling for refugees, and it is one that can sustain them through the harshest conditions.

Although arriving in these situations as refugees, once settled in the host country, people often develop a dual sense of belonging (Clopot 2018), straddling attachments for both the place of departure and their new home. In *Narratives of Place, Language and Belonging*, this is reflected in discussions of languages that refugee writers use in their everyday lives and in their writing. One such writer is John Semprún, who had fled the coercive political regime in Spain under Franco to settle in France. While this is just an example, there are many other refugees who become such '"in between" writers' (Nic Craith 2012: 6) navigating their lives through bi- or multilingualism.

Difference

The example of the refugees presents perhaps an acute example of the difficulties of belonging. Considering other forms of migration leads to exposing new layers of complexity in our analysis of belonging. One of the core themes outlined in *Narratives of Place* is that of difference: 'There is always some attribute which will identify the migrant as different – and even as children, the migrants are aware of a strong sense of difference and often hostility' (Nic Craith 2012: 139). Difference often triggers negative reactions in the host society, as the quote suggests. Yet, preserving difference and enabling spaces of inclusion where migrants can rejoice in their difference can also lead to positive effects. Fortier's (1999) study of Italians in London, for instance, shows the importance of symbolic buildings and institutions for fostering a sense of belonging. Such places allow migrants to dwell in their nostalgia; they can interact with members of their community and enable dual processes of reasserting belonging to the past – the 'longing' part of the word – and place attachment in England: rooting in place, the 'be-' part. Immigrants' experiences, such as those of the Italian community in England, show how change and continuity can go hand in hand, the liminality of individual lives (Clopot 2016; Clopot and McCullagh 2019) is configured through adaptation processes.

Belonging also has a temporal dimension, and 'memories of past belonging can be used to create a sense of belonging in the present' (May 2017: 409). The case of Russian Old Believers in Romania, a small religious and ethnic group that fights to preserve its heritage and identity shows this (Clopot 2017; Clopot and Nic Craith 2018). This is not a case of refugees, first- or second-generation migrants; rather, the example shows the long end of migration: how, once settled in a place, descendants of migrants meet new challenges in sustaining community belonging. Belonging is an ongoing process; assessing what to hold on to from this past and what to adopt from the host society is a continuous challenge throughout one's life. Moreover, communities that have migrated a long time ago face the challenge that difference might be erased altogether. The Russian Old Believers in Romania, and other historical migrant groups, are acutely aware of this, and see the danger of adaptation processes that threaten to erase inner-community belonging. To avert this, Old Believers mobilise notions of duty to-wards their ancestors who had defended the right to preserve their faith with their lives. These discourses are necessary to ensure adherence to the commu-nity in the future. Anchoring arguments of belonging in the mythical past of the ancestors also leads to a resistance movement against globalisation, bordering processes (Barth 1969) that are necessary to ensure the sustainability of their heritage and their identity.

Multicultural societies?
Having looked at newer and former forms of migration and displacement, we thus come full circle. What are we to make of these examples more generally? It could be argued that the case studies presented outline how belonging is con-tingent and fragile, it can be easily denied and later on becomes more difficult to sustain without great loss.

There are some bigger reflections in order though, and the themes of inter-culturality and multiculturality featured in this book that has served as a refer-ence point are apt for this discussion. In *Narratives*, Máiréad presents argu-ments in favour of embracing multiculturality across Europe. As the problematic cases presented here suggest, multiculturalism has shown its shortcomings. It has even led some people to proclaim that it might be 'dead' (Modood 2014). Claims for recognition from different groups are combined with efforts to re-dress inequalities, and account for gaps in representation as national heritage narratives often seek to erase or silence minority or immigrant heritages.

At this present time, there is no other case more salient than that of the UK. With a Brexit process finally confirmed and a transitional period in place, questions of identity and belonging are ever more relevant, both for British (Scottish/Northern Irish/Welsh) citizens, but also for the millions that have made these islands their home. Migration was one of the thorny issues that led to the Brexit vote, and as the transition period is going forward, new narratives of belonging to Europe will be created for both majority and minority groups. For the most vulnerable groups, this is likely to lead to more rejections of claims of belonging, and difficulties in expressing difference. While there is a growing recognition that feelings of belonging are essential for people's well-being, for the most vulnerable groups in the UK and in Europe, such as migrants and refugees, claims to belong are not always easily settled. In this light, Máiréad's earlier conclusions on the lived experiences of migrant writers become ever more important and can be extrapolated to other migrants also. There is a lot to be gained from accepting and fostering difference. As she concludes in her study, this can lead to new reservoirs of creative expression and enriched intercultural encounters, as well as an increased empathy for the other.

References

Abani, C. (2018), 'The Road', in: V. Thanh Nguyen ed., *The Displaced: Refugee Writers on Refugee Lives* (New York: Abrams).

Antonsich, M. (2010), 'Searching for Belonging: An Analytical Framework', *Geography Compass* 4(6): 644–59.

Barth, F. (1969), 'Introduction', in: F. Barth ed., *Ethnic Groups and Boundaries: The Social Organization of Culture Difference* (London: Allen & Unwin), 9–38.

Boym, S. (2001), *The Future of Nostalgia* (New York: Basic).

Christou, A. (2011), 'Narrating Lives in (e)Motion: Embodiment, Belongingness and Displacement in Diasporic Spaces of Home and Return', *Emotion, Space and Society* 4: 249–57.

Clopot, C. (2016), 'Liminal Identities within Migrant Groups: The Russian Old Believers of Romania', in: D. Downey, I. Kinane and E. Parker (eds), *Landscapes of Liminality: Between Space and Place* (London: Rowman & Littlefield), 153–76.

Clopot, C. (2017), 'Ambiguous Attachments and Industrious Nostalgias', *Anthropological Journal of European Cultures* 26(2): 31–51.

Clopot, C. and C. McCullagh (2019), 'The Construction of Belonging and Otherness in Heritage Events', in: U. Kockel, C. Clopot, M. Nic Craith and B. Tjarve (eds), *Heritage and Festivals in Europe: Performing Identities* (London: Routledge), 47-62.

Clopot, C. and M. Nic Craith (2018), 'Gender, Heritage and Changing Traditions – Russian Old Believers in Romania', in: W. Grahn and R. Wilson (eds), *Gender and Heritage: Performance, Place and Politics* (London: Routledge), 30–43.

Cressey, G. (2006), *Diaspora Youth and Ancestral Homeland: British Pakistani/Kashmiri Youth Visiting Kin in Pakistan and Kashmir* (Leiden: Brill).

Fortier, A-M. (2006), 'Community, Belonging and Intimate Ethnicity', *Modern Italy* 11(1): 63–77.

Hill, E., M. Nic Craith and C. Clopot (2018), 'At the Limits of Cultural Heritage Rights? The Glasgow Bajuni Campaign and the UK Immigration System: A Case Study', *International Journal of Cultural Property* 25(1): 35-58.

Logan, W. (2012), 'Cultural Diversity, Cultural Heritage and Human Rights: Towards Heritage Management as Human Rights-Based Cultural Practice', *International Journal of Heritage Studies* 18(3): 231–44.

May, V. (2017), 'Belonging from Afar: Nostalgia, Time and Memory', *Sociological Review* 65(2): 401–15.

Modood, T. (2014), 'Understanding "Death of Multiculturalism" Discourse Means Understanding Multiculturalism', *Journal of Multicultural Discourses* 9(3): 201–11.

Nic Craith, M. (2012), *Narratives of Place, Belonging and Language: An Intercultural Perspective* (Basingstoke: Palgrave).

Nic Craith, M., U. Kockel and K. Lloyd (2018), 'The Convention for the Safeguarding of the Intangible Cultural Heritage: absentees, objections and assertions', in: N. Akagawa, and L. Smith (eds), *Safeguarding Intangible Heritage* (London: Routledge), 132-146.

Wernesjö, U. (2015), 'Landing in a Rural Village: Home and Belonging from the Perspectives of Unaccompanied Young Refugees', *Identities* 22 (4): 451–467.

Yuval-Davis, N. (2006), 'Belonging and the Politics of Belonging', *Patterns of Prejudice* 40(3): 197–214.

(Re-)Making Heritage
Biblical Theatre and Ecology in *Noah and His Ship*

Kerstin Pfeiffer

Some sentences stick with you long after they have been uttered – for better or for worse. *'Zukunft braucht Herkunft'* is one of those for me, and it is forever associated with my former history and philosophy teacher, although he was citing the philosopher Odo Marquard (2003). I still blame Mr Henn somewhat for sending me on a path of mild obsession with the relationship between past, present, and future. 'Oh, what's the point of *that* in this day and age?' is another one of those 'sticky' sentences - *'that'* being my PhD on medieval English theatre. True, medieval literature and drama is not exactly where the money is, and for many, it is the *hic sunt dracones* section on the Arts and Humanities map. But it opens up more potential research avenues and paths through an academic career then even many a senior academic in English Studies might be able to think of. All it takes sometimes is a slight shift of perspective. For me, an impetus to think differently about medieval theatre came from one of my first research conversations with Máiréad Nic Craith. Hitherto, no one had yet responded to my musings on medieval English mystery plays and their relationship to their post-World War II reincarnations with 'that's a really interesting example of intangible cultural heritage'.

If one comes at medieval theatre via literature, it is sometimes easy to forget that the (admittedly few) late medieval plays we still have, were conceived to be performed and experienced together with others, not read in solitude. It is equally easy to lose sight of what makes modern productions of medieval plays not only popular but relevant in the here and now. It is not primarily whether or how carefully they excavate (fossilised) relics of the medieval mystery playing tradition. The latter does, of course, have its uses, for example in academic contexts, where trying to recreate medieval staging practices has helped us to understand better how mystery plays were performed in the fourteenth and fifteenth centuries. Yet the strength of theatre and drama as an art form lies in its immediacy and contemporaneity. Theatre (and performance more generally) is an event that always occurs in the present because it is incomplete without its witnessing participants, i.e. the audience, with whom it is in a constant 'autopoietic feedback loop' (Fischer-Lichte 2004: 284). Consequently, a different viewership – more secular, more socially and culturally heterogeneous than in the late Middle Ages – necessarily makes biblical or mystery plays a very different enterprise today from what they once were.

Thinking about modern performances of medieval biblical plays as a performing art that is 'constantly recreated' (UNESCO 2003) by communities in response to their social and physical environments turns the focus on the sociocultural work they do in the present. Here, I would like to focus on a brief example from the Chester Mystery Plays in the summer of 2018 to illustrate how exploring such plays as an element of intangible cultural heritage practice allows us to focus more closely on how their (symbolic) meanings can be adapted and reshaped depending on the needs of the diverse communities they address today (Kockel 2007). The example that I use, *Noah and His Ship*, is not intended to provide some sort of paradigmatic case; nor would I like to claim that my brief thoughts on this matter here answer all the questions that the scene, let alone the entire production, raises about ideas of community, identity, authority and heritage. Rather, the 2018 Chester version of the Flood is simply one among many possible examples that illustrate how older theatrical forms are not only adaptable enough to respond to present needs and preoccupations, but that it can provide an experiential form of dialogue between actors and audiences, present and past, reality and performance (Haldrup and Bærenholdt 2015). I was drawn to this particular scene because it engages with something at the forefront of my mind in the summer of 2018 – the human impact on nature.

The Chester Mystery Plays are produced every five years, by Chester Mystery Plays Limited, a charitable company. They are based on a collection of pageants dating to the first half of the 17th century, which narrate biblical stories in 24 episodes from the Fall of Lucifer to the Coming of the Antichrist, with some additions and creative expansions from the anonymous playwright(s) (Lumianski and Mills 1974). Each of these was associated with a local guild (the Ironmongers, for example, produced the Crucifixion) and was likely staged in processional performance on pageant wagons, which stopped at specific points along a pre-determined route through the city. There is no unbroken performative tradition, as the performances of the Chester plays were suppressed after 1575 and only resumed again as part of the 1951 Festival of Britain festivities (Mills 1998). Since then, they have been produced in regular intervals at changing venues in Chester and involving different numbers of people. Yet, as Tyler points out, 'presenting [...] essentially medieval plays occupies a complex and problematic place within [a] modern city's cultural landscape' (2010: 322). At their inception, the Chester plays served as a celebration of shared civic identity and heritage, as well as a didactic vehicle for the central tenets of Christianity.

They were performed by local members of the trade and craft guilds in the city streets and associated with specific points in the pre-Reformation religious calendar such as Whitsun. Their twentieth and twenty-first century incarnations are instead now integrated into modern frameworks of celebration, be this nationally (such as the 1951 Festival of Britain) or locally.

The 2018 production of the Chester Mystery Plays was a large-scale undertaking, involving around two hundred local volunteers as actors and musicians, as well as a production team led by artistic director Peter Leslie Wild and music by Matt Baker. Performances took place between 27 June and 14 July inside the nave of Chester Cathedral, where a thrust stage with an elaborate multi-level set had been specially constructed against the backdrop of the choir's stained-glass windows. Writer Deborah McAndrew had selected material from nineteen of the Chester plays, which she combined to a seamless performance, using recurring images and musical elements to create a continuous narrative. The actor playing Cain at the beginning of the evening, for example, re-appeared as the Antichrist later. Part one of the 150-minute performance covered Old Testament materials such as the Fall of Lucifer, the Creation and the Flood, as well as the Nativity and the Slaughter of the Innocents. Part two starts with the Temptation of Christ, and ends with the last Judgement, but focuses mainly on sequences associated with the Passion. McAndrew's editorial choices were guided by the aim 'to make the story clear for someone who'd never heard of Adam, or Noah, or even Jesus' (Chester Mystery Plays 2018: 14).

Unlike their fifteenth- and sixteenth-century counterparts, modern producers cannot necessarily presume knowledge of Christian doctrine among their increasingly diverse audiences. Consequently, there is a clear tendency to focus on conceptual readings of the existing play-texts and to 'secularise' the plays in modern productions through concentration on universal themes such as death or grief and re-imagining them in modern settings (Normington 2007; Tyler 2010; McGavin 2010). The 2018 Chester Mystery Plays are no exception to this rule. The presence of universal themes in the material goes some way to help answer the question why the mystery plays, steeped as they are in medieval lay piety and urban communities, have been finding vast audiences over the past nearly 70 years. I have argued elsewhere that the continuing popularity of biblical plays raises questions about what images of heritage and of community are presented in these (Pfeiffer 2019), but I will leave these aside here for now. Deborah McAndrew identified two themes in the sixteenth-century material that she says, 'chime with our modern world' (Chester Mystery Plays 2018: 14): human conflict and humankind's relationship with nature. They provide the lens not only for selecting but also for organising material into coherent narratives through staging decisions. The nature theme stands out in three sequences in particular: *The Creation of the World*, *Noah and His Ship*, and the coming of the *Antichrist*, in the form of the fifteen signs of the end of the world associated with the Antichrist's prophets. I want to focus here on a couple of scenes in the *Noah and His Ship* sequence, the third sequence in part 1 of the 2018 production.

Noah's Flood, traditionally produced by the Waterleaders and Drawers of Dee, is one of the best-known plays from the Chester cycle, due to its inclusion of the gossiping, drinking and quick-witted Mrs Noah, who remains resolutely unconvinced by her husband's warnings of the great flood and eventually has to be forcibly carried into the Ark by her sons. Even though McAndrew's script retains much of the original dialogue, the somewhat misogynistic humour is considerably toned down. The 2018 production reframes Mrs Noah's reluctance to believe that the flood is coming as disbelief about the consequences of human behaviour for the planet. Yet like its late medieval precursors, this production also uses contemporary clothing to highlight continuities and to make connections between the biblical past and the present. Cain probably provides one of the clearest examples. After his exile for the murder of his brother Abel, Cain, or more to the point the actor playing Cain, returns to the stage dressed as a suicide bomber and carrying a backpack full of weapons which he hands out to Herod's soldiers just before the Slaughter of the Innocents which concludes part 1 of the performance. In the second half, he returns as the Antichrist in a black leather trench coat and army boots – a costume which for many Germans like me almost inevitably conjures up images of Gestapo officers. However, Noah's costume also makes a point. Noah makes a first, unassuming appearance as a street cleaner with a high-vis vest and litter-picker at the end of a lively party that humanity throws (mostly for itself), picking up the litter left behind by the revellers. Polystyrene food containers of the type used in fast food outlets up and down the country, single use plastic bottles have all been carelessly thrown on stage. The street cleaner quietly tut-tuts as he goes about his work and soon after changes the high-vis vest for a beige multi-function one and a tool belt to return as Noah at the beginning of the *Noah and His Ship* sequence.

As part of the sequence, God appears on stage and looks around in disgust at what humanity has done to the earth. Picking up a plastic bottle carelessly dumped by another member of the cast at the end of the party, he looks at it wearily, pensively, before venting his anger about humankind to the audience. The party and particularly this single use plastic bottle, which is later on passed between characters 'as gingerly as an unexploded bomb' (Green 2018), become symbols of humankind's reckless mistreatment of the planet. While a result of God's wrath, the Flood and therefore the destruction of humanity are clearly marked out as the consequence of human behaviour in McAndrew's and Wild's production: the sea around Noah's ark is full of plastic waste.

Many of the scenes in Noah and His Ship were reminiscent of images in the BBC documentary film series *Blue Planet II,* presented by David Attenborough, which had been broadcast in October and November 2017. A couple of episodes showed oceans choked with plastic waste; images of a turtle tangled in a plastic sack until it is rescued by the film crew, and albatrosses feeding their chicks a lethal diet of plastic waste in the last episode illustrated the threat of plastic pollution to wildlife. The programmes provided powerful images that catapulted the problem of plastic pollution into public awareness (Thompson 2019). While the performance made no overt reference to *Blue Planet II,* at least none that I was able to hear, the similarities between the plastic-chocked waters of the Flood and those that had captivated an audience of around 14 million viewers (BBC, 2018) were not lost on the audience, including the elderly lady sitting next to me in the cathedral. 'Did you see that David Attenborough programme about the plastic waste?' she asked me at the start of the interval, looking pensively first at her own and then at my single use plastic water bottle. It was a blister-ingly hot evening on 6 July when we watched the performance, and with hun-dreds of bodies in the audience, even the nave of Chester Cathedral provided little relief from the heat, so water was very much required. 'I think I might buy one of those reusable ones they sell now, you know, one of the metal ones,' my neighbour continued. I simply nodded, feeling increasingly guilty for having for-gotten to bring my own.

The decision by the 2018 artistic team to revise the play of the Flood through an ecological lens brings to mind Lavery's (2019: 258) call to revisit the dramatic canon and to reread, analyse, and revise it for its ecological potential. *Noah and His Ship* does not provide what Lavery (2019) refers to as an 'ecologi-cal image'. An 'ecological image', for Lavery, is one that foregrounds its own ma-teriality, that gives the spectator time for reflection, that has a political dimen-sion and that 'refuses to be fathomed and exhausted' (2019: 261). Yet *Noah and his Ship* provides 'images of ecology' in cultural historian Andrew Ross' sense of the term (1994: 172), that is images which represent the human impact on na-ture. Ross (1994) distinguishes between 'images of ecology' such as burning oil fields or starving polar bears and an ecology of images. The latter is a term he borrows from Susan Sontag's *On Photography* (1977); it refers to the produc-tion, distribution and consumption of images. Where they come together, Ross argues, images of ecology and the ecology of images can act as a powerful mo-biliser for public awareness about the impact of human activity at the expense of natural ecosystems. The images presented in *Blue Planet II* provide a memorable example in that they resulted in a step change in interest and awareness of plastic ocean pollution (Thompson 2019). The staging of *Noah and His Ship* seems to consciously tap into the affective power of the images of plastic pollution, and it would certainly be worthwhile to examine the contexts and the image community in this particular ecology of images further, but I will have to leave this for another day. Suffice to say here that if the artistic team's intention had been to use the story of the Flood to invite the audience to question our throwaway culture and exploitation of the planet, anecdotal evidence in the form of my own response and that of my seat neighbour would suggest that they succeeded.

The biblical story of the Flood lends itself to an environmental makeover not only because of its subject matter. Our engagements with the natural environment in performance (and perhaps more generally) always involve engagement with the past, present and future in that present performance can help us understand our past transgressions against nature, and towards future change and improvement. Similarly, biblical or mystery plays of the type that are still performed in Chester or York operate on a threefold temporal plane. They stage what is considered the biblical past (e.g. the Flood) in the medieval or twenty-first century present, but always draw a link to an imagined future – the Last Judgment or the Apocalypse. The 2018 Chester *Noah and His Ship* complicates matters further in that the Flood acts as a visual representation of the biblical past that could be our dystopian future.

In reframing of the Flood as a result of human transgressions against the planet rather than (primarily) as a transgression against divine will, *Noah and His Ship* exemplifies the tendency in modern productions of medieval biblical plays to secularise or universalise the subject matter mentioned earlier. While this may be understood as a necessary response to the changed needs and preoccupations of modern audiences, we should not lose sight of the fact that even plays with ostensibly biblical subject matter are always products of social interactions – between audiences and performers, between actors and characters, and their contexts and environments. For all that, late medieval biblical plays had a religious and didactic dimension, they also provided an opportunity for engagement with social realities. For example, the Towneley play of the *Slaughter of the Innocents* presents the killing of the first-born children on King Herod's orders as theft, thus making a point about violence as an aspect of feudal rule as an underpinning of the urban economy (Sponsler 1997). And documentary evidence suggests the characters such as Herod himself could function as a projection screen for commentary on contemporary rulers and dignitaries (Pfeiffer 2015: 118-19).

The 2018 Chester *Noah and His Ship* and its reimagination of the biblical Flood as an ecological catastrophe of human making reminds us that no matter in which era, local people actively own and modify their heritage and culture, and that the social significance of heritage places and practices can and does change over time (Byrne 2008). Through the decision to avoid the ritualised heritage performance that still characterises many productions of the York Mystery Plays, for example, *Noah and His Ship* invites the audience to form new responses to the story of the Flood and to define for themselves its meaning centred on their own present and future. Ritualised heritage performance is here to be understood as fairly strict adherence to late medieval play texts and performance styles (see also Tyler 2010). The play texts we have for medieval biblical plays like those of Chester are, of course, at best blurry snapshots of what might have gone on in performance. Reimaging the Flood as the result of the (present) human destruction of nature avoids the past of the Chester Noah play (both its medieval and its twentieth century past) persisting as a kind of performance residue or ruin, regularly displayed and rediscovered and yet always distant. 'Ruins provide us with ancestors not with descendants,' Sarah Beckwith notes (2001: 10). Approaching performances like the 2018 Chester *Noah and His Ship* with an eye to both performance aspects and its status as an example of intangible cultural heritage guides our eye away from the ruins of the text and the performance heritage which offer themselves up as 'fetish to our nostalgia' (Beckwiths 2001:10) and sharpens, instead, our eye for the descendants. It allows us to focus more closely on *how* a heritage practice like mystery playing can function as a vehicle for present priorities and concerns by shifting our gaze towards the people in whom the heritage practice is embodied (Nic Craith and Kockel 2015; Taylor 2003) and reminds us of the importance of the experience of the performance event (Fischer-Lichte 2004) and of heritage itself. Or, as Smith put it, 'heritage has to be experienced for it to be heritage' (Smith 2006: 47).

References

BBC (2018), *Blue Planet II tops 2017 TV ratings*. Available at www.bbc.co.uk/news/entertainment-arts-42641146 (Accessed: 29 November 2019).

Beckwith, S. (2001), *Signifying God: Social Relation and Symbolic Act in the York Corpus Christi Plays* (Chicago: University of Chicago Press).

Byrne, D. (2008), 'Heritage as Social Action', in Fairclough, G., R. Harrison, J. Jameson and J. Schofield (eds), *The Heritage Reader* (London: Routledge), 149-173.

Chester Mystery Plays (2018), *Chester Mystery Plays*, 6th July 2018, programme (Chester Cathedral: Chester).

Fischer-Lichte, E. (2004), *Die Ästhetik des Performativen* (Frankfurt: Suhrkamp).

Green, M. (2018), 'Review: Chester Mystery Plays 2018 at Chester Cathedral' *Cheshire live*, 9 July. Available at https://www.cheshire-live.co.uk/whats-on/theatre/review-chester-mystery-plays-2018-14870351 (Accessed: 30 November 2019).

Haldrup, M. and J. Bærenholdt (2015), 'Heritage as Performance', in Waterton, E. and S. Watson, S. (eds), *The Palgrave Handbook on Heritage Research* (Basingstoke: Palgrave Macmillan), 52-68.

Kockel, U. (2007), 'Heritage versus tradition: cultural resources for a new Europe?', in Demoissier, M. (ed.), *The European Puzzle: The Political Structuring of Cultural Identities at a Time of Transition* (Oxford: Berghahn), 85-101.

Lavery, C. (2019), 'How Does Theatre Think Through Ecology?', in Bleeker, M., A. Kear, J. Kelleher and H. Roms (eds), *Thinking Through Theatre and Performance* (London: Methuen), 257-269.

Lumiansky, R. and D. Mills (1974), *The Chester Mystery Cycle,* vol 1 (London: Oxford University Press).

Marquard, O. (2003), *Zukunft braucht Herkunft. Philosophische Essays* (Stuttgart: Reclam).

McGavin, J. (2010), 'Performing Communities: Civic Religious Drama', in Treherne, E. and G. Walker (eds), *The Oxford Handbook of Medieval Literature in English* (Oxford: Oxford University Press), 200-218.

Mills, D. (1998), *Recycling the Cycle: The City of Chester and its Whitsun Plays* (Toronto: University of Toronto Press).

Nic Craith, M. and U. Kockel (2015), '(Re-)building Heritage: Integrating Tangible and Intangible', in Logan W., M. Nic Craith and U. Kockel (eds) *A Companion to Heritage Studies* (Malden, MA: Wiley), 426-442.

Normington, K. (2007), *Modern Mysteries: Contemporary Productions of Medieval English Cycle Dramas* (Cambridge: Brewer).

Pfeiffer, K. (2015), '"A stroke schalt thow beyre": Staging Anger in Plays of the Massacre of the Innocents', *The Mediæval Journal* 5(2): 109-130.

Pfeiffer, K. (2019), 'Re-Writing the Script: Updating the Massacre of the Innocents for the Twenty-First Century', *Skenè Journal of Theatre and Drama Studies* 5(1): 189-196.

Ross, A. (1994), *The Chicago Gangster Theory of Life. Nature's Debt to Society* (London: Verso).

Smith, L. (2006), *Uses of Heritage* (London: Routledge).

Sontag, S. (1977), *On Photography* (New York: Farrar, Straus and Giroux).

Sponsler, C. (1997), *Drama and Resistance: Bodies, Goods, and Theatricality in Late Medieval England* (Minneapolis: University of Minnesota Press).

Thompson. R. (2019), 'Has Blue Planet II had an impact on pollution?', *Science Focus*, 12 April. Available at https://www.sciencefocus.com/nature/has-blue-planet-ii-had-an-impact-on-plastic-pollution/ (Accessed: 29 November 2019).

Taylor, D. (2003), *The Archive and the Repertoire: Performing Cultural Memory in the Americas* (Durham, NC: Duke University Press).

Tyler, M. (2010), 'Revived, Remixed, Retold, Upgraded? The Heritage of the York Cycle of Mystery Plays', *International Journal of Heritage Studies* 16(4-5): 322-36.

UNESCO (2003), *Convention for the Safeguarding of the Intangible Cultural Heritage* (Paris: UNESCO).

Vergangenheitsbewältigung at a Distance
Rachel Seiffert's *The Dark Room*

Maggie Sargeant

The relationship between past and present, between the events of the Second World War and the sociopolitical condition of contemporary Germany continues to be explored today. The debate around Angela Merkel's early open-door response to the migrant crisis in August 2015, for example, was often framed around the notion that Germany had a unique humanitarian responsibility in light of the Holocaust. But it was not just the victimised 'other' which stimulated the reaction to migrants seeking refuge in the west, but also the victimised 'self' at the end of the war: Taberner (2017), for example, points to this phenomenon in a *Zeitonline* interview with historian Andreas Kossert on the refugee crisis: 'Doch kann die deutsche Erfahrung von Flucht und Vertreibung nach 1945 vielleicht auch ein Schlüssel für Empathie sein' (Florin 2015).

Literary presentations have also continued to re-ignite the debate around the appropriateness of conferring victim status on Germany. *Im Krebsgang* (2002) by Günter Grass provoked warnings about the danger of relativising German suffering with that of Germany's victims, and *Beim Häuten der Zwiebel* (2006), an account of the period between Grass's adolescence and the publication of *Die Blechtrommel* in 1956, led to an outcry in the German press and the feuilletons as he made public the previously suppressed fact of his membership of the Waffen-SS in the closing months of the war. Grass, like his fellow member of the literary Gruppe 47, Heinrich Böll, had been regarded as the 'conscience of the nation' and so the reception of this 'admission' was at times bitter. Grass's claims that post-war writers had failed to engage with German suffering during the Second World War, with *Im Krebsgang* filling this gap, also attracted criticism from literary critics and writers, not least by Walter Kempowski, whose second volume of a four-part masterpiece, *Das Echolot* (1999), describes Germans fleeing from eastern Germany as the Red Army advanced. Four years before the publication of *Im Krebsgang*, W. G. Sebald published his essay *Luftkrieg und Literatur* (1999), which accused post-war German writers of self-censoring through their silence about the bombing of German towns because conferring victimhood on the German population was taboo. Consequently, '[d]er wahre Zustand der materiellen und moralischen Vernichtung, in welchem das ganze Land sich befand, durfte aufgrund einer stillschweigend eingegangenen und für alle gleichermaßen gültigen Vereinbarung nicht beschrieben werden' (Hage 1998).

The term *Vergangenhbeitsbewältigung* (mastering or overcoming the past) was initially applied to early fictional representations of the Second World War and came to refer more generally in the late 1950s to a past that had not been mastered (Peitsch 1995). There is some evidence, however, that Germany's relationship with its National Socialist past, although undoubtedly still complex, had been 'normalised' to some extent by the early part of the new century, for example, in the publication of a series of articles on the bombing of German cities in 2003 (Der Spiegel 2003). Today, there is a political impetus in some quarters, particularly on the right, to allow the Third Reich past to become history, seen to some extent in the condemnation of the culture of remembrance by the AfD in the Bundestag in the last twelve months (Deutsche Welle News 2019). However, there is an unabated hunger for movies and books about the Holocaust and the Second World War, which film-makers and writers have satisfied in the last thirty years: blockbusters such as Spielberg's *Schindler's List* (1994) and Polanski's *The Pianist* (2002) have been succeeded by productions as different as the Hungarian concentration camp film *Son of Saul* (2015) and Waititi's comedy *Jojo Rabbit* (2019). Indeed, the latest offering, *The Painted Bird* (2019) by the Czech director, Václav Marhoul, caused an outcry because of its staged brutality in the images of a child wandering alone through a bleak warworn eastern Europe. Like Seiffert, Marhoul also draws a direct line from the Second World War to current world conflicts and to the rise of the right (Rose 2020). Literary presentations of the 1933-45 period also offer a similar range in tone, style and assumed audience to the cinema, including the picaresque detective novels by Philip Kerr (1989, 1990, 1991), the autobiographical *Am Beispiel meines Bruders* by Uwe Timm (2003), and the quasi-genealogical *The Book of Dirt* (2017) by Bram Presser.

Rachel Seiffert's Booker prize-nominated work, *The Dark Room*, which was published in 2001 and translated into German in the same year, did not provoke much discussion in Germany despite the fact that it deals specifically with the perpetrator-victim binary and the relationship that grandchildren of German soldiers have with their grandfathers. Contemporary German identity is at the heart of this work, and yet, reviews published in Germany were much more concerned about the age of the writer (30 at the time of publication) and her family background, which is seen as her motivation for setting her first fictional work in Germany. There are no recriminations that the writer's biographical distance (she is an English-speaking writer educated in Australia and the UK) necessarily deny her the right to place the Third Reich at the heart of her work. Such a neutral reception would have been beyond German society in the fifties, when publishers were aware that the relationship of the author to that period in Germany's recent history could affect sales, as was the case with Erich Maria Remarque's fictional Second World War novels, *Der Funke Leben* (1952) and *Zeit zu leben und Zeit zu sterben* (1954). The publisher expressed concerns about the antipathy which would arise, given that Remarque had found it necessary to flee from Germany during the Nazis' rise to power and had, therefore, not experienced the events at the heart of these novels. Indeed, only a censored version of the latter novel was available in German until 1989 (Sargeant 2005: 73-74). It seems that the passage of time has all but eradicated such sensitivities.

The Dark Room is a collection of three novellas whose narratives are each concerned with an aspect of the Second World War. The order of the narratives shows the chronological progression towards war under the National Socialists, the privations experienced by the German population during the war and in its immediate aftermath, and the influence which that period continues to have on German society at the end of the twentieth century. Rather like the characters in Heinrich Böll's early prose works, Seiffert's main characters are victims of circumstances over which they have no control, at least superficially. The first story, 'Helmut', tells of a boy born in 1921 with a minor disability, the effects of which push him to the periphery of the groups to which he wants to belong: he is refused entry to the community of boys playing in the street, unable to raise his right hand above his shoulder (and perform the Hitler salute) and unfit for service in the Wehrmacht. The local photographer to whom Helmut is apprenticed encourages Helmut's talent for photography, and he observes Berlin as it changes over the war years through the lens of the camera. Seiffert uses the camera motif (a little obviously) to underline the isolation of the boy. The obsessive precision with which he documents the dwindling population is the device that transforms the reader into a witness of the effects of the war on the city's population. The second story, 'Lore', portrays the weeks after the war as Germany is occupied by the Allies and the process of denazification begins. Lore's father, a Nazi officer, has been arrested by the Allies, while her mother is interned in a camp run by the Americans. The adolescent is instructed by her mother to take her four siblings on a journey through Germany, from Bavaria to Hamburg where her maternal grandmother lives.

The story details the privations of the children, their feelings for their parents, and the developing symbiosis with a putative concentration camp victim whom they meet on their travels. The final novella, 'Micha', is set at the end of the 1990s and portrays the ambivalent feelings that develop in a young teacher for his beloved deceased grandfather when he finds out that he was a member of the Waffen-SS stationed in today's Belarus. The desire to establish whether his grandfather was actively involved in atrocities becomes an obsession and threatens the stability of his family. The uneasy truce that Micha makes with his deceased grandfather and, therefore, with the past at the end of the novel, represents perhaps the most important message about Germany's modern relationship with the legacy of the Third Reich. Seiffert avoids the simplistic suggestion through her protagonists that Germany was as much victim as perpetrator. Susanne Baackmann suggests that the Lore narrative 'navigates the perpetrator's point of view through the lens of a young protagonist who invites empathy as a victim of personal and historical circumstance', but that the Lore figure is exposed as 'nonetheless ideologically biased' and, therefore, an 'implicated witness' (Baackmann 2017: 166). This could also be said of Helmut, who uses his photographic work to dissociate himself from the events around him, and of Micha, who believes Germans continue to be implicated by the actions of their forefathers.

As the title suggests, the photographic image is the principal leitmotif which binds the stories. A number of academic accounts of the work take up the photography theme. Rau, for example, argues that Seiffert 'repeatedly contests that photographs are effective mnemonic devices or unequivocal pieces of evidence. At best, they are a version of 'reality' or merely a synecdochal representation' (Rau 2006: 297). This view is indeed reflected in all three stories; for example, Lore has to conceal photographs of the family with her Nazi father in uniform since anyone seeing these images in the changing political landscape at the end of the war is unlikely to view them as simple family portraits. While Lore is a child who suffers, she is also aware (sometimes only vaguely) of how the victors of this war will interpret the recent past.

Reviewers of Seiffert's work in both Germany and the UK tended to focus on the containment of both 'good' and 'evil' within the same individual:

> Wie ist es möglich, dass jemand gut und böse zugleich sein, recht und unrecht haben kann? [...] Dass Familienväter, Onkel und Großväter während des Nationalsozialismus gleichzeitig Mörder und liebevolle Verwandte waren, ist nur scheinbar ein Widerspruch, der Psychologen und Historiker seit langem beschäftigt (Schubert 2001).

And this aspect is most marked in the Lore and Micha narratives. Micha's story is the closest in time to the current day (set between 1997 and 1999). He struggles to reconcile the barbarous images he finds during lengthy periods of re-search in the library with his childhood memories of his grandfather, especially since he attributes responsibility for the atrocities committed on the Eastern Front to a Germany to which he still feels linked through the family line. He is unable to identify with the emotions of his fellow teachers and the pupils in his school during the annual commemorations of the liberation of the concentra-tion camps because he sees their reactions to history as a selfish attempt to identify with the victims of Nazism and so disengage themselves from the events of the Holocaust. Micha's criticisms reflect the psychology described by Buruma (1994) in his comparison of Japan's and Germany's relationship with the Second World War. Buruma describes a sizeable group of people in Germany at the out-break of the first Gulf War who expressed themselves as *betroffen* because they made a specific personal connection between the Second World War and the Gulf War and were, therefore, unable to support the war in the Middle East. Buruma attributes to the notion of *Betroffenheit* 'a sense of guilt, a sense of shame, or even embarrassment. To be "betroffen" is to be speechless, but it also implies an idea of moral purity. To be "betroffen" is one way to "master the past", to show contriteness, to confess, and to be absolved and purified' (Bu-ruma 1994: 21).

Fulbrook also reflects on this phenomenon among the post-war genera-tions in the reactions to Daniel Goldhagen's controversial *Hitler's Willing Execu-tioners* (1996), which 'played both on their desire to wallow in a degree of public guilt on behalf of their forebears, and at the same time vindicated their sense that, since 1945, they had made a clean and final break with the past' (Fulbrook 1999: 230). Seiffert clearly recognises the contradictions of this phenomenon and uses a discussion between Micha and his Turkish-German partner to exam-ine it critically (Seiffert 2001: 289-290):

> - Every year it's the fucking same. The students read survivors' accounts. Everyone cries these 'we didn't do it' tears. Then the essays get marked, the displays are packed away, and we move right on with the next project. [...]
> - It's taboo, untouchable. It says our school is open and good.
> - I think it is. I think it's good. The students should learn about it.
> - But it's perverse, Mina. They identify with the survivors, with the victims. [...]
> - And they shouldn't cry?
> - Yes, they should cry! But they should cry that we did this. We did this, it wasn't done to us. [...]

- They are being taught that there are no perpetrators, only victims. They are being taught like it just happened, you know, just out of the blue people came along and did it and then disappeared. Not the same people who lived in the same towns and did the same jobs and had children and grandchildren after the war.

Micha's attitude changes by the end of the novel as a result of the knowledge he gleans from Jozef Kolesnik, a Belarussian whom he interviews in order to try and establish his grandfather's involvement in atrocities. To Micha, Jozef is the personification of the innocent victim, and so the revelation that he acted as an interpreter for the SS, and was also guilty of killing innocent Jews, is all the more shocking. Micha's unequivocal moral view, revealed in his remorse about a past to which he feels shamefully linked, is shaken by the knowledge that Germans were not the only perpetrators. For his part, Jozef accepts responsibility and acknowledges that any excuses he can provide are inadequate (Seiffert 2001: 345):

> - I made the choice, you see? I watched the Germans kill the Jews for almost two years and then I killed, too. It was my choice, do you see?
> [...]
> - It is hard to say this, Herr Lehner, even after so many years. It is difficult to know this about myself, do you see? I can give all these reasons. I lost my father, I was hungry, I wanted to help my family, orders were orders, I was not responsible, they said the Jews were Communists, Communists caused my pain. Over and over I can say these things. Nothing changes. I chose to kill.

This confession has a force beyond the narrative. Although Seiffert places Jozef on solid moral ground through his rejection of excuses, there are nevertheless echoes of the justifications commonly used by soldiers as criminal acts came to light in the decades after the war. The reactions to the 1995 touring exhibition *Vernichtungskrieg. Verbrechen der Wehrmacht 1941 bis 1944*, in which shocking photographs were shown of ordinary soldiers committing barbarous acts, resulting in significant public controversy, is a case in point (Heer and Kaplan 1998). For Micha, the discovery that those whom he has regarded as victims of Germany were also perpetrators leads him to reconcile himself with the grandfather's past, a somewhat unlikely development given the strong views he had expressed about the disengagement inherent in Holocaust commemorations. It is this 'equivalence strategy' that reveals a certain helplessness in dealing with such a complex issue.

Seiffert uses the relationship between Micha and his Turkish-German partner to provide a counterweight to Micha's obsession with Germany's past: this democratic multicultural society is proof that the past has indeed become history. The birth of a daughter is instrumental in reconciling Micha with his grandmother (and, through her, with the memory of his grandfather): 'Micha looks into his daughter's face, watches her accept another family member without a flicker. Her family map spreads out; unproblematic, curious, unhesitant' (Seiffert 2001: 390). Micha's struggle is the conduit through which Seiffert demonstrates her belief that Germany's modern identity emerges through the painful process of acknowledging its National Socialist past in order that it can move forward positively. Nevertheless, the transformation of the victim into perpetrator, the notion that all human beings have the capacity for evil, is a strategy that gives credence to the theory that the Second World War was 'a war like any other', as expounded, for example, by neo-revisionist war veterans who justify the actions of German soldiers by setting them in the context of warfare in general. An article published in *Die Zeit* in 1995 exemplifies this approach in which the writer, a war veteran, states that this war was 'ein Stück Barbarei, was er immer war und bleiben wird', in which atrocities occurred, '[a]uf allen Seiten' (Schmückle 1995: 48). Certainly, Seiffert's presentation has moved on from the attitudes of the fifties and early sixties in which the notion of the guilty German soldier was firmly denied. In fact, the Micha story evidences the phenomenon described as follows (Messerschmidt 1995: 49):

> dieses Verdrängen, dieses Nicht-Wahrhaben-Wollen dessen, was dieser Krieg wirklich war, [ist] beinahe so etwas wie eine psychische Notwendigkeit für die Nachkriegsgesellschaft gewesen. Es gab in fast jeder Familie einen Vater, einen Bruder, einen Sohn, der Soldat war, und sich vorzustellen, daß die nun alle an einem verbrecherischen Krieg beteiligt waren, geht für eine Gesellschaft einfach über deren Kraft.

Micha's determination to reveal his grandfather's past has the capacity to destroy relationships within the family, and, by extension, to rupture society.

It was suggested by one reviewer that 'Seiffert tiptoes around controversy by keeping the political context vague' (Hopkin 2001). The story of Helmut, however, does not entirely support this criticism. In this narrative, Seiffert explores the economic roots of the support for Nazism. His development from child to adult is traced against the background of the political events of the time. Helmut is born in 1921 to a family characterised as poor and hardworking, who simply want to improve their economic circumstances. However, the family's early and growing contentment is based on a dual lie, the concealment of Helmut's disability in the photographs taken by his photographer employer annually and the economic stability resulting from the father's promotion as *Zwangsarbeiter* arrive to support the German war effort. Helmut's story supports the idea, used successfully by the NSDAP, that the Treaty of Versailles created an impoverished and weakened Germany. Seiffert calibrates Germany's economic recovery (and the better financial situation of the family) to *Kristallnacht* in November 1938 and to the National Socialist imperial ambitions, couched in propagandistic euphemisms: 'To the east, new land is found; old land found again. So many things are better now: brighter, cleaner. Helmut sees it in his parents' faces, knows it is enshrined in law' (Seiffert 2001:16). Both Helmut and his parents appear naïvely to accept that support for Hitler will improve their lot, and the reader never learns whether the consequences for those German citizens who do not fit the Nazi template are ever discussed. The parents join the NSDAP and 'the Führer joins the family portraits on the wall [...]' (Seiffert 2001: 17). The National Socialist movement is seen at first to create a cohesive society whose aims, to act 'in the service of the next one thousand years' (Seiffert 2001: 28), bring advantages to those who belong. However, Helmut, by virtue of his disability, does not fit the blueprint of National Socialist youth and he is, in time, alienated from his family through the influence of the all-pervasive regime. This emerges when his parents return from an outing to greet Hitler after the occupation of Paris: Helmut 'feels their pride, knows he isn't part of it, turns away from their faraway eyes' (Seiffert 2001: 29). Thus, the cohesion which the process of *Gleichschaltung* provides also results in splitting the family. Hitler's portrait symbolises the supplanting of Helmut at the centre of his parents' lives. Although historical events provide the timeline in this narrative, there is no discussion by the characters of the political context, a vacuum the reader is expected to fill from a position of anachronistic knowledge. Only those events which affect the lives of the characters directly are reported: neighbours experience bereavement as male relatives are killed at the front, and women and children leave for the countryside.

Helmut's forced dissociation from society imposes on him the role of witness which he fulfils by obsessively keeping a record of the number of trains which pass through the nearby station and by developing the technical aspects of photographing the reducing number of people on the streets of Berlin. He is, however, a naïve witness unable to draw any conclusions from the records he maintains. He has an accidental encounter with an SS unit rounding up a group of Gypsies, but the imperfect photographs taken fail to reflect the true nature of the event. Without a good image to reflect the discomfort and fear he has experienced first-hand, he is unable to interpret the scene and can only see the photographs through the eyes of his photographer employer, a witness once removed, and the prints are discarded in disgust. The focus on the minutiae of the photography process contributes to the self-delusive way in which Helmut experiences the world. However, the reader is never invited to condemn Helmut – he has been shaped by his parents and the society in which he has become an adult.

The story of Lore contains elements present both in the Helmut and Micha narratives. Lore and her siblings are also victims; they are separated from their National Socialist parents and forced to survive alone as her mother is interned in a camp run by the Americans and her father is arrested by the Allies. Lore is faced with a dilemma – she loves her father, but she begins to understand that this new society rejects him. For the sake of survival, the parents must be disavowed. This suppression of the relationship is presented in the symbolic burying of photographs of her father 'as deeply as she can [...] and before she goes back to the barn, she takes care to wash her hands clean again in the stream.' (Seiffert 2001: 140). She is aware that Nazi emblems must be hidden forever and hears mixed opinions about the veracity of publicity disseminated by the Allies on the barbarity of the concentration camps. Despite her vague understanding of the atrocities committed in the name of Germany, Lore's subconscious connectedness to the barbarity is revealed by her half-waking dreams of the skeletal images of the concentration camps displayed to the public. The role of Thomas, the putative ex-concentration camp inmate who befriends the children, is at first unclear. It emerges towards the end of the story that he has adopted someone else's identity by using a tattooed number and stolen papers in order to dupe the occupying authorities. Despite Lore's distrust of him at first, the children learn to rely on him and he is added to the list of adults who symbolise both 'good' and 'evil' (Seiffert 2001: 210):

> She tries to unravel Thomas and prisons and skeleton people; lies and photographs; Jews and graves; tattoos and newspapers and things not being as bad as people say and the badges in the bushes and the ashes in the stove and the sick feeling that Thomas was both right and wrong; good and bad; both at the same time.

A changed Hamburg – 'the old being buried by the new again' (Seiffert 2001: 215) – allows Lore to look forward to a future when 'she won't remember any more how it was before' (Seiffert 2001: 217), prefiguring the emergence of a *Wirtschaftswunder* that will provide a camouflage for the past. Micha's story, in contrast, ends with the painful acceptance that his efforts to engage in a truthful *Vergangenheitsbewältigung* are inevitably diluted by the distance of time.

References

Baackman, S. (2017), 'Lore or the Implicated Witness: Seiffert's Postmemory Work', in: M.J. Martínez-Alfaro and S. Pellicer-Ortín (eds), *Memory Frictions in Contemporary Literature* (Cham: Palgrave Macmillan), 165-186.

Berberich, C. (2011), '"We Shall Be Punished": Positionality and Postmemory in Rachel Seiffert's The Dark Room and Uwe Timm's In My Brother's Shadow', *Holocaust Studies: A Journal of Culture and History* 17(2–3), 261–82.

Buruma, I. (1994) *The Wages of Guilt: Memories of War in Germany and Japan* (New York: Farrar, Strauss and Giroux).

Der Spiegel (1993), 'Als Feuer vom Himmel fiel', *Der Spiegel*, 6 January. First part available at https://www.spiegel.de/spiegel/print/index-2003-2.html (accessed 5 March 2020).

Deutsche Welle News (2019), 'Germany's culture of Holocaust remembrance irks right-wing AfD', 23 April. Available at https://www.youtube.com/watch?v=wgfEjM-BH_M (accessed 13 March 2020).

Florin, C. (2015), 'Flüchtlingstrecks wecken kollektive Erinnerungen', *Zeitonline*, 23 October. Available at http://www.zeit.de/2015/43/flucht-fluechtlinge-zweiter-weltkrieg-vertreibung-kirche (accessed 8 March 2020).

Fulbrook, M. (1999), *German National Identity After the Holocaust* (Cambridge: Polity).

Goldhagen, D. (1994), *Hitler's Willing Executioners* (New York: Knopf).

Grass, G. (2002), *Im Krebsgang* (Göttingen: Steidl).

Grass, G. (2006), *Beim Häuten der Zwiebel* (Göttingen: Steidl).

Hage, V. (1998), 'Feuer vom Himmel', *Der Spiegel* 3. Available at https://www.spiegel.de/spiegel/print/d-7810012.html (accessed 12 March 2020).

Heer, H. and Kaplan, J. (1998), 'The Difficulty of Ending a War: Reactions to the Exhibition "War of Extermination: Crimes of the Wehrmacht 1941 to 1944"', *History Workshop Journal* 46: 187-203.

Hopkin, J. (2001), 'The Healing Process', *The Guardian*, 28 July. Available at https://www.theguardian.com/books/2001/jul/28/fiction.reviews (accessed 18 March 2020).

Kempowski, W. (1993) *Das Echolot. Fuga furiosa. Ein kollektives Tagebuch. Winter 1945* (Munich: Knaus)

Kerr, P. (1989) *March of Violets* (London: Viking).

Kerr, P. (1990) *The Pale Criminal* (London: Viking).

Kerr, P. (1991) *A German Requiem* (London: Viking).

Lüddemann, S. (2015), '"Luftkrieg und Literatur": Sebalds Anklage gegen Autoren', *Neue Osnabrücker Zeitung*, 18 June. Available at https://www.noz.de/deutschland-welt/kultur/artikel/586616/luftkrieg-und-literatur-sebalds-anklage-gegen-autoren#gallery&0&0&586616 (accessed 13 March 2020).

Messerschmidt, M. (1995), 'Hitlers ehrenhafte Komplizen', *Zeit-Punkte* 3: 49–53.

Peitsch, H. (1995), 'Towards a History of Vergangenheitsbewältigung: East and West German novels of the 1950s', *Monatshefte* 87(3): 287-308.

Presser, B. (2017), *The Book of Dirt* (Melbourne: Text).

Rau, Petra (2006), 'Beyond Punctum and Studium: Photography and Trauma in Rachel Seiffert's The Dark Room', *Journal of European Studies* 36(3): 295-327.

Remarque, E.M. (1952), *Der Funke Leben* (Cologne: Kiepenheuer und Witsch)

Remarque, E.M. (1954), *Zeit zu leben und Zeit zu sterben* (Cologne: Kiepenheuer und Witsch)

Rose, S (2020), 'The Painted Bird: 'My film isn't depraved. It's truthful', *The Guardian*, 16 March. Available at: https://www.theguardian.com/film/2019/sep/03/the-painted-bird-review-vaclav-mahoul (accessed 16 March 2020).

Sargeant, M. (2005), *Kitsch und Kunst: Presentations of a Lost War* (Pieterlen: Peter Lang).

Schmückle, G. (1995), 'Was es heißt, Soldat zu sein', *Zeit-Punkte* 3: 45-48.

Schubert, E. (2001), *Süddeutsche Zeitung*, 19 March, 17.

Sebald W.G. (1999), *Luftkrieg und Literatur* (Munich: Hanser).

Seiffert, R (2001), *The Dark Room* (London: Heinemann).

Seiffert, R (2017), *A Boy in Winter* (London: Virago).

Seiffert, R (2017), 'Rachel Seiffert: My grandparents were Nazis. I can't remember a time when I didn't know this', *The Guardian*, 27 May. Available at https://www.theguardian.com/books/2017/may/27/grandparents-nazis-inspired-my-novel-about-holocaust#img-1 (accessed 8 March 2020).

Taberner, S. (2017), *Transnationalism and German-Language Literature in the Twenty-First Century* (Cham: Palgrave Macmillan).

Timm, U. (2003), *Am Beispiel meines Bruders* (Cologne: Kiepenheuer und Witsch).

The Lightness of Heritage

Katerina Strani

> When we want to give expression to a dramatic situation in our lives, we tend to use metaphors of heaviness. We say that something has become a great burden to us. We either bear the burden or fail and go down with it, we struggle with it, win or lose. (Kundera 1984: 64)

Heritage as a Duty

Where I come from, heritage is something very heavy. It is a load that you carry, but which also defines you. It explains things about you that you cannot. You cannot escape it. You have to carry it, acknowledge it, honour it, protect it, preserve it. You have to pass it on exactly as it was passed on to you. You can't change it; you don't have the right. It is sacred. If you do, the bones of your ancestors will creak, and the sound will haunt you forever.

My heritage is heavy: 5,000 years of art, science, philosophy and literature. Even though it's part of me, I'm still learning about it. It defines me, yet I still don't know it. I feel it in songs, in theatre, in my language. My language is the language of about 15 million people (10 million at home and about 5 million abroad). Like all languages, it has many variations. They speak it differently on the mainland, in the Ionian islands, in the Aegean islands, in Cyprus, in Southern Italy, in Melbourne, in New York. My language, the Northern Greek variant with its heavy 'L's, its Ottoman and Balkan influences, its refugee soul, is not just my heritage, it is me. Three of my grandparents were refugees, Ottoman Greeks who were displaced from their homelands during the infamous 'population exchanges' when the empire was collapsing. *Yaya* Maria from Roda, now Narlı on the western shore of the Erdek Peninsula on the Marmara Sea. *Pappou* Nikolas from Peristasi, now Şarköy in Tekirdağ Province on the north coast of the Marmara Sea. *Pappou* Kostas, from Stenimahos, now Asenovgrad in southern Bulgaria. Thessaloniki, my hometown, was full of refugees like my grandparents, who brought back their own dialects in the beginning of the 20th century and helped transform the language into a spicy blend of Ottoman and Balkan Greek. There's a reason why the region of Macedonia, which has Thessaloniki as its capital, has come to mean a 'mix'. And there's a reason why our last name is Strani, which means 'strange' or 'foreign'.

And yet it was my grandmother (*yaya*) Katina, my only grandparent who was not a refugee, who was most proud of her language and her local heritage.

My beloved *yaya* Katina died in April 2019 at the age of 97, and with her died, among other things, a source of rural family dialect. She came from a gorgeous mountain village named Galatista in Northern Greece and was one of seven surviving children of the village priest. She spoke the local dialect, but because of her large family with many siblings and cousins, they soon developed their own family vernacular, or *familect* (Wertheimer 1973; Giménez Moreno and Skorczynska Sznajder 2015). She was very interested in language, wrote for the local paper, meticulously documented vocabulary and phrases from her village, but most of this was really the family code.

When I was about 16 or 17, *yaya* Katina gave me a folder with her archive work. Her notes, her lists, her home-made, handwritten dictionary, her anecdotes, newspaper clippings from the local paper with her stories and articles. As one of the priest's daughters, her columns always had a prominent place in the local press. I looked through the folder and gave it to my mum. It was put in the storage cupboard. Yaya never asked me about it, and we never discussed it. As a teenager, I was focused on other things at that time.

Language as Heritage

I never really thought about the link between language and heritage until I had my daughter. True to my name, I married an Englishman and settled in Scotland. My brother too married a Cypriot and settled in Dubai (if that is ever possible). Stranis must always be foreigners. Suddenly, the weight of language as heritage, and of heritage as a duty, became real. My (Northern) Greek heritage had to be acknowledged, unpacked and passed on. I wanted my daughter to be bilingual and bicultural, I had to stay true to my ancestors, those I knew and those before them who I never met.

What happens to heritage when it is passed on through language? What happens to language when it is passed on for heritage preservation?

Academics have been grappling with these questions, and with the link between language and heritage, for a long time. Nic Craith (2012a) has written broadly about language in its cultural context, but also specifically about the significance of language for belonging, nationhood, statehood and citizenship: 'Language can be as important, if not more important than territory or history for the generation of a sense of belonging' (Nic Craith 2006: 21). Indeed, as Nic Craith demonstrates using the examples of Sámi and Roma/Gypsy people (2006: 126-146), there are cases where language is not strictly tied to a specific territory at all. When we detach language from territory, we move to the intangible realms of heritage and to the notion of heritage as something that is passed on, as opposed to something monolithic that is meant to be admired and consumed.

When heritage is passed on through language, in the form of storytelling or schooling, it cannot possibly remain unchanged. Much to the chagrin of my fellow Greeks, I don't think I can assume this responsibility in a worthy manner, and as the only Greek parent, it is up to me to do this. My husband's role is passing on centuries of Yorkshire pride blended with London cosmopolitanism and the great Cumbrian outdoors. It will be interesting to see how much of this our daughter will decide to keep, and what to pass on in her turn. Language can only be passed on alongside other forms of heritage, otherwise it doesn't work. Religion is a huge part of the Greek psyche. Some 90% of Greeks are Orthodox (on paper, at least), and the rest are Muslim, a recognised minority that lives mostly in North-East Greece, Jewish,[1] Catholic and other. The Greek Orthodox faith is passed on through rituals and practices, smells and bells, but its language is so archaic and incomprehensible that it has become meaningless. You learn psalms by heart without having any idea what they mean, but it's the Byzantine chants and the smell of incense that makes you feel at home. That's precisely what your heritage is meant to do – make you feel at home, whatever or wherever home is.

And yet Kockel (2007: 96) writes:

> Culture becomes 'heritage' only when it is no longer current, that is, when it is no longer actively used. In other words, 'heritage' is culture that has dropped out of the process of tradition. The term 'tradition' literally refers to cultural patterns, practices and objects that are 'handed down' to a later generation, for use according to their purposes, as appropriate to their context.

The term 'tradition' makes me feel uneasy. In my case, it is something that you need to follow because of your heritage, otherwise you don't stay true to your identity (which in my case is defined by that heritage in the first place). I can't think of the word 'tradition' without having the image of Topol in my head as Tevye the Dairyman in *Fiddler on the Roof*, scolding his daughters when they

---

[1] Thessaloniki has had a sizeable and important Jewish community since the arrival of Sephardic Jews from Spain following their expulsion in 1492. In the 16th century, the Jewish population was the largest in the city, surpassing in numbers the Muslim and Christian populations (Mazower 2005: 45). Thessaloniki always had the largest Jewish population in Greece. Sadly, today this has significantly diminished (there are only about 1,200 Jewish people living in the city) but there are three Synagogues and an active Jewish Community. The multicultural roots and soul of the city are beautifully unpacked in Mazower's 2005 book *Salonica, City of Ghosts: Christians, Muslims and Jews, 1430–1950*.

decide to marry the men they love as opposed to the ones chosen by the match-maker. What I'd like to pass on is language as heritage; not as my heritage, but as my daughter's.

What happens to language when it is passed on as heritage?
There is an abundance of interesting research on family language policy in single and mixed language families. Family language policy is broadly defined as 'explicit and overt planning in relation to language use within the home among family members' (King and Fogle 2017: 315). Scholars such as Garcia (2003), Schwarz and Verschik (2013), Tannenbaum (2012), Park and Sarkar (2007), Smith-Christmas (2016), and many others have written about such family language policies and offered useful insights on the following questions (Curdt-Christiansen 2009: 353):

> Why do members of some immigrant groups maintain their languages, while members of other groups lose their language? Why do some children, growing up in a monolingual environment, become bilinguals while other children, growing up in a bilingual environment, become monolinguals? To what extent do language policies at governmental and institutional levels impede and prevent or support and promote family language policies? And what is the overarching role of the society at large?

These scholars agree on the centrality of language use at home between parents and children in determining whether the (minority) language will be maintained or lost over the generations. Spolsky (2012:7) also considers cases where 'heritage-language-speaking elders [...] pass the language to their grandchildren in a common situation where the parental generation had already given it up.' Overall, parents' and grandparents' attitudes towards a heritage/minority language is proven to be a crucial factor in language maintenance, along with family and community (see Park and Sarkar's 2007 study of Korean-Canadian immigrants).

Perhaps I should mention at this point that I don't like the term heritage language, because of the connotations that heritage has for me as something heavy, mystical and elusive, together with an inescapable duty. A heritage language implies that the language is a thing of the past (see Kockel's critique above), and that you are trying to revive it and pass it on, out of duty. García (2005: 601) seems to agree:

> [H]eritage languages [...] speaks to what was left behind in remote lands, what is in one's past. By leaving the languages in the past, the term heritage

languages connotes something that one holds onto vaguely as one's re-membrances, but certainly not something that is used in the present or that can be projected into the future.

Selim (2019) also challenges the terms 'heritage language' and 'heritage language learner' when discussing Arabs learning Arabic in diaspora or non-Arab Muslim learners of Arabic. The latter do so for religious reasons. Selim sees heritage as something monolithic and obsolete, which has a negative impact on motivation and perpetuates the linguistic hegemony of English with the binary construction of dominant/heritage language. She instead suggests the terms 'Arab learner of Arabic (ALA) and Muslim learner of Arabic (MLA)' (Selim 2019: 23) as possible alternatives. This excludes those who learn Arabic as a foreign language.

Of course, one's heritage language is not a foreign language. Even if people don't speak one of their languages from an early age and they learn it later on in life, the language can never be regarded as foreign. Doerr (2010: 55) argues that 'naming a language one's "heritage" changes an individual's relationship with his/her linguistic practices, other individuals, and an imagined ancestral homeland' (p. 55). This can be a double-edged sword. Firstly, it implies that an ethnic or cultural identity is rigidly associated with a specific language, which is what Blommaert (1996) calls 'the ethnolinguistic assumption'. Secondly, it reinforces the view that heritage languages are passed on in a sterile fashion, where language is stripped of all its zest, all its nuances, connotations, colloquialisms, playfulness, humour, and all its pragmatic functions, and it is reduced to every-day vocabulary and obscure or obsolete phrases. When languages are separated from their speakers and are seen as something to be passed on like an old watch in an unopened box, which you've inherited with pride, kept it safe in your drawer, taken it out every now and then, promised to pass on to your own children, but have no idea where it came from, who it belonged to, what it means, and whether you can use it or not, they are soul-less. If language stays dormant in your brain, even if you dust it and use it every now and then, if you don't explore it, experiment with it, make mistakes in it, have fun with it, sing with it, dance with it, laugh with it, tell stories with it, create with it, you will never make it your own. As Kockel poignantly observes, 'language, unlike many other resources, is enhanced rather than diminished by its use' (Kockel 2007: 96). And this is why for the most part people don't speak heritage languages as well as their dominant ones (Montrul 2010).[2]

Moreover, let's not forget that the choice of what can be regarded a heritage language is largely a political one (Strani 2020). When you speak a heritage language, you make a political statement about the relevant imagined ancestral homeland, but also about the status and relation to the country's dominant language. When you just speak one of your mother tongues, you make a statement about yourself and your own identity. There is no burden, no duty of displaying your heritage, just the wish, or need, to express yourself in your mother tongue – to be understood, to share a joke, to tell a story, to make a specific cultural reference.

But language as heritage is different from a heritage language. In Japanese, language as heritage has such high value and status that it also has its own term – *keishōgo*. Doerr and Lee, who have conducted studies on the role of schooling in terms of 'inheriting' the Japanese language, explain that there are two distinct types of Japanese language learning: *kokugo* and *keishōgo*. According to the authors, *kokugo* focuses on the national language and arts curriculum which is part of compulsory education in Japan, while *keishōgo* is an independent programme developed in some US cities as locally produced curricula (Doerr and Lee 2010: 194). The real difference between the two, is that parents

> do not consider the kokugo instruction [...] to be heritage language education: they argued that it was more about learning Japanese as a school subject (language arts) — as 'Japanese children do in Japan' — than about inheriting the Japanese language as Japanese Americans' (Doerr and Lee 2010: 195).

Interestingly, a similar approach is followed in my daughter's Greek complementary school, which she attends every Saturday for 90 minutes. The school follows a broad Greek curriculum, but the textbooks they use are not the same as the ones used in schools in Greece. On their cover, the textbooks have an Acropolis, a map of Cyprus and Big Ben, together with a Greek, Cypriot and British flag, and the contents of the books are full of references to British society and transliterated UK place names. I don't like it. I bought the books used in Greek schools and we look at these in parallel. Let's face it, she will probably not

---

[2] Montrul notes the term 'incomplete acquisition' used to describe the ultimate attainment of many adult heritage language speakers, alongside other 'less felicitous" terms used by researchers to describe the imperfect language abilities of heritage speakers, such as reduced, partial, truncated, deficient, and atrophied language acquisition (Montrul 2010: 19n3).

be speaking Greek with British-born kids like her. But she does speak Greek with her cousins and friends back home, so she needs to have the same points of reference with them (schoolbooks, music, contemporary social references). Some scholars have challenged the language-as-heritage approach in schooling by investigating children's views of heritage language that emerge within the classroom (Doerr and Lee 2010). Children may engage in creative practices 'which appear to contest and subvert schools' attempts to impose upon them 'heritage' identities' (Blackledge et al. 2008: 533), or they may challenge the use of heritage languages in classrooms (in this example Bengali schools in Birmingham) by arguing that 'it should be possible to choose which language to speak in a particular context' (Creese and Blackledge 2010: 558). In making these languages their own, these children seem to reject the tag of 'heritage language' attached to them, probably for the same reasons I am not comfortable with it.

Against this backdrop, to come back to parents' attitudes towards their own language, mine has always been that Greek is the language we speak with *mama*, with other Greeks in the family and at the Greek complementary school, because it's part of who we are. This is where heritage and identity get conflated. I will not attempt to offer clear definitions of either concept, not only because these don't exist, but also because heritage scholars have investigated this nexus already and I have nothing academic to add. Kockel, Nic Craith, Clopot and Tjarve (2019) offer a succinct analysis of both concepts and their interplay, including a detailed schematic representation of home and public identities, divided into self- and other-identification, and performance and heritage respectively. Clearly, heritage is part of identity (and performance is part of both), but the concepts are so multifaceted that language-as-heritage cannot be linear and straightforward. Language as heritage is who we are, so my daughter learns Greek because it's part of who she is. And this is where I fall into the trap of perpetuating the notion of heritage, and language-as-heritage, as a duty. Who am I to define her? Sure, her mother is Greek, but her father is English, and she was born and raised in Scotland. She can define herself as she pleases.

So, I went down the route of heritage as an asset, not in the way that it is used in tourism, but in the sense of Bourdieu's 'cultural capital', to increase motivation. Bourdieu recognised the social value of linguistic competence and its 'capacity to function as linguistic capital' (Bourdieu 1991: 57). The term linguistic capital is based on his concept of cultural capital as 'knowledge, skills and other cultural acquisitions, as exemplified by educational or technical qualifications' (Bourdieu 1991: 14). In line with this, my daughter should learn and speak Greek because it's useful. A lot of medical, scientific and philosophical terminology is Greek, for example. Learn how to speak it now, and you will have a Greek SQA

Higher or GCE A-Level in your pocket. It can also be fun; Greek is the language of the summer, of beaches, music and laughter, and speaking it means that we make more friends.

This approach has opened a different can of worms, however. If Greek is an asset that will help my daughter expand her social circle, gain additional qualifications and get a job, then why not invest in more useful languages such as French or Spanish? These have more resources, and therefore can be easier to learn, and there is a higher chance that her peers will be learning these languages as well. Furthermore, seeing Greek as an asset rather than as heritage seems to almost surgically remove identity from language. It ceases to be one of her languages, and instead it becomes one of the languages she can speak. If I want to pass on language as heritage, but make it *her* language and *her* heritage, I need to try something different.

What would yaya Katina do?

Her language was admittedly uninteresting. A strong rural Northern Greek dialect like many others, nothing like the Ottoman-Balkan-refugee fusion that my other grandparents offered. Yet she always spoke it with pride, talked about her family, her village, and shared their stories. Her grandkids all know the village of Galatista, its inhabitants, their families, their daily activities and the gossip, even though we only went once as young children. I personally don't remember the village at all. Her storytelling was vivid and hilarious, her humour was witty and sometimes rude (double entendres were her favourite) and the familect terms meant that it was impossible to translate any of these jokes to anybody outside the family. Yaya Katina was above all a storyteller, but the audience were strictly family members. When it comes to language as belonging, or what anthropologists sometimes call a 'sense of place' (Nic Craith 2003), she managed to create a hearth around which we would all gather to listen to her stories and feel at home, with a language that was not our own, of a village that we barely knew. It's been a year since she died, and we all still use her jokes between us, in the same language as she did. We keep asking my mum and uncle to tell us more, or to remind us of those that we may have forgotten. My daughter doesn't understand a word of it.

The Lightness of Heritage

When discussing European heritage, Nic Craith (2012b: 24), in her post-universalist thesis against singular narratives, ideals and stories, strongly argues for the use of the plural, 'heritages', rather than heritage:

Maybe it's time to begin promoting the cultural heritages of a contested continent and think more explicitly about what we choose to remember and what we choose to discard when promoting those heritages. Maybe it is time to acknowledge that there is no one collective memory in which we all share and even recognise. Instead we have multiple heritages, multiple traditions and multiple memories at different geographical levels which sometime unite – and sadly sometimes divide us.

This could be true of individuals as well. We don't have to have one heritage and certainly not have one language that represents it. That's all well and good, but how on earth can I translate my heritages into languages that I can pass on to my daughter, as her own? My own Greek language with its Thessaloniki accent (a rather stagnant variant, as I have been living in Scotland for more than half my life), yaya Katina's familect, with its brio, its fun, and its taste of the mountains of Chalkidiki, or the language of a British Greek (a *keishōgo* equivalent)? I am neither capable nor worthy of making such a decision. Heritage becomes not only a burden but a herculean task.

Moreover, if heritage is a burden, and language is dynamic, the task of 'passing on' language as heritage is near impossible. Perhaps heritage should be porous, and its boundaries should be able to filter in (and out) stimuli and elements from their environment (see Luhmann 1995: 178ff.). If, in Luhmann's terms, heritage can be considered a system that is only interested in its autopoiesis and its self-reference, but its boundaries are also porous, then can it self-reproduce with a different result each time? In theory, yes, especially if language is part of its soul – or its code, as Luhmann would probably describe it. But then what happens to its sacred and profane elements? Luhmann would say that meaning has nothing to do with human beings, but it is a systemic function and it refers to a series of selection procedures. Social systems create meaning through past selections of communications, and these selections can be categorised and stored for future (self-)reference (see Strani's 2010 critique). If we follow this thinking, then some meanings, considered sacred and normative, are retained as vital for the system's autopoiesis, others are discarded into the environment, and others are introduced and categorised as new meanings from the changing environmental contexts, or from other systems. What is considered heritage changes. Intangible cultural heritage, for example, did not exist as a UNESCO category before 2003 – an example of a Luhmann-style systemic change.

Unlike Luhmann, I believe in human agency and the capacity of people to make these selections themselves for their own heritages. I've always considered the Byzantine chanting of my church to be part of my heritage, for example, but I had no idea that it is now officially inscribed into the UNESCO Representative List of the Intangible Cultural Heritage of Humanity.[3] This is great news, but it makes no difference to how I feel about it. Systemic (state and INGO) meanings and functions are important for external recognition, but it is personal experiences of belonging, 'home' and 'sense-of-place' constructions that make the cut in the end.

Perhaps I am guilty of overthinking a process that should be simple. In *The Unbearable Lightness of Being*, Milan Kundera (1984) starts from the premise that we only live one life, which underpins the lightness of our being. Life and experiences are fleeting. Experiences and language are situated, and it is up to us to make the connections and manage this lightness which, as part of our heritage, is heavy at the same time. We cannot use language in the same way as our ancestors, or even in the same way as other people around us. The Galatista familect, the Roda, Peristasi and Stenimahos dialects from Eastern Thrace and Eastern Rumelia, the Thessaloniki blend of Greek, Balkan, Jewish and Muslim flavours, it's all been already filtered. I cannot use these in the same way, and I've contaminated them with the 'standard' modern Greek I need to use with Greeks in the UK. It's not an old watch stuck in the drawer, but a recipe that has changed because I can't source all the ingredients. The taste is still reminiscent of the old flavours, but my daughter should still be able to make it.

Language as heritage doesn't need to be heavy. It never was for yaya Katina. It never is in the writings of Máiréad Nic Craith. Language as heritage is uncomplicated yet valuable (and sometimes sacred) when it constitutes a form of storytelling and when the purpose is not to pass anything on. Through the lens of literary anthropology, Nic Craith has shown, seemingly effortlessly, that literature, art and music, as a form of self-expression and identity, communicates far more in terms of language in its context of politics, nostalgia, trauma, emotion or personal experiences than any systemic, institutionalised or otherwise formal medium. Storytellers' voices in the literary sense of the term are carriers but also conduits of language and heritage. In her latest book, *The Vanishing World of the Islandman* (2020), Nic Craith looks at the writing of Tomás Ó Criomhthain, a native of Ireland's remote Great Blasket Island, who documented his life on the island for generations to come. Tomás's language was similar to

---

[3] Decision of the Intergovernmental Committee for the Safeguarding of Intangible Cultural Heritage 14.COM 10.B.9 https://ich.unesco.org/en/decisions/14.COM/10.B.9.

that of my yaya in the sense of remoteness (one on an island, the other on the mountains) and confinement, yet his memoir gained international recognition. He didn't have a mission to pass on his language as people's heritage. But he wanted to tell his story in his own way, in the form of memoirs, so that people can remember the island and its life. And it worked

After yaya Katina died, my mum dug out her files and archives and gave them to me once again. I told her to keep them for now. I don't want to look at them. It would spoil all her stories and incomprehensible rude jokes. Language can only be passed on alongside other forms of heritage, otherwise it doesn't work. I don't want a map of my sense of place. Despite being a foreigner by default, I know where my home is. Through my own stories, I hope that my daughter finds hers.

References

Blackledge, A. Creese, A. Baraç, T., Bhatt, A., Hamid, S., Wei, L., Lytra, V., Martin, P., Wu, C., Yağcioğlu, D. (2008), 'Contesting "Language" as "Heritage": Negotiation of Identities in Late Modernity', *Applied Linguistics* 29(4): 533–554.

Blommaert, J. (1996). 'Language Planning as a Discourse on Language and Society: The Linguistic Ideology of a Scholarly Tradition, *Language Problems & Language Planning* 20(3): 199-222.

Bourdieu, P. (1991), *Language and Symbolic Power* (Cambridge: Polity).

Creese, A., Blackledge, A. (2010), 'Towards a sociolinguistics of superdiversity', *Zeitschrift für Erziehungswissenschaft* 13: 549–572.

Curdt-Christiansen, X. (2009), 'Invisible and visible language planning: ideological factors in the family language policy of Chinese immigrant families in Quebec', *Language Policy* 8: 351–375.

Doerr, N. (2010), 'Introduction: Heritage, Nationhood and Language', *Critical Asian Studies* 42(1): 53-62.

Doerr, N. and Lee, K. (2010), 'Inheriting "Japanese-ness" diversely: Heritage practices at a weekend Japanese language school in the United States', *Critical Asian Studies* 42(2): 191–216.

Garcia, M. (2003), 'Recent research on language maintenance', *Annual Review of Applied Linguistics* 23: 22–43.

García, O. (2005), 'Positioning Heritage Languages in the United States', *The Modern Language Journal* 89(4): 601-605.

Giménez Moreno, R., Skorczynska Sznajder, H. (2015), 'Family register in British English: The first approach to its systematic study', *Procedia – Social and Behavioral Sciences* 173: 222-227.

King K., and Fogle L. (2017), 'Family Language Policy', in: McCarty, T. and May, S. (eds), *Language Policy and Political Issues in Education. Encyclopedia of Language and Education* 3rd ed. (Cham: Springer), 315-327.

Kockel, U. (2007), 'Heritage Versus Tradition: Cultural Resources for a New Europe?', in Demossier, M. (ed.), *The European Puzzle: The Political Structuring of Cultural Identities at a Time of Transition* (Oxford: Berghahn), 85-101.

Kockel, U., Nic Craith, M., Clopot, C., and Tjarve, B. (2019), 'Heritages, Identities and Europe: Exploring Cultural Forms and Expressions', In U. Kockel, C. Clopot, B. Tjarve and M. Nic Craith (eds), *Heritage and Festivals in Europe: Performing Identities* (London: Routledge), 1-17.

Kundera, M. (1984), *The Unbearable Lightness of Being* (New York: Harper Collins).

Luhmann, N. (1995), *Social Systems. Writing Science* (Stanford/CA: Stanford University Press).

Mazower, M. (2005), *Salonica, City of Ghosts: Christians, Muslims and Jews, 1430–1950* (New York: Vintage).

Montrul, S. (2010), 'Current Issues in Heritage Language Acquisition', *Annual Review of Applied Linguistics* 30: 3–23.

Nic Craith M. (2003), *Culture and Identity Politics in Northern Ireland* (London: Palgrave).

Nic Craith, M. (2006), *Europe and the Politics of Language: Citizens, Migrants and Outsiders* (London: Palgrave).

Nic Craith, M. (2012a) *Narratives of Place, Belonging and Language: An Intercultural Perspective* (London: Palgrave).

Nic Craith, M. (2012b), 'Europe's (Un)common Heritage(s)', *Traditiones* 41(2): 11-28.

O'Grady, W. (2005), *Syntactic carpentry: An emergentist approach to syntax* (Mahwah/NJ: Erlbaum).

Park, S. and Sarkar, M. (2007), 'Parents' Attitudes Toward Heritage Language Maintenance for Their Children and Their Efforts to Help Their Children Maintain the Heritage Language: A Case Study of Korean-Canadian Immigrants', *Language, Culture and Curriculum* 20(3): 223-235.

Schwarz, M. and Verschik, A. eds (2013), *Successful Family Language Policy: Parents, Children and Educators in Interaction* (New York: Springer).

Selim, N. (2019), 'Arabic Should Not Be Cast as Heritage: Arabic Lives', *Ulum Islamiyyah – Malaysian Journal of Islamic Sciences* 27(1): 18-25.

Smith-Christmas, C. (2016), *Family Language Policy: Maintaining an Endangered Language in the Home* (London: Palgrave).

Spolsky, B. (2012), 'Family language policy – the critical domain', *Journal of Multilingual and Multicultural Development* 33(1): 3-11.

Strani, K. (2010), 'Communicative rationality and the challenge of systems theory', in C. Grant (ed.), *Beyond universal pragmatics: studies in the philosophy of communication* (Oxford: Peter Lang), 123-148.

Strani, K. (2020), 'Multilingualism in/and politics revisited: the state of the art', in Strani, K. (ed.), *Multilingualism and Politics: Revisiting Multilingual Citizenship* (London: Palgrave).

Tannenbaum, M. (2012), 'Family language policy as a form of coping or defence mechanism', *Journal of Multilingual and Multicultural Development* 33(1): 57-66.

Wertheimer, M. (1973), 'Toward a Phenomenological Psycholinguistics of Multilingualism', in: Krech, D. (ed.), *The MacLeod Symposium* (Ithaca: Cornell University).

Keeping an Ear to the Ground While Gazing at Things
Unravelling Textiles Heritage in the Scottish Borders

Britta Kalkreuter

In a world where climatic and neo-colonial challenges are rightly traced back to our unsustainably resource-hungry practices of production and consumption, Don Norman's hopeful characterisation that '[d]esigners are creators of preferred futures' demands that 'they (...) see the world as changeable and have to make decisions about how designs influence situations that are complex' (Norman 2016). He prefaces his observations on the future of design by saying that 'Designing focuses on the interactions between people and things', and it is in this context that Máiréad Nic Craith's and my own professional paths converge.

Well before Don Norman formulated these thoughts, most design professionals would readily accept the fact that design satisfies, above all, human needs, and many have happily argued that good design constitutes appropriate objects and systems that work for people as well as the ecologies around them. The measure of successful design practice could be presumed then to fulfil human needs, at the time of creation, but even more so in a preferred future, a better time ahead shaped by design's great continuous inventions. Surprisingly, however, a design attitude that puts users centre-stage of the creative process, that moves away from the 'designer as guru', that understands the value of deep intellectual enquiry alongside instinctive practice has languished for decades as much practice shuns the various versions of the often divisive field of 'design thinking'. And while anthropology long held an interest in material practices of design users, the connection of such systematic enquiry into human habits with professional designers was only very recently formalised into the field of design anthropology, as Gunn et al. (2013) have traced. Even now, as the twenty-first century enters its third decade with much frightening clarity about the devastating effects of existing design industry paradigms, a design focus on users of material culture remains patchy outside of the disciplines of systems and product design, and more practitioners seek to tame the known challenges of current design production with new technology and novel materials, than dare to rethink entirely our patterns of consumption (Payne 2017).

In this climate, this essay makes the case for cross-disciplinary approaches to design, and specifically reaffirms that design anthropology can add aspects of user centeredness to technology focused design innovation in a way that closes the loop between the innovation culture of much professional design practice and the commitment to human rituals so prevalent in crafts. Following Don Norman (2016: 348), the essay argues that '[w]hen you come to the fork in the road [of design futures]: Take it!' Some background on how our approaches to making have developed might be of use here.

Amongst concerns over increasing social disparities, in our era of peak stuff and an existential environmental crisis, voices have once more become more critical of design's original 19ᵗʰ century raison d'être of providing blueprints for manufacturing goods for competitive advantage, so as to design objects that generate human wants and feed corporate growth rather than satisfying reasonable needs, as Naomi Klein amongst others critiqued two decades ago (Klein 1999). In this scenario, scholars from design to economics are increasingly questioning continuous growth as a maker's key measure of success, and when many argue instead in favour of the paradigm of life quality, nobody does so more than Mikko Jalas (2006) in his doctoral study on temporalities of consumption. In it, he ponders the practice of wooden boat building to ascertain where quality and satisfaction in making might originate, and what the positive impact on widespread environmental concerns for design might be. He posits that 'the temporality of economic action constructs time as a scarce resource to be allocated optimally. However, it is equally conceivable that human action unfolds as intrinsically meaningful and self-legitimizing action' (Jalas 2006). We may regard his observations as a turn towards intangible heritage of making, something that has become a popular consideration in peak stuff design practice and theory, as he implores us to consider what time-consuming practices of making by hand have to offer in a world of over consumption. So once more, in the hundredth' year of the Bauhaus foundation and in the second century after the Arts and Crafts' rediscovery of the artisan in the industrialised world, design disciplines are being asked to take a turn towards heritage practices of making as an antidote to unsustainable production practices.

The above snapshots of current design debates and a (re)new(ed) proximity to anthropology and heritage studies very much sum up why the presence of Máiréad Nic Craith and her colleagues at the Intercultural Research Centre has had such a profound influence on design research at Heriot-Watt University, where heritage is much less now a historical account of the past 'as it has been', but rather represents, with Walter Benjamin, a present value to inform preferable futures, where anthropological enquiry is seen as an active factor in design, as part of empathy with users via ethnographic enquiry (Wasson 2000), vital in order to make a better future together, as, in Ingold's (2017: 22) words, 'we cannot be content with things as they are' and need to 'make a conversation of life itself'.

My professional journey from an art historical and largely object based research focus on design towards a wider anthropological enquiry into its heritage came after about two (happy) decades of iconographic and archival study of medieval and then modernist architecture, later somewhat opportunistically extended into architectural motifs in archival textiles as I joined the School of Textiles and Design at Heriot-Watt University. The move from forensic examination of medieval monuments across Europe to an interest in near contemporary cloth whose manufacturers often still reside in the Scottish Borders already marked a noticeable shift towards anthropology: Added to the customary contextual knowledge an art historian gleans from archival and iconographic considerations now were the accounts of breathing stakeholders eager to add their narratives to inform my analysis. So, as well as gazing at things, as I had done from many a ladder and in many a ruin, I was keeping an ear to the ground as I walked the Scottish Borders in search of its textiles heritage. I quickly gained an appreciation that contemporary making could only truly be understood while communicating and sharing experiences with the makers and other stakeholders, and the practice of approaching material culture research in this way was deepened once I had been introduced to thriving craft communities in India during visits at Design institutes, to establish student exchange partners. My enthusiasm for living practice was matched, ironically, by some of our Indian NGO partners' zest for archiving past achievements, in European style drawers and cabinets, and with the same eagerness in which colonial visitors to the continent once attempted to catalogue a vibrant and evolving field.

These experiences turned into more systematic enquiry, resembling anthropology in a rather tentative way at first, after my Head of School Alison Harley introduced me to some social sciences colleagues at a graduation ceremony. Thinking back now, the importance of that encounter with Máiréad Nic Craith and Ulli Kockel was perfectly staged by the academic gowns we all donned; they signalled to a (German) first time wearer of such sumptuous robes that seriously good academic work might follow the encounter! Exchanging findings from some recent research experiences we soon found common ground in our understanding of heritage; heritage that I might simply describe as history that looks forward as well as back. The initial trading of past experiences soon turned into a strong working relationship that greatly expanded our school's research focus towards wider societal relevance of design, welcomed our postgraduate students into a much wider community of cultural enquiry and resulted in a number of tangible research projects that combines our expertise and interests in a spirit of transdisciplinary openness.

In terms of research focus and methods, the links to the Intercultural Research Centre and its members mean continuous encouragement to look beyond buildings and cloth, to not only focus on the objects of material culture as art historians do, but practice the 'generous' and 'open ended' enquiry of anthropology (Ingold 2017) in order to include multiple perspectives on what heritage may offer for contemporary design. Working with Máiréad always inspires to give greater sensitivity to the 'human/non-human-nexus', to see heritage studies as a collaborative venue involving people, material objects and the environment (Nic Craith, Böser and Devasundaram 2016).

The best testimony for Máiréad's importance on research in the School of Textiles and Design can be found in a number of research projects that staff and students in our school have been, and still are, working on:

Grassroots engagement to increase impact of intercultural design encounters
From 2011 to 2014, the ReSIde project, with support from Creative Scotland, funded extended making exchanges for two Scottish and two Indian textile practitioners. The journeys of the participants were facilitated and chronicled by the ReSIde team of two applied arts curators and one design academic with a view to establishing differences in individual textiles making in environments of pervasive living heritage practices (India) and post-industrial designer-makers (Scotland). The project provided many enriching and often unexpected experiences to the four practitioners, but had limited measurable impact beyond the immediate participants, as is often, and almost unavoidably, the case in such expert focused programmes.

Following conversations at the IRC between Máiréad Nic Craith, myself and PhD student Chamithri Greru, this changed however, as the latter led a series of ambitious workshops with school and non-professional makers in the Scottish Borders in order to capture Scottish grassroots voices, and in turn to expose these grassroots makers to international perspectives on textiles practice. These engagements allowed actors who are frequently marginalised in official heritage discourse to connect to internationally visible expressions of textiles making; by including participants ranging from teenage art students to pension age amateurs, and by giving voice to accomplished makers as well as enthusiastic dilettantes, it was a truly 'generous' enquiry that forged an international community of textiles makers whose members continue to connect via the ReSIde–Scotland/India textiles residency social media platform.

Non-hierarchical co-design amongst varied stakeholders

The successful experience of providing a platform for interaction between official and non-authorised actors of textile making encouraged us to pursue a similar format in 2016 in order to co-design practices. A basket making charrette in June 2016 brought together textile actors in mixed multidisciplinary groups that were instructed to co-create objects through the medium of basket making. No participants were specialists in this craft, but with backgrounds ranging from design students to design theory lecturers, textile designers to technicians, from curators to historians, some very specific hierarchies were present. As part of a wider enquiry into design and craft interactions, Greru and Kalkreuter here wanted to investigate what the role of 'making' might be in design's potential move from individual practice to co-creation (Sanders and Stappers 2014). Using ethnographic observation and interviews helped understand the complex relationships people build with each other and with the material and object cultures in the fuzzy front of end of the design processes (Sanders and Stappers 2008), and a resulting paper discussed how new communities of practice emerge from people with different ways of knowing and doing. It thereby added to understanding of how co-creational and participatory methods contribute to convergences between heritage and design (Greru and Kalkreuter 2017).

Collaborative research on heritage and identity, gender and conflict

Over a number of years, Máiréad Nic Craith and Ulli Kockel have generously contributed their expertise in heritage and conflict studies to a nascent project that investigates the potential role of Palmyrah craft practice in bridging ethnic divisions in Sri Lanka's northern province. An important step in realising the project objectives has been taken in mid-2019 when a GCRF network grant allowed some 20 participants to attend a workshop in Colombo to determine the best focus for research regarding heritage crafts' use for conflict resolution, with female empowerment and sustainability emerging as surprise centres of interest amongst local partners. The local participants included Sri Lankan academics from three institutions and across the areas of integrated design, economics and geography, as well as professionals from NGOs and government organisations involved in Palmyrah craft. The day long workshop was followed by planned field visits to United Nations Development Programme (UNDP) craft projects where grassroots stakeholders offered input to our plans, before serendipitously a visit to a mine clearing site of UK charity MAG was secured where a very different kind of employment project and a fresh set of concerns for the Tamil community at the heart of the project was voiced. As we are looking forward to shaping the project further with an expanded team and our wider appreciation of local concerns and agendas, we have benefitted from the 'open' and 'generous', even 'speculative' nature of anthropology once more, with Máiréad Nic Craith guiding our collaborative project design approach all the way.

Developing distributed archives with a maximum of voices

Our last example returns closer to home, but again is characterised by inviting a wide range of expertise, whether official or grass roots. Textiles heritage in the Scottish Borders has left indelible footprints both in the built environment and in the archival collections of the region. It also features prominently in the marketing copy of many businesses where rather romantic notions of local manufacturing heritage can mask contemporary challenges of the textiles industry, and it continues to attract students and non-professional practitioners working with cloth to the region. The distributed archive project 'Spinning Yarns' seeks to hear the voice of varied stakeholders in the manufacture of textiles that continues to play a big part in the official and lived identity of the Scottish Borders despite its steep industrial decline since the 19th century. Developed by a team that counts cultural geography, design practice, anthropology, heritage studies, archival and curatorial practice amongst its areas of expertise, Máiréad's participation in it is set to greatly enhance its spirit of 'open ended' enquiry into a story told in many voices. The project seeks to document and analyse the great variety of tangible manifestations of Scottish textiles but also study intangible aspects, to elicit cherished memories alongside less comfortable recollections, and always in the firm belief that heritage is history looking forward as well as back. It has the ultimate aim of exploring what honoured customs actually have to offer contemporary textiles and fashion practice, how heritage may positively influence an industry in relative crisis as its wasteful practices has brought it to the heart of sustainability and climate change debates. The focus in exploring such heritage then is both on its significance for the life worlds and identity of past and present makers, and as to its merit for businesses seeking to weather the challenges of a global textiles industry, whether as designer-makers, as micro-entrepreneurs, or as global players in the niche luxury market for textiles. The oral history accounts and dispersed archival collections will further be decoded in order to clarify what effect changing making practices have not just on the environment and economics of places, but also on the social relations between those involved in the production and consumption of a changing industry. It is the telling of a story then that is alive and with relevance to the preferred futures that design seeks to enact.

By way of conclusion, we might remind ourselves that '[d]esign is everywhere' (Clark and Brody 2009: 1):

> Arguably, nothing today, has a greater impact on human beings. The modern world is artificial, it is a world that we have made and designed and keep on remaking and redesigning. Professional designers have been important in this process from the early twentieth century on, but so are we all, as users, consumers, interrogators, and recipients of designed environments, objects, images, experiences, services and messages.

It is in no small part through Máiréad's generosity in sharing expertise and contributing ideas on heritage and anthropology that research in the School of Textiles and Design at Heriot-Watt University is now in a better position than ever to rise to this challenge, to see the user as central to design and to see heritage as a history that impacts the past as well as the present.

References

Clark, H. and D. Brody (2009), *Design Studies. A Reader* (Oxford: Berg).

Greru, C. and B. Kalkreuter (2017), Design Charrette: Co creating design possibilities for the future', in C. Kung, E. Lam and Y. Lee (eds), *Cumulus Hong Kong 2016: Open Design for E-very-thing.* Cumulus Working Papers (Hong Kong: Hong Kong Design Institute), 283-290.

Gunn, W., T. Otto and R. Smith (2013), *Design Anthropology. Theory and Practice* (London: Bloomsbury).

Ingold, T. (2017), 'Anthropology contra Ethnography', in *HAU: Journal of Ethnographic Theory* 7(1): 21-26.

Jalas, M. (2006), *Busy, wise and idle time: A study of the temporalities of consumption in the environmental debate* (Helsinki: Acta Universitatis Oeconomicae Helsingiensis).

Klein, N. (1999), *No Logo* (London: Picador).

Nic Craith, M., U. Böser and A. Devasundaram (2016), 'Giving voice to heritage: a virtual case study', *Social Anthropology* 24(4): 433-445.

Norman, D. (2016), 'When You Come to a Fork in the Road, Take It: The Future of Design', *She Ji: Journal of Design, Economics, and Innovation* 2: 343-348.

Payne, A. (2017), 'Fashion Futuring in the Anthropocene: Sustainable Fashion as "Taming" and "Rewilding"', *Fashion Theory* 23(1): 5-23.

Sanders, E. and P. Stappers (2008), 'Co-creation and the new landscapes of design', *CoDesign* 4(1): 5-18.

Sanders, E. and P. Stappers (2014), 'Probes, toolkits and prototypes: three approaches to making in codesigning', *CoDesign* 10(1): 5-14.

Wasson, C. (2000), 'Ethnography in the Field of Design', *Human Organization* 59(4): 377-388.

Homage à Máiréad

Sophia Labadi

I met Máiréad in person twice. I remember these times vividly. The first time was in Montreal, Canada at the 2016 conference of the Association of Critical Heritage Studies. We had both been invited to give a short 'provocation' to promote the UK Chapter of this association. Máiréad enthusiastically talked to me about my 2013 book *UNESCO, Cultural Heritage and Outstanding Universal Value*. She had written a review of it for *American Anthropologist*. I was not aware of this review that had been published in December 2015. In any case, I did not want to know about or read reviews that had been written on my publications. I had just changed career and moved, from being an international consultant on heritage and culture, to academia. As an emerging academic, talking about my work or reading reviews about my books was nerve racking. I doubt my abilities, particularly as a young woman and a BAME academic, in a world that is predominantly white and where those who usually thrive, get praised and are cited, as I ironically discuss in my 2013 book, are men. I did not think that I knew the codes of the trade and had the necessary social and cultural capitals.

I still remember Máiréad's enthusiasm about my work. She talked highly of my book and told me about the very positive review she had written on it. Our encounter in Montréal, our discussion and her review massively boosted my confidence. Of course, the review was written for American Anthropologist, a key publication with over 12,000 readers with each issue. But what mattered to me is that it had been written by Máiréad. So many of her ideas, as an authoritative voice in the field of heritage, had inspired and shaped this particular work: the constructed nature of heritage and history and their uses for nationalistic endeavours; the need to find connections between intangible and tangible heritage, to dwell into the particularisms of intangible heritage; the issues with European heritage and Eurocentrism; the uses and representations of heritage and history for the constructions of national and individual cultural identities; as well as the empowerment of girls and women and their ability to shake and alter stereotypes. Her opinion as someone who had written on so many similar topics validated my scholarship; gave it credibility, legitimacy and authority. It changed the way I looked at my own work and eased some of my self-doubts. Our first meeting, Máiréad's praiseworthy words and her book review gave me much needed assurance to pursue my academic career.

The second time I saw Máiréad was in Edinburgh. She had invited me for a conversation on my book *UNESCO, Cultural Heritage and Outstanding Universal Value*. Entitled *Valuing Living Traditions—Challenges and Opportunities*, I felt privileged that the event was right on High Street, open to anybody and was attended by a diverse people, even by interested tourists! It was a series of questions that reflected the diversity of our common research interests on heritage, from a gender perspective, to Eurocentrism, to local communities' perspectives to cultural tourism, to post-authenticity or the future of the World Heritage Convention and the Intangible Heritage Convention of UNESCO. Many past and current students of Máiréad attended this event. I learnt a great deal from Máiréad about leadership and about leading the young generations during this event. She is obviously a great supervisor, able to nurture her students but also to challenge them. During discussions, it became obvious that she motivated her students to read key texts, but most importantly, in a critical manner. Research was fun for students, who were able to meet the authors of the books they read, and discuss ideas directly with them. She also encouraged her students to meet us, the older generation and not to be afraid to talk to us about their own research, to sharpen their own research questions, expand their literature and their network. She gave students a set of key skills, the ability to reach out to source people, to discuss their own work and ask them key questions that could guide them on their own research journey. She was thus able to form the academic leaders of tomorrow, able to network and reach out to others, be confident, but also to be critical and not to accept any scholarship at face value. During that meeting, I also met a number of postdocs who had been carefully guided by Máiréad through the difficult water of the world post PhD and were enthusiastically discussing their new research projects.

My next project, the book *Museums, Immigrants and Social Justice*, was very different from anything that I had done before. It was about museums; up to then I had only published on heritage. And I ventured into the topic of social justice, which was also a first for me. The method of work was in-depth ethnographic work with immigrants, in Denmark, England and France. I had never conducted an interview before the start of the project. This new project was daunting, because everything was so new. I actually did not get major funding for the project, because it was felt that I did not have the right competences and background to complete it and write a book. During these challenging times, I needed a role model. I could not dream of a better one than Máiréad. Not only has she been a prolific writer and academic, but she also has written skilfully on many different subjects: from Irish language, to immigrants, to Wim Wenders, literature, cultural diversity, human rights, media, living heritage and traditions, memory, translations, languages, anthropology and indigenous concepts. Máiréad is a living testimony of the importance of tackling a multiplicity of academic topics. Her prolific work is an antidote to what can be hyper-specialism, stale and bounded academic work. She inspired me to be daring, to explore new academic territories and to draw connections between academic publications, literature, films and current affairs. Her work convinced me that I could be interdisciplinary in my approach and plural in the themes of research I considered, without lacking in depth and rigor. It was not only her open approach to scholarship that inspired and guided me, but also her ideas. I found her long-term approach to European migration fascinating, as well as her analyses of the negative stereotypes and 'deficit theory' that affect so many migrant communities. Máiréad poetically and forcefully writes about the importance of multilingualism for immigrants, which is a key topic of my book, although she tends to focus on great novelists and I on more mundane people. How languages form identity, are ways of expressing identity and the tactical approaches to language learning and switching are also common topics shared between our publications. But maybe one of the most significant concepts I borrowed was that of 'linguistic capital', the fluency in high status languages, such as English, French or Danish and how such capital provides speakers with new powers and opportunities in life. In my research, I demonstrate how learning Danish, French and English is often considered a priority by immigrants and the role of museums in delivering such service.

Like any great scholar and mentor, her work encouraged me to expand my intellectual horizon and my mind. Her intellectual openness and her willingness to explore new intellectual horizons is the reason why I asked her to be External Examiner of the interdisciplinary MA that I launched at the University of Kent on International Heritage and Law. I asked her to examine the two modules I have developed and taught: 'Heritage and Human Rights' and 'International Heritage, Archaeology, and Development'. Not only had she the appropriate seniority and level of experience in the field, but she was surely one of the only UK scholars able to review the diversity of topics covered in this course.

Above all, Máiréad is a genuinely kind and caring academic. Academia as a discipline has been documented as thriving on hostility, aggressions, rivalries, backbiting and racism. Máiréad is none of that. She has shown openness to my work and its eclectic approach, support when I was a young and unknown academic and helpful when I needed her. As both a great academic and human being, she is definitively a role model to emulate.

References

Labadi, S. (2013), *Cultural Heritage, and Outstanding Universal Value: Value-Based Analyses of the World Heritage and Intangible Cultural Heritage Conventions* (Lanham: AltaMira).

Langfield, M., W. Logan and M. Nic Craith eds (2010), *Cultural Diversity, Heritage and Human Rights: Intersections in Theory and Practice* (London: Routledge).

Nic Craith, M. (2020), *The Vanishing World of The Islandman. Narrative and Nostalgia* (Basingstoke: Palgrave).

Nic Craith, M. (2015), Review of *UNESCO, Cultural Heritage, and Outstanding Universal Value: Value-Based Analyses of the World Heritage and Intangible Cultural Heritage Conventions* by Sophia Labadi. Lanham: AltaMira, 2013. 204 pp. *American Anthropologist* 117(4): 844-845.

Nic Craith, M. (2012), 'Heritage Politics and Neglected Traditions: A Case-Study of Skellig Michael', in R. Bendix, A. Eggert and A. Peselmann (eds), *Heritage Regimes and the State: Nomination, Implementation, Regulation* (Göttingen: Göttingen University Press), 157-176.

Nic Craith, M. (2010), 'Citizenship, Culture and the Nation-State: a European Perspective', in W. Ommundsen, M. Leach and A. Vandenberg (eds), *Cultural Citizenship and the Challenges of Globalization* (New York: Hampton), 111-26.

Nic Craith, M. (2007), 'Languages and Power: Accommodation and Resistance', in M. Nic Craith (ed.), *Language, Power and Identity Politics* (Basingstoke: Palgrave), 1-20.

Fields Elysian

Patrick Corbett

You were like many, in a sense homeless,
Seeking a place to seed a new family,
When Riccarton became your address.

You have earned this little homily.
You speak such intercultural sense
When we meet and lunch, daily

Arts today is so inter-sectional, whence
I'm so glad your group joined us,
Piling in and not sitting on the fence.

We say 'Per scribendum, sumus'.
Students have long valued insight and vision,
Now you are here, clear air will not leave us.

Together, on one more Geddesian mission,
Lead us from semi-comfort to green fields *elysian*.

Máiréad Nic Craith has been a source of wise words of encouragement at Heriot-Watt University, as I have experienced as a student-poet, and I dedicate this *terza rima* to her.

It is very fitting that Geddes' 'By leaves, we live' should be the inspiration for this collection—'Per scribendum, sumus!'—in her honour. The University, for which we have both worked, defies simple classification whilst addressing the universal challenges. A rich heritage as precursor Institution of Arts, then a Mechanics Institute, and now a Global University, defines the institution as one unencumbered by the constraints of rigorous science, engineering, and arts disciplines—no pigeonholes. In this environment, Máiréad has sought to be a point of reference for Intercultural Studies; this volume celebrates her contribution.

Mairéad Nic Craith's Academic Publications

2020

Narrative and Nostalgia: The Vanishing World of the Islandman, Palgrave.

Heritage and Festivals in Europe (ed. with U. Kockel, C. Clopot and B. Tjarve), Routledge.

'From Bengal to Scotland: Hybridity, Borders and National Narratives', in Cicilie Fagerlid & Michelle A. Tisdel (eds), *A Literary Anthropology of Migration and Belonging: Roots, routes, and rhizomes*, Palgrave, 157-180.

'Performing Scots-European Heritage, "For A' That"' (with Mairi McFayden), in Ullrich Kockel, Cristina Clopot, Baiba Tjarve and Máiréad Nic Craith (eds), *Heritage and Festivals in Europe*, Routledge, 141-155.

'Heritages, Identities and Europe: Exploring Cultural Forms and Expressions' (with Ullrich Kockel, Cristina Clopot and Baiba Tjarve), in Ullrich Kockel, Cristina Clopot, Baiba Tjarve and Máiréad Nic Craith (eds), *Heritage and Festivals in Europe*, Routledge, 1-17.

'A Sense of Place in Irish-Language Memoirs: the West Kerry Gaeltacht, 1929-1939', in Maurice Bric (ed.), *Kerry: History and Society*, Geography Publications (Dublin), 509-524.

2019

'Linguistic Recognition in Deeply Divided Societies: Antagonism or Reconciliation?' (with Philip McDermott), in Gabrielle Hogan-Brun and Bernadette O'Rourke (eds), *The Palgrave Handbook of Minority Languages and Communities*, Palgrave Macmillan, 159-179.

'The Convention for the Safeguarding of the Intangible Cultural Heritage: Absentees, Objections and Discourses' (with Ullrich Kockel and Katherine. Lloyd), in Laurajane Smith and Natsuko Akagawa (eds), *Safeguarding Intangible Heritage*, Routledge, 118-32.

2018

Cultural Heritage Conservation and Sustainability (ed. with U Kockel). Special Issue, *Sustainability* [online journal]

'At the Limits of Cultural Heritage: the Glasgow Bajuni Campaign and the UK Immigration System. A Case-Study' (with E. Hill and C. Clopot), *International Journal of Cultural Property* 25(1): 35-58.

'Gender, Heritage and Changing Traditions: Russian Old Believers in Romania' (with Cristina Clopot), in Wera Grahn and Ross Wilson (eds), *Gender and Heritage*, Routledge, 30-43.

'Homo Hibernicus Rusticus' (with U. Kockel), in Regina Bendix and Dorothy Noyes (eds), *Terra Ridens,* Vandenhoeck & Ruprecht, 220-42.

2017

Anthropology and Literature (ed. with L. Fournier). Special Issue, *Anthropological Journal of European Cultures* 23(2).

'The Representation of "Building Events" in Wim Wenders' Cathedrals of Culture' (with U. Böser and A. Devasundaram), *Studies in Documentary Film* 11(1), 1-15.

2016

A Companion to Heritage Studies (ed. with W. Logan and U. Kockel), Wiley-Blackwell.

'The New Heritage Studies: Origins and Evolution, Problems and Prospects' (with W. Logan and U. Kockel), in William Logan, Máiréad Nic Craith and Ullrich Kockel (eds), *A Companion to Heritage Studies*, Wiley-Blackwell, 1-26.

'(Re-)Building Heritage: Integrating Tangible and Intangible' (with U. Kockel), in William Logan, Máiréad Nic Craith and Ullrich Kockel (eds), *A Companion to Heritage Studies,* Wiley-Blackwell, 426-442.

'Medium and Narrative Change: The Effects of Multiple Media on the "Glasgow Girls" Story and Their Real-Life Campaign' (with E. Hill), *Narrative Culture* 3 (1), 87–109.

'Giving Voice to Heritage: A Virtual Case Study' (with U. Böser and A. Devasundaram), *Social Anthropology* 24, 433-445.

'The Anglicization of Anthropology: Opportunities and Challenges', in Helena Wulff (ed.), *The Anthropologist as Writer: Genres and Contexts in the 21st Century*, Berghahn, 73-90.

'Scottish identity is moving too fast to keep up, as Edinburgh play shows', *The Conversation* <https://theconversation.com/scottish-identity-is-moving-too-fast-to-keep-up-as-edinburgh-play-shows-63978>

'The Manchester terror drill – and why we must stop linking Arabic with fanatics', *The Conversation* <https://theconversation.com/the-manchester-terror-drill-and-why-we-must-stop-linking-arabic-with-fanatics-59334>

2015

Anthropology and Language (ed. with B. O'Rourke). Special Issue, *Anthropological Journal of European Cultures* 22(2).

'Forum Rethinking Euro-Anthropology' (multi-authored), *Social Anthropology* 23(3) 330–364.

'Public Space, Collective Memory and Intercultural Dialogue in a (UK) City of Culture' (with P. McDermott and K. Strani), *Identities* 23(5), 610-627.

'Migrant' Writing and the Re-Imagined Community: Discourses of Inclusion/Exclusion', *German Politics and Society* 33 (1-2), 84-99

'Tangible and intangible heritage' (with Ullrich Kockel), *Context* 140, 2015, 30-32.

'Re-locating the Ethnographic Field: From Being "There" to "Being" There' (with E. Hill), *Anthropological Journal of European Cultures* 24 (1), 42-62

'Anthropology and Language in Europe: Setting the Context' (with B. O'Rourke), *Anthropological Journal of European Cultures* 24 (1), 1-6

'Hybride Ethnologien des Eigenen, Anderen und Dritten: Toposophische Erkundungen am Beispiel der Pfälzer in Irland (with U. Kockel), in F. Jacobs and I. Kellers (ed.), *Das Reine und das Vermischte*, Waxmann, 73-90.

2014

'Blurring the Boundaries between Literature and Anthropology: a British Perspective' (with U. Kockel), *Ethnologie française* 44 (4), 689-697

2013

History, Heritage and Place-Making (ed. with M. Fenske). Special Issue, *Anthropological Journal of European Cultures* 21(1).

'Living Heritage and Religious Traditions: Reinterpreting Columba/Colmcille in the UK City of Culture', *Anthropological Journal of European Cultures* 21(1), 42-58.

'Introduction: History as a Resource in Postmodern Societies' (with M. Fenske), *Anthropological Journal of European Cultures* 21(1), 1-6.

2012

Narratives of Place, Belonging and Language: An Intercultural Perspective, Palgrave Macmillan

A Companion to the Anthropology of Europe (ed. with U. Kockel and J. Frykman), Wiley-Blackwell.

'Europe's Uncommon Heritage(s)', *Traditiones*, 41/2, 11-28.

'Heritage Politics and Neglected Traditions: a Case-Study of Skellig Michael', in R. Bendix, A. Eggert and A. Peselmann (eds), *Heritage Regimes and the State: Nomination, Implementation, Regulation*, Universitätsverlag Göttingen, 157-179.

'Legacy and Loss: The Great Silence and its Aftermath' in J. Crowley, W. J. Smyth and M. Murphy (eds), *Atlas of the Great Irish Famine, 1845-1852*, Cork University Press, 580-88.

'Language, Power and Politics in Europe', in U. Kockel, M. Nic Craith and J. Frykman (eds), *A Companion to the Anthropology of Europe*, Wiley-Blackwell, 373-88.

'Introduction, The Frontiers of Europe and European Ethnology' (with U. Kockel and J. Frykman) Europe', in U. Kockel, M. Nic Craith and J. Frykman (eds), *A Companion to the Anthropology of Europe*, Wiley-Blackwell, 1-10.

2011

'Europa Schreiben: Yoko Tawada und Emine Sevgi Őzdamar' in R. Johler, M. Matter and S. Zinn-Thomas (eds), *Mobilitäten. Europa in Bewegung als Herausforderung kulturanalytischer Forschung*, Waxmann, 520-28.

'Kulturen im Gespräch', *Kulturen* 5(1), 55-58.

2010

Cultural Diversity, Heritage and Human Rights: Intersections in Theory and Practice (ed. with M. Langfield and W. Logan), Routledge.

'Linguistic Heritage and Language Rights in Europe: Theoretical Considerations', in M. Langfeld, W. Logan and M. Nic Craith (eds), *Cultural Diversity, Heritage and Human Rights*, Routledge, 45-62.

'Intersecting Concepts and Practices' (with W. Logan and M. Langfield), in M. Langfeld, W. Logan and M. Nic Craith (eds), *Cultural Diversity, Heritage and Human Rights*, Routledge, 3-20.

'Citizenship, Culture and the Nation-State: a European Perspective', in W. Ommundsen, M. Leach and A. Vandenberg (eds), *Cultural Citizenship and the Challenges of Globalization*, Hampton, 111-26

'Language and Belonging in Ireland: Exploring Intercultural Memoirs', in B. Schmidt-Lauber and G. Schwibbe (eds), *Alterität: Erzählen vom Anderssein*, Schmerse Media, 169-84.

'Ulster-Zyklus', in *Enzyklopädie des Märchens*, Walter de Gruyter, 1147-51.

2009

'Writing Europe: a Dialogue of Liminal Europeans', *Social Anthropology* 17(2), 198-208.

'Giving Voice to Africans: West of the Bann'(with E. Odhiambo and K. Moyo), in CRC (eds), *Challenges of Peace – Research as a Contribution to Peace-building in Northern Ireland*, Community Relations Council, 191-206.

2008

Everyday Cultures in Europe: Approaches and Methodologies (ed. with U. Kockel and R. Johler), Ashgate.

Anthropology /European Ethnology in Northern Ireland (ed. with F. Magowan). Special Issue, *Irish Journal of Anthropology* 11(1).

Migration and Cultural Encounters in Northern Ireland (ed.). Special Issue, *Shared Space* 5.

'Intangible Cultural Heritages: The Challenges for Europe', *Anthropological Journal of European Cultures* 17(1), 54-73. [Derry Inaugural]

'From National to Transnational: a Discipline *en route* to Europe', in M. Nic Craith, U. Kockel and R. Johler (eds), *Everyday Culture in Europe: Approaches and Methodologies*, Ashgate, 1-17.

2007

Language, Power and Identity Politics (ed.), Palgrave Macmillan.

Cultural Heritages as Reflexive Traditions (ed. with U. Kockel), Palgrave Macmillan.

'Traditions, Symbols and Languages in Contemporary Northern Ireland' (with Anthony Alcock), in K. Kujawińska Courtney and M. A. Łukowska (eds), *Multiculturalism at the Start of the 21ˢᵗ Century: the British-Polish Experience, Australian Theory and Practice*, Łódź University Press, 83-96.

'Rethinking Language Policies: Challenges and Opportunities', in C. Williams (ed.), *Language and Governance,* University of Wales Press, 159-84.

'Languages and Power: Accommodation and Resistance', in M. Nic Craith (ed.), *Language, Power and Identity Politics*, Palgrave Macmillan, 1-21

'Sichtbarer Unterschied oder unsichtbare Gleichheit? Ethnische Minderheiten in Nordirland', in E. Tschernokoshewa and V. Gransow eds, *Beziehungsgeschichten. Minderheiten-Mehrheiten in europäischer Perspektive*, Domowina, 169-79.

'Cultural Heritages: Process, Power, Commodification', in U. Kockel and M. Nic Craith (eds), *Cultural Heritages as Reflexive Traditions*, Palgrave Macmillan, 1-19.

2006

Europe and the Politics of Language: Citizens, Migrants, Outsiders, Palgrave Macmillan

'Boundaries of Europe: Towards a Political Anthropology of the Baltic States' in R. Sliuzinskas and V. Ciubrinskas (eds), *Defining Region: Socio-Cultural Anthropology and Interdisciplinary Perspectives*, Klaipéda University Press, 117-128

'From the Local to the Global (and Back): Political Anthropology in Europe', in K. Poehls and A. Vonderau (eds), *Turn to Europe: Kulturanthropologische Europaforschungen*, LIT, 146-57.

'A Spatial Analysis of In-Migration: A Case-Study of Northern Ireland' (with Amanda McMullan), in U. Kockel and R. Byron (eds), *Negotiating Culture. Moving, Mixing and Memory in Contemporary Europe*, LIT, 121-42.

2005

'Discussion: Anthropology and Citizenship. A Rejoinder', *Social Anthropology* 13(2), 211-3.

2004

Communicating Cultures (ed. with U. Kockel), LIT.

'Culture and Citizenship in Europe: Questions for Anthropologists', *Social Anthropology* 12 (3), 289-300.

'Conceptions of Equality: the Case of Northern Ireland', in A. Finlay (ed.), *Nationalism and Multiculturalism: Irish Identity, Citizenship and the Peace Process*, LIT, 111-30.

'Local Cultures in a Global World', in U. Kockel and M. Nic Craith (eds), *Communicating Cultures*, LIT, 279-99.

2003

Culture and Identity Politics in Northern Ireland, Palgrave Macmillan.

'Facilitating or Generating Linguistic Diversity: the European Charter for Regional or Minority Languages', in S. Wolff and G. Hogan-Brun (eds), *Minority Languages in Europe: Frameworks – Status – Prospects*, Palgrave Macmillan, 59-72.

2002

Plural Identities: Singular Narratives – the Case of Northern Ireland, Berghahn. [joint winner of 2004 Ruth Michaelis Jena-Ratcliff Research Prize]

'The Tiger No Longer Speaks Celtic: Economic Conditioning and the Irish Language', in U. Kockel (ed.), *Culture and Economy: Contemporary Perspectives*, Ashgate, 175-95.

'Culture and Economy: Towards an Agenda for Further Research' (with Ullrich Kockel), in U. Kockel (ed.), *Culture and Economy, Contemporary Perspectives,* Ashgate, 231-40.

2001

'Politicised Linguistic Consciousness: The Case of Ulster Scots', *Nations and Nationalism* 7(1), 21-37.

2000

'Contested Identities and the Quest for Legitimacy', *Journal of Multilingual and Multicultural Development* 21(5), 399-413.

'Irish' in J. Wirrer (ed.), *Regional and Minority Languages in Europe*, Westdeutscher Verlag, 27-35.

1999

'Irish Speakers in Northern Ireland, and the Good Friday Agreement', *Journal of Multilingual and Multicultural Development* 20 (6), 494-507.

'Primary Education on the Great Blasket Island 1864-1940', *Journal of the Kerry Historical and Archaeological Society* 28, 77-137.

'The Irish Language in Britain: A Case Study of North West England' (with J. Leyland), *Language, Culture and Curriculum* 10 (3), 171-85.

'Linguistic Policy in Ireland and the Creation of a Border', in M. Anderson and E. Bort (eds), *The Irish Border: History, Politics, Culture*, Liverpool University Press, 175-200.

1998

'Culture and Economy: Issues for the 21st Century' (with U. Kockel), in A. Kilday (ed.), *Culture and Economic Development in the Regions of Europe*, European Centre for Traditional and Regional Cultures, 185-99.

1996

Watching One's Tongue: Issues in Language Planning (ed.), Liverpool University Press.

Watching One's Tongue: Aspects of Romance and Celtic Languages (ed.), Liverpool University Press

'Irish in Primary and Post-primary Education: North and South of the Border', *Irish Studies Review* 17, 35-39.

'Irish in Northern Ireland: the 1991 Census' (with I. Shuttleworth), in M. Nic Craith (ed.), *Watching One's Tongue: Aspects of Celtic and Romance Languages*, Liverpool University Press, 163-76.

1995

'Tomás Ó Criomthain and the English Tongue', *The Celtic Pen* 3 (1), 21-25.

'The Symbolism of Irish in Northern Ireland', in U. Kockel ed., *Landscape, Heritage and Identity: Case Studies in Irish Ethnography*, Liverpool University Press, 11-46.

1994

'The Irish Language in a Comparative Context', *Oideas* 42, 52-67.

'The Irish Language: Problems and Prospects', *Chimera* 9, 49-54.

'The Role of Language in Cultural Tourism', in J. Munro (ed.), *Cultural Tourism*, Gateway Europe, 15-22.

'Irish Language and Tourism; Problems and Prospects', in U. Kockel (ed.), *Culture, Tourism and Development: The Case of Ireland*, Liverpool University Press, 149-60.

1993

Malartú Teanga: An Ghaeilge i gCorcaigh sa Naoú hAois Déag, European Society for Irish Studies. [repr. 1994]

'Dátheangachas agus Malartú Teanga', *Oideas,* 40, 35-47.

1988

An tOileánach Léannta, Research Series, Clóchomhar (bestseller)

European Studies in Culture and Policy

edited by Prof. Máiréad Nic Craith (Heriot-Watt University, Edinburgh) and Prof. Ullrich Kockel (Heriot-Watt University, Edinburgh)

Sandra Johnston
Beyond Reasonable Doubt
An Investigation of Doubt, Risk and Testimony Through Performance Art Processes in Relation to Systems of Legal Justice
Bd. 13, 2013, 248 S., 29,90 €, br., ISBN 978-3-643-90440-9

Adriënne Heijnen
The Social Life of Dreams
A Thousand Years of Negotiated Meanings in Iceland
Bd. 12, 2013, 296 S., 29,90 €, br., ISBN 978-3-643-90238-2

Pia Olsson
Women in Distress
Self-understanding among 20th-century Finnish rural women
Bd. 11, 2011, 288 S., 29,90 €, br., ISBN 978-3-643-90133-0

Victoria Walters
Joseph Beuys and the Celtic Wor(l)d
A Language of Healing
Bd. 10, 2012, 416 S., 39,90 €, br., ISBN 978-3-643-90105-7

Philip McDermott
Migrant Languages in the Public Space
A Case Study from Northern Ireland
Bd. 9, 2011, 320 S., 29,90 €, br., ISBN 978-3-643-90158-3

Ann Kennard
Old Cultures, New Institutions
Around the New Eastern Border of the European Union
vol. 8, 2010, 240 pp., 39,90 €, br., ISBN 978-3-643-10751-0

Christa-Maria Lerm Hayes; Victoria Walters
Beuysian Legacies in Ireland and Beyond
Art, Culture and Politics
vol. 6, 2011, 248 pp., 29,90 €, br., ISBN 978-3-8258-0761-0

Thomas M. Wilson; Hastings Donnan (Eds.)
Culture and Power at the Edges of the State
National support and subversion in European border regions
vol. 3, 2005, 376 pp., 29,90 €, br., ISBN 3-8258-7569-5

Susan Mazur-Stommen
Engines of Ideology
Urban Renewal in Rostock, Germany 1990 – 2000
vol. 2, 2005, 240 pp., 29,90 €, br., ISBN 3-8258-6892-3

Ullrich Kockel; Máiréad Nic Craith (Eds.)
Communicating Culture
vol. 1, 2004, 320 pp., 29,90 €, br., ISBN 3-8258-6643-2

LIT Verlag Berlin – Münster – Wien – Zürich – London
Auslieferung Deutschland / Österreich / Schweiz: siehe Impressumsseite